OPERATION GARBO

THE PERSONAL STORY OF THE MOST SUCCESSFUL SPY OF WORLD WAR II

JUAN PUJOL GARCÍA & NIGEL WEST

Biteback Publishing

First published as 'GARBO' in Great Britain in 1985 by
George Weidenfeld and Nicolson Limited

This edition published in 2011 by
Biteback Publishing Ltd
Westminster Tower
3 Albert Embankment
London
SE1 7SP

ISBN 978-1-84954-107-7

10 9 8 7 6 5 4 3

A CIP catalogue record for this book is available from the British Library.

Printed and bound in Great Britain by
CPI Group (UK) Ltd, Croydon CR0 4YY

MIX
Paper from
responsible sources
FSC FSC® C020471
www.fsc.org

Contents

GARBO'S NETWORK OF NATIONAL SUBAGENTS

GARBO/ARABEL
Juan Pujol

	Agent ONE	Agent TWO	Agent THREE	Agent FOUR
	KLM steward	William Gerbers	BENEDICT	CHAMILLUS
			Venezuelan student	Gibraltrian NAAFI waiter
	Resigned in 1943	Died in Bootle in 1942	'Carlos' in Glasgow	based at Chilehurst
J(2)	KLM pilot and courier	2(1) WIDOW Mrs. Gerbers	3(1) Pilot Officer	4(1) ALMURA radio operator
J(3)	Head of Spanish MOI Section		3(2) Officer in British 49th Infantry Division	4(2) Guard based at Chislehurst
J(4)	Censor in MOI		3(3) Greek seaman and deserter	4(3) US NCO based in London
J(5)	Secretary in Cabinet Office			

Agent FIVE	Agent SIX	Agent SEVEN
MOONBEAM	Field Security NCO, died in 1943	DAGOBERT
Venezuelan in Ottawa (brother to Agent THREE)		Ex-seaman in Swansea
5(1) Agent FIVE's cousin in Buffalo, USA		7(1) British soldier in 9th Armoured Division
		7(2) DONNY Leader of World Aryan Order
		7(3) Wren in Ceylon
		7(4) DICK Indian fanatic
		7(5) DRAKE in Exeter
		7(6) Welsh fascist in South Wales
		7(5) DORICK in Harwich

About the authors

Nigel West is a military historian and journalist specialising in intelligence matters. He has researched books for a number of authors and is an acknowledged expert on his subject. He has worked on several television programs, including the BBC's 'Spy!' and 'Escape!' series. His previous books include *MI5: 1909–1945*, which led to the exposure of two previously unknown spies, *The Circus: MI5 Operations 1945–1972* and *MI6: British Secret Intelligence Service Operations 1909–1945*. Most recently, Nigel West co-authored *Snow: The Double Life of a World War II Spy*.

Juan Pujol García was born in Barcelona in 1912. After the war Garbo faked his own death and moved to Venezuela where he later opened a book store. He died in Caracas in 1988.

Acknowledgements

This book could not have been completed without the kind assistance of the following, to whom we owe a debt of gratitude:

Colonel Roger Hesketh, who gave generous access to his authoritative *FORTITUDE, A History of Strategic Deception in North-Western Europe, April 1943 to May 1945*. This important book, published in 1999 as *FORTITUDE: The D-Day Deception Campaign*, is an essential reference work for any student of wartime intelligence operations.

Tony Tobella, who spent many hours with GARBO translating his experiences from Catalan and Castilian Spanish into English.

Bill Risso-Gill, who allowed us to reproduce his father's photograph and offered invaluable information concerning his father's wartime activities as GARBO's first British case officer.

Major General P. R. Kay of the Ministry of Defence's D Notice Committee, who gave us his guidance.

Various former members of the wartime Security Service (MI5) and Secret Intelligence Service (MI6) who were directly concerned with GARBO's case. For obvious reasons none can be publicly thanked for their contribution.

Introduction

Late in May 1984 a group of retired intelligence officers gathered in the drawing room of the Special Forces Club in London to be reunited with a spy reported dead in 1959. None was certain that the man they hoped to meet would really be the double agent they had known by his wartime code name, GARBO.

GARBO's extraordinary contribution to the Allied victory is well documented. There is hardly a textbook on the subject of strategic deception that fails to mention this remarkable individual. But no author has ever succeeded in penetrating the wall of secrecy that MI5, the British Security Service, constructed around their star performer. His true identity remained as closely guarded in 1984 as it was at the end of the war, when elaborate arrangements were made to protect him for the rest of his life.

My own search for GARBO began in 1972 when I read Sir John Masterman's account of MI5's double agents, *The Double Cross System in the War of 1939–1945* (Yale University Press, 1972), and I was impressed by his observation that GARBO had been 'something of a genius' and had displayed a 'masterly skill'. Indeed, GARBO was the agent singled out for particular praise: 'Connoisseurs of double-cross have always regarded the GARBO case as the most highly developed example of their art.' Unfortunately, Masterman gave only minimal clues as to his true identity, so there was little opportunity to pursue the matter further.

Nevertheless, I was intrigued by the Spaniard known only as GARBO. Why that choice of code name? What had become of him after the war?

According to Sefton Delmer, the veteran journalist who recounted GARBO's adventures in *The Counterfeit Spy* (Hutchinson, 1973), 'he set up a prosperous public relations firm along with an import and export business' in Angola. But 'suddenly in 1959...' GARBO 'succumbed to another attack of malaria. And this time it killed him'. Or did it? Was it really likely that such an expert in self-preservation would die, ignominiously, running a small business in a corner of Portuguese Africa? I had my doubts, and whenever I tracked down a former wartime MI5 officer I always inquired about GARBO's whereabouts. Unfortunately, GARBO's principal MI5 case officer, Tomás Harris, had been killed in a car accident in Majorca in January 1964. His wife Hilda, who had also known GARBO well, had died soon afterwards. Sefton Delmer was also dead, and although his son, Felix, told me that he believed his father had discovered GARBO's real name, he had evidently confided in no one. Nor had he committed it to paper. Even those officers who had spent most of the war supervising double agent operations knew GARBO only by his code name. The 'need-to-know' rule had worked perfectly. All had been aware of GARBO's extraordinary achievements, but none seemed to know his real identity, or what had become of him. It was not until I interviewed Anthony Blunt, in May 1981, that I was at last put on the right track.

Eighteen months earlier the distinguished art historian had been exposed publicly as a former Soviet spy and had been stripped of his knighthood. Apart from attending a short press conference, Blunt had avoided discussing his treachery with anyone. In April 1981, while putting the finishing touches to my history of the Security Service, I had written to him requesting an interview. Blunt had spent five years serving in MI5 during the war and I was anxious to hear his version of events. I knew that even before Blunt's exposure he had always refused to talk about his work for the Security Service. His usual excuse had been his fear of the Official Secrets Act. But to my surprise,

Blunt had agreed to meet me and invited me to his London flat. Apparently, some of his former colleagues in MI5 had urged him to see me. He imposed only one condition: that our meetings should remain secret until his death, as should certain items of information which he undertook to confide in me.

I knew that Blunt had been a close friend of Tommy Harris and had known something of his collaboration with GARBO. That much was clear from an introduction he had written in 1975 to an exhibition of Harris's art at the Courtauld Institute Galleries. Blunt, who had then recently retired as director of the Courtauld Institute, had offered a brief biography of Harris, and, in doing so, had mentioned his involvement with GARBO:

> At the outbreak of war Tomás joined the war office, where his intimate knowledge of Spain was of great value. His greatest achievement, however, was as one of the principal organis-ers of what has been described as the greatest double-cross operation of the war – 'Operation GARBO' – which seriously misled the Germans about the Allied plans for the invasion of France. ... After the invasion of France one of the high-est commanders said that the GARBO operation was worth an armoured division.

I had a series of lengthy conversations with Blunt during which he recalled his war work and, without prompting, he told me of the single occasion he had dined with GARBO. The two men had been introduced by Tommy Harris in 1944, at Garibaldi's Restaurant in Jermyn Street. Blunt still enjoyed a tremendous memory for detail. He even remembered that GARBO had been using the name Juan or Jose García. This was no great help as García is a very common name in Spain, but nevertheless I felt some progress had been made.

My hunt for GARBO stalled temporarily, but only until March 1984 when I received a fascinating note from a retired British Secret Intelligence Service officer living abroad. He wrote to elaborate on an incident I had mentioned briefly in my history of MI5. I acknowledged his letter and, since I knew he had once served in a wartime counter-intelligence section dealing with Spanish matters, I included my customary query concerning GARBO.

To my delight, the officer replied that he had actually met GARBO and knew his true name. He added that he had no idea whether GARBO was alive or dead, or where he might be located. Dropping everything, I flew to meet my contact and explained what Anthony Blunt had disclosed to me. My new informant told me that GARBO's full name was Juan Pujol García and confirmed that he had only used his mother's maiden name, García, while in England during the war. Unfortunately, he could shed little light on his possible whereabouts, but suggested Barcelona as a starting point, because the Pujol García family had originated from the Catalan capital.

The Barcelona telephone directory contains the names of literally hundreds of Pujol Garcías so, undaunted, I employed a local researcher, Jose Escoriza, to do some detective work for me. He and his family had given me invaluable assistance with my research in the past, and on this occasion he undertook to ring every number listed in the telephone book and ask two short elimination questions, concerning the age and the wartime occupation of every Juan Pujol García listed. Was he in his late sixties or early seventies, and had he spent some time in London during the war? A negative to either of these two queries would rule out the candidate. In case of a positive result, I had a longer list of supplementary questions. Had he known someone named Tommy Harris? Had he received a decoration from the British government? Did he recognise the code name GARBO? Answers to these questions would surely identify the right Juan Pujol García. After a week of repetitive calling no result had been achieved, and we had exhausted all the Pujol Garcías with the initial J. But, before going further, my resourceful helper made a significant comment: 'Every time I call I ask the same question, and I usually get the same response,' he explained. 'But there was one exception. I spoke to one person, who I could tell was too young to be our target, who kept on asking me questions. After so many abortive conversations, this one stands out in my mind as being quite different, but I can't explain how.'

I asked Jose to trace his notes on this particular Pujol García and to talk to him again. On the second call the recipient behaved in a very suspicious manner. He demanded to know who was delving into the past, and why. Escoriza explained that he was trying to trace a wartime hero for a friend from England. This news went down well, and on the third approach the young Catalan confirmed that his uncle, Juan Pujol García, now in his early seventies, had indeed spent much of the war in London. Unfortunately, he had not seen his uncle for twenty years. And at that time he had been living somewhere in South America.

To me, this was excellent news. It meant that if the uncle was truly GARBO, he had been seen alive some years after his officially reported demise. Further persuasion elicited the information from the nephew that Juan Pujol García had last been heard of in Venezuela, but there was no address or telephone number. I immediately engaged a television researcher based in Caracas to find GARBO and, ten days later, after a laborious search, he supplied me with a telephone number belonging to Pujol's son. If I rang at a prearranged time I could speak to the elusive Juan Pujol García. This I did, and I asked the voice at the other end my series of prepared questions, the answers of which I believed would only have been known to GARBO. Juan Pujol García answered them all correctly and even volunteered some additional information. Certainly, he had spent much of the war in London ... in Hendon. Yes, he had been a good friend of Tommy Harris and had known his three sisters, Violetta, Conchita and Enriqueta. Yes, he still possessed the medal awarded to him by the British government in 1944. So this was indeed GARBO, albeit several thousand miles away.

Somewhat hesitantly, he agreed to meet me the following week. Our rendezvous was to be New Orleans. There, on Sunday 20 May 1984, I first met my quarry, the spy I had spent over a decade tracing. It was only a matter of days away from the fortieth anniversary of the D-Day landings, the invasion that GARBO had done so much to help.

The rest of what transpired is now well known and was reported in dozens of newspapers around the world. Later in the month he flew to London to attend a private audience with HRH The Duke of Edinburgh at Buckingham Palace, and then went on to see some old comrades at the Special Forces Club. Among those present were Colonel T. A. Robertson, the MI5 officer who had been responsible for the Security Service's wartime double agent operations; Colonel Roger Hesketh, the mastermind behind GARBO's campaign of strategic deception; Cyril Mills, GARBO's first MI5 case officer (whom he only knew as Mr Grey); and Desmond Bristow, a retired SIS man who had attended GARBO's initial interrogation upon his arrival in England. On 6 June 1984, GARBO travelled to Normandy to tour the invasion beaches and pay his respects to those who gave their lives to free Europe from the Nazis. Both the reunion in London and the visit to France were profoundly emotional experiences. Wherever GARBO went he was thanked for his unique contribution and asked the same questions: Why did you do it? How did you manage it? What follows is the full story.

GARBO has written chapters one to four, then I have explained the London end in chapter five; GARBO has then continued in chapters six and eleven and I have filled in the details in chapters seven, eight, nine, ten and the epilogue. Finally, in an appendix, Roger Hesketh has detailed the full significance of GARBO's outstanding achievement.

Nigel West

1

Childhood

The history of the world is our image of the world, not the image of mankind.

Oswald Spengler

My first forty years were full of adventure and I have found it very interesting to put them down on paper, but I would like first to ask for the reader's understanding and sympathy, for I am neither subtle nor learned. I agree with the Roman philosopher who said, 'All I know is that I know nothing'; my aim is simply to tell the story of my life.

I was born on 14 February 1912 in Barcelona, in the city which they call 'the Unrivalled'. In those days Barcelona was still trying to recover from the bitter memories of the *Setmana Tràgica*, that Tragic Week in 1909 when radicals, socialists and anarchists collaborated in organising a strike during which churches, homes and convents were burnt and political agitators and demagogues incited the people to take to the streets, unleashing a week of rioting. Although the authorities soon restored order, unrest still lay close to the surface and, during my childhood, Barcelona was the scene of frequent street battles, strikes, attempts on people's lives and revolutionary coups. Every morning, when my father left for work, he would say goodbye to us as if for the last time; each parting was heartrending.

We lived in the first-floor flat at 70 Carrer Muntaner near the corner of Arago Street. At that time the Madrid-Saragossa-Alicante railway line ran in a deep cutting along Arago Street to Barcelona's main station. I never tired of peering through the railings to watch the powerful steam engines hissing by with their endless wagons and carriages. My imagination would travel with them as they sped away to remote destinations to the echoing sound of a whistle. I dreamed of getting to know the world and am convinced that my passionate enthusiasm for travel stems from those years of living so close to the railway line. Later, as our social standing improved, we moved to grander houses, but I missed the trains which had so stimulated my fantasies about far-off countries and unknown lands.

My mother was called Mercedes García. From the photographs I still have of her as a young woman, it is clear that she had been very good-looking. She came from Motril, a town in the southern province of Granada, and all her life she preserved the lilting yet elegant stride of an Andalusian. She kept her fine figure, and to see her walk down the street when she was nearing seventy and had snow-white hair, one would have taken her for forty.

As her parents had brought her to Barcelona when she was only eight, she spoke Catalan without a trace of an accent and used it constantly at home, resorting to Castilian only when we had visitors. She loved all things Catalan: the songs, the music, the dances and the idiosyncrasies of the people. But although the atmosphere at home was so strongly Catalan, neither my parents nor anyone else felt the sting of separatism for we were first and foremost Spaniards.

Sometimes my mother would tell us about her childhood in Motril, a town with seven sugar mills which lay in a beautiful, fertile valley covered in huge plantations of waving sugar cane. She would tell us about the town's festivals, its home-made sweets, the famous *torta real* or royal pie, the delicious *pan de aceite* bread which substitutes oil for lard, the ring-shaped rolls and tropical fruits. Her parents were strict Catholics who received Holy Communion every day, a show of piety which their neighbours considered to be excessively sanctimonious. My mother was, therefore, brought up in an austere atmosphere of considerable harshness. Her rigid attitudes remained with her even after her marriage, and she stayed an unyielding disciplinarian with a relentlessly Christian outlook to the end of her life.

My father, Juan Pujol, was a Catalan through and through. His family came from Olot, a town near La Garrotxa in the province of Girona, but they later moved to Barcelona where my father was born and went to school. Goethe once said: 'Talent is shaped in seclusion and character in the torrent of the world.' My father had no chance of studying in seclusion, but his character was certainly shaped in the daily struggle to earn his keep. By dint of saving and working hard, he was able to set up his own little factory and eventually it became the most important dye-house in Barcelona, well known for the superb black it produced.

My parents had four children. First came my brother Joaquin, a sturdy, straightforward character whose favourite hobbies were photography and stamp collecting. He was followed two years later by my sister Buenaventura, who still is, and always has been, a true second mother to me. I was born two years after her and then came my younger sister Elena. All of us followed Spanish custom and called ourselves by our Christian names, followed by our father's surname of Pujol, followed by our mother's surname of García. We were considered what they, in the beleaguered Barcelona of those days, called a well-to-do family. Far removed from the risk of poverty, we did not have to worry about our daily needs; we lacked nothing, not even the pleasures for which we would have yearned, had we not had them.

My father deserves a very special mention; indeed he almost warrants a whole chapter to himself, for to write about him is to understand my subsequent actions. He was my progenitor, the head of the family; he saw to my everyday needs and to my moral upbringing, and he instilled in me, by instruction and advice, the attitudes and ideas, the very spirit that made me. Step by step, throughout my childhood and early youth, his precepts guided and taught me.

I have no qualms in asserting that he was the most honest, noble and disinterested man that I have ever known. His affability was such that not only his friends, but also his enemies – if he had any – saw in him a protector and a refuge. He was always ready to listen to people's worries and to offer help with their problems and solace for their sorrows. Unquestionably a man of ideals, he was always prepared to assist those in trouble.

Perhaps such a description gives the impression that I over idealised my father. But even if I were to stand back and take a detached view, I would still describe him exactly as I have done, even though he cannot unfortunately read what I am saying. If he could read the praises that my poor but enthusiastic pen has written, he would probably have been made a happy man. Two episodes from my early life will illustrate what a straight-forward, generous and loving father he was.

My older relations used to say that as a boy I was somewhat difficult to control. I not only broke my own toys but often those of my brother and sisters as well; they used to guard theirs with great care, lest they fall into my hands. From what I have been told, I was indeed fairly unmanageable; so, when I was seven years old, my mother decided to send me away to a well-known boarding school run by the Marist Fathers at Mataró, about twenty miles from Barcelona. My brother was also sent at the same time so that he could look after me and stop me from feeling homesick.

The school was called Valldèmia and I remember it well. It had spacious classrooms, large gardens and playing fields, and an education with a decidedly French feel to it, which was not surprising as most of the fathers teaching there were of that nationality.

I spent four interminable years there as a boarder; they seemed particularly endless because we only went home for Christmas, Easter and the summer holidays. During the rest of the year, we were only allowed out on Sundays if a relative came to visit us. And this is precisely what my father did, week after week for four long years; he did not miss a single Sunday during the whole of my time at Mataró. He would arrive by train early on Sunday morning, fetch us from school and take us for long walks along the beach, ending up in one of the town's many restaurants for lunch. Then in the afternoon we would invariably call in at a patisserie, where he would buy cakes and sweets for us to take back to school. During our time together he would tell stories, give advice and encourage us in our studies. Even now I can remember the exhortations, admonishments and gentle reproaches with which he regaled us during our long walks by the sea.

A second example of my father's affectionate nature occurred when I was about nineteen. One day I suddenly began to feel stabbing pains in my stomach. The doctors diagnosed acute appendicitis and arranged for me to be taken to the hospital immediately. I was rushed into the operating room, where they gave me an anaesthetic. Three days later, when the incision became infected and refused to heal, I developed a high temperature and became delirious. In between my bouts of delirium I was aware of my father's presence; all night long he sat there, holding my hand, weeping. It was the only occasion I ever saw my father cry. I have never forgotten either his tears, his unhappiness or his tenderness.

My father belonged to no political party: he was apolitical. He was deeply steeped in liberalism and believed implicitly in freedom. He abhorred oppression. He never attended political gatherings or party meetings; he cared neither for Right nor Left. If anything, he gravitated towards the Centre, where he found common ground with those who held his own ideas on liberalism and economic freedom. He taught me to respect the individuality of human beings, their sorrows and their sufferings, be they rich or poor, good or evil, black or white. He despised war and bloody revolutions, scorning the despot, the authoritarian, those prepared to take advantage of others and those filled with prejudice. So strong was his personality and so powerful his hold over me and my brother that neither of us ever belonged to a political party. Politics, he said, were for the politicians, although he always exercised his duty as citizen and voted for one or another of the groups seeking power.

My father never got into an argument; as far as he was concerned, everyone was entitled to his own beliefs: it was not for him to butt into a discussion. As a result, he felt himself free to condemn misgovernment and equally free – if a vote was available – to give his vote to those he considered good patriots. Holding such liberal ideas, he was deeply depressed by the Carlist Wars, the Spanish–Moroccan War and, bloodiest of all, the First World War, all of which occurred in his lifetime. He could not understand why mankind had embarked on such an orgy of self-destruction, why so many young lives should be sacrificed, so many people shorn of all their vitality and virtue. Was history unable to check such dismemberment, such a violent rout of humanity? Spain had taken a neutral position in the First World War, although the country leant toward the Allied cause. Catalan industry had increased its export trade with France, Spain's nearest neighbour, and other parts of Spain had also produced a flood of goods which were in great demand throughout the Entente Cordiale. There was no unemployment; instead, there was prosperity and plenty, but this did not make my father happy. He would recall Tolstoy's words condemning hostilities: 'War is so horrendous, so atrocious, that no man, especially one of Christian principles, should feel able to undertake the responsibility of starting it.'

How then was it possible that those who did start it presumed themselves to be Christians? My father did not criticise the army for existing, but directed his anger against those who gave the orders, the politicians: those who send thousands upon thousands of simple townsfolk and labourers to their death, having first taught them to hate the enemy. My father did not bear a grudge against the military uniform, nor against the man wearing it: his revulsion was directed exclusively toward the spirit of war. He recognised that officers, generals, military commanders and even the troops in the barracks were indispensable for they guaranteed national order and independence. But he found it very hard to understand why politicians had seized upon the assassination of the Archduke Francis Ferdinand and his wife in Sarajevo on 28 June 1914 as an excuse for the holocaust that followed. Artius, the Roman orator, said: 'The pig feeds on acorns, the stork on snakes and history on human lives.' This may be true, but my father could not stomach it and taught me to loathe the violence and the utter destruction of the battlefield.

A great number of friends and acquaintances – including a great many of those who fought on the Allied side during the Second World War – have asked me at different times why I threw myself, wholeheartedly, totally and completely, with all my strength and determination, behind the Allied cause. What harm had the forces of the European Axis done to me to make me want to put all my energies into disrupting their ambitions? The Duke of Edinburgh, who honoured me with a long private audience at Buckingham Palace, asked me, after I had told him of my wartime exploits: 'Why were you, a Spaniard, so keen to help the British during the Second World War?'

The answer lies in my beliefs, the same beliefs that my father instilled in me during my childhood, beliefs which urged me to fight against all tyranny and oppression. I have never borne, nor indeed do I bear now, any grudge against the German people. In fact, I have always admired their industry and their love of tradition. They suffered a crushing defeat in 1918 and no one was there to give them a helping hand. They had been deeply humiliated and left with no friends to comfort them. It was at this point, at this decisive moment when the lack of understanding on the part of their neighbours left them dispossessed, scorned and offended, that an ambitious and cruel human being – a maniac, an inhuman brute – arose and cajoled them with his empty verbosity. He made them believe in what was not believable, in what was irrational, unlikely, impossible and inadmissible, namely the strength of the Prussian army and the greatness of the German people. Both these nations were decisive in bringing about that stubborn arrogance which fuelled the Nazi leader's provocative talk. How could the German people have fallen victim to such stratagems? What sophistries and snares had those devious, despotic rabble-rousers used to enable them to indoctrinate the minds of intelligent and resourceful Germans so successfully?

The man's name was Adolf Hitler; his doctrine, *Mein Kampf*. Hitler hated both the political parties of the Left, as well as those which supported the Hapsburgs. His greatest spite, though, he reserved for the Jewish people, whom he managed to nearly exterminate by the most perverse, malignant and evil means ever witnessed in history. Many millions were his victims and their deaths were upon his conscience. Mankind would not tolerate such satanic splendour. Nor would I. That was why I fought against injustice and iniquity with the only weapons at my disposal.

2

Barcelona

A historian is a prophet that looks back.

F. von Schiegel

'**O**n reading a biography, bear in mind that the truth can never be published.' I do not accept this dictum of George Bernard Shaw's, but would rather claim that there is an exception to every rule. I intend in these pages to refute the famous Irish writer's comment by directing every effort toward exploring all that I can unearth about the double identity that became ARABEL—GARBO.

When I look back at the past, I seem to be watching a documentary which, despite the whirlwind of time, has not become blurred. After four years at Valldèmia, I returned to Barcelona to attend a primary school less than half a block away from home, run by the De La Salle Brothers. The four of us also received private French lessons three days a week from a teacher from Marseilles, for French in those days was what English is today, the universal language of tourism, diplomacy and business. But what I remember most when I feel nostalgic is my beloved father, my friend and mentor. I remember the smell of his stinking, black tobacco, for which he had a passion. He particularly liked long, thin cigars, similar to those blended in Tuscany, which we in Catalonia call *caliquenyes*; in no time at all a room would reek so foully from the stench that we would all be forced to leave, so he usually did his best to smoke them out of doors where he would not inconvenience those around him. He frequently tried to give them up, but never succeeded.

He was eventually so poisoned by them that they contributed in no small way to his death.

I remember too his love of cards, a distraction which he particularly enjoyed on Sunday afternoons. His favourite game was Manilla, for which four people were needed. The group usually consisted of my father; a family friend; the headmaster of the local secondary school, who was a priest called Mossen Josep; and myself. Eventually, my father decided that my brother and I should attend Mossen Josep's school. But if the truth be told, I soon found both the school and its headmaster extremely tedious. The lessons seemed endless and dull and I attended them most unwillingly. After three years there I had become a hefty fellow of fifteen, with an incipient beard. Soon I was shaving and thought myself every inch a man. Going out with girls accounted for a fair bit of my time and the rest I devoted to sports, gymnastics and hiking.

One day I had a row with one of my teachers: he had it in for me and I didn't think much of him. I came home and told my father that I did not want to stay at school any longer. He took my decision calmly and replied that if I was not going to study anymore, I must get a job. I accepted the challenge and went to work in a hardware shop in the old Carrer Comte d'el Asalto, in the old quarter of Barcelona near the famous promenade or *Rambla*.

As an apprentice, I had to keep the shop clean, run errands and return to their rightful places all those tools which the shop assistants left out on the counters after they had shown them to prospective clients. Gradually, the dreariness of the routine and the hard work involved in having to sweep out such huge premises every day undermined my show of bravado. I gave up my job.

I decided I wanted to read for an arts degree and began to spend hours in my father's library. In particular, I was fascinated by the origins of words and spent my days perusing book after book. It was during this period that my appendix burst and I was rushed into the hospital, as I have already explained. When I had recovered from the operation, I decided not to read for an arts degree after all, but to become a chicken farmer. I made up my mind to enter the Royal Poultry School at Arenys de Mar as soon as I was well enough.

It was 1931, General Primo de Rivera's long dictatorship had ended and a new government had been sworn in under General Berenguer, who had promised democracy and municipal elections.

Most of the large cities voted Republican, but in the country people voted overwhelmingly in favour of the Monarchist Party. Despite being in the minority, the Republicans claimed a victory because they had gained the cities and the provincial capitals. To avoid bloodshed, King Alfonso XIII left the country, but without formally abdicating. Power was then transferred into the hands of the centrist leader of the Republic, Niceto Alcalá Zamora.

All I could make out from the tangled web of proclamations, announcements and acclamations that followed was that Spain's stability was swiftly coming to an end. It seemed to me that those who had endured a dictatorship backed by the king were now in revolt against the prevailing judicial and national unity. My father had a premonition that hard days were looming over the horizon for his countrymen, which worried him greatly. However, as fate would have it, he never knew what followed, for he died a few months after the birth of the Second Republic in 1931.

His death left a great vacuum in the family, and the flight of his soul from the world left me oppressed and overwhelmed, my heart gripped by deep sorrow. I had lost the one I loved most, for ever. His coffin was borne on the shoulders of his factory workers and accompanied by some of the patients from the Saint John of God Hospital for Sick Children, to which he had been a great benefactor. Many other mourners also followed this kind and generous man to his body's last resting place. Fifty years after his death, I feel that providence had been right to remove him from the scene before he could see the tribulation and suffering which his beloved country was to suffer.

After I had finished training to be a poultry farmer, it was time for me to report to barracks for compulsory military service. In those days it was possible for a conscript to buy himself out after serving for six months. This scheme, known as the Fee-Paying Military Service Scheme, had the additional advantage that those who joined it could spend their nights at home. Moreover, if a recruit took all the necessary military training courses and studied hard during those six months, he was allowed to graduate with a star as a second lieutenant.

I decided to join the scheme and so avoid some of the more onerous chores of military life. I was drafted into the Seventh Regiment of Light Artillery, which had its barracks near Barcelona's harbour, in the *drassanes* or old dockyard area. Unfortunately, it turned out to be a cavalry regiment so I had to learn to ride. The captain who taught us was extremely harsh, so that I returned to barracks more than once with my buttocks on fire. The accepted cure for this was to apply a cloth to the raw part that had been soaked in vinegar and sprinkled with salt; when I did this, it made me see all the stars in the firmament. Such tough training left me with little love for the cavalry by the time I had won my spurs. I ended my military service without any enthusiasm whatsoever for my companions or my mount; I lacked those essential qualities of loyalty, generosity and honour that the cavalryman is meant to possess; I had no desire to stay in the army.

I was lucky not to have been called upon to quell any civil disturbances while doing my national service. In January 1933 anarchists took over the village of Casas Viejas near Cádiz and were ruthlessly put down by the security forces at the instigation of Manuel Azaña Diaz's left-wing government: fourteen prisoners were shot. All our leave was cancelled, but thankfully it was too far away from Catalonia for us to be sent there.

In October 1934 there was a revolt in Asturias, which was put down by the then centre-right government. After that, transitions from one government to another were swift. Bad news travelled around the country even faster. Every day newspapers reported more violent deaths. Passions were unleashed in bloody fashion. Debates in Parliament degenerated into insults and diatribes; politicians quarrelled endlessly among themselves. One day a right-wing faction sitting outside a coffee-bar would be machine-gunned; the next day it was the turn of the Left. Shots were exchanged daily. To make matters worse, governments took part in reprisals, lashed their opponents and claimed powers never granted them by the constitution. The police force, swamped by endless acts of private retaliation, ended up contravening the laws themselves. Finally, there came a black day in the annals of the country, 18 July 1936, an ill-fated date that changed the course of Spanish history, for it saw the beginning of a bloody civil war.

3

Civil War

There is no joy comparable to that of regaining one's lost freedom.
                                                            Cervantes

I have stumbled across dictatorships all too often during my life, albeit with different characteristics and aims; it almost seems as though they were following me around. Perhaps in trying to avoid them I have inevitably strayed into their orbits. Fortunately, I have never had any personal misadventures with such regimes because I have been careful never to give cause for anyone to take action against me. Let me emphasise, once again, my apolitical stance. This does not mean that I have no interest in politics, which are inevitably all around us; indeed, politics are so much part of our everyday life that they even turn up in our soup, as we say in Spain. When I say I am apolitical I mean, if I may make myself absolutely clear, that I have never belonged to any political party, nor have I ever given a penny to further the cause of any of them. I have never held a party membership card, nor do I feel strongly about any specific faction or group.

If one looks at two or three recent dictatorships, one sees that they have certain facets in common. Franco's dictatorship, for example, was a direct result of blindness, disunity and disagreement among all the political parties before his rise to power. These parties were all too ready to talk about their own freedom while oppressing that of their neighbours. They were willing to defend their doctrinaire and absolutist ideas by fire and the sword, but they were not open to rational argument, nor did they show any tolerance for the opposition. When the

Right was in power it took advantage; when the Left dominated it would trample autocratically over its opponents. As a result, a third force emerged which overcame both the Left and the Right with its motto 'Order, peace and respect'. Salazar's dictatorship in Portugal occurred for the same reasons, as did Marcos Pérez Jiménez's coup d'état in Venezuela, where endless battles between the Adecos and Copeyanos, the nation's two most prominent political parties, brought about such a confused state of affairs that Jiménez had to intervene to restore order.

Those who impose a totalitarian regime argue in the same breath about their love for their country, their faith in its destiny and their hope for 'peace, progress and bread'. But they hate an adversary who gets in their way, who detracts from their own glory. Authoritarian by nature, they detest opposition and will not accept censure or criticism. They are all for efficiency and obedience: crime has to be punished unceremoniously and at once. Unfortunately, this is a relief to many people, who then support the dictator, for the great majority crave law and order, which can be harder to achieve in a democracy – where punishment is tempered with justice – than under a dictatorship.

The Count of Maistre once said, 'Every nation has the government that it deserves,' which is a profound truth. But if only the politicians who governed us would concentrate more on their democratic role, not just with honeyed words but with specific deeds, then we would not have to deplore the way they curtail our freedom. Philosophers and writers such as Seneca, Goethe and Cervantes, to name but a few, clearly define the guilt incurred by any free man who unwittingly crushes freedom. Once a man has lost his freedom through incompetence, dogmatism, sectarianism or lack of appreciation, he will mourn that loss like Abderramán, the last Moorish king on Spanish soil, 'who cried like a child over what he did not know how to defend as a man'.

There are various ways of fighting absolute rulers: man to man, by clandestine methods, in dumb silence and finally

through retreat. But dying in battle does not bring down tyrannies. The efforts of those who give their lives to regain lost
freedom is never enough. Violence breeds further violence.
Those who have sacrificed their lives are followed by others
who are tortured and persecuted.

Despite all this fighting and dying, it is my firm belief that
no liberating changes occur until and unless men use their
brains, teach, argue and produce practical solutions for regaining the freedom that has been lost. Pio Baroja once said: 'The
sublime moment, the heroic act is more of an exaltation of the
intellect than of the will.'

Balzac wrote a brief note, which he put under a picture of
Napoleon, which read: 'What he was unable to secure by the
sword, I will attain by the pen.' Such an outlook has greatly
influenced mankind. For it is not enough to fight with weapons
of destruction and annihilation; it is essential to fight with ideas:
powerful arguments can destroy whole empires, dominions and
tyrannies. History is full of examples showing that the pen is
indeed mightier than the sword. I too believe this sincerely
and absolutely. I have devoted the greater part of my life to
this ideal, using all my talents, all my convictions, all possible
schemes, machinations and stratagems. The Second World War
was a decisive moment in the human epic: it gave birth to the
story of GARBO, the central character in this book.

I can assert with pride and a clear conscience that I have
never fired a rifle, nor any other gun for that matter, with an
enemy in front of me. My feelings, my scruples, even my morals
would not allow me to take the sublime gift of life away from
my neighbour.

In 1936 I was managing a poultry farm twenty miles north of
Barcelona, at Llinars del Vallès. On that ill-fated day, Sunday 18
July, I had arranged to go on an excursion to Mont Montseny
with some friends of mine from the Catholic Club in Plaça
Trilla, but all my plans kept collapsing like a house of cards.

Early in the morning I learned from my radio that there had been an attempted military coup. I rang my friends and relations to try to find out what was happening. 'People are fighting and killing each other in the streets,' said one. 'They are putting up barricades of paving stones in the main square and in the avenues,' said another. News spread like wildfire. Many, who were frightened, did not dare come out onto the streets. Others hung white sheets over their balconies, ostensibly to show their neutrality. Most of us stayed glued to our radios, which were transmitting messages and speeches from both sides, from the Nationalist rebels and from the Republicans.

I plucked up courage and decided to walk to my girlfriend's house in Carrer Girona. I spent the whole of that Sunday with her and her family, listening intently to the radio and hoping that order would soon be restored. However, the situation grew worse as the hours went by; it was clearly no ordinary military coup d'état, but nobody had yet realised that it was the beginning of three long years of civil war.

The days that followed were filled with fear. Columns of smoke rose everywhere: convents, churches and local party political headquarters were being set on fire all over Barcelona. No one reported for work as all the unions had decreed an indefinite general strike. We were afraid to walk down the streets as armed militia were shooting at random at anything that moved. Food soon became scarce; people were forced to go out to augment their rapidly dwindling larders. They would creep to the nearest shop after careful reconnoitring only to find that many shopkeepers had put up their shutters; others only opened to those they knew. If a car loaded with militia happened to be passing just as the owner opened the door, the soldiers would dash in, ransack the shop and then drag off the shopkeeper, charging him with strike breaking.

Utter confusion reigned. Neighbour denounced neighbour, paying off old scores. Some accusations were made in order to earn the 'right' to become a revolutionary, others to obtain a union card or in order to be thought a political radical. In this suspicious atmosphere everyone mistrusted everyone else: threats bred bewilderment and insecurity.

Catalans had backed the dictator General Primo de Rivera until he had tried to curtail Catalonia's desire for autonomy; after that they had tried to undermine his rule. Now, six years later, the people were tired of dictatorships and coup d'états; they longed for stability and, with this in mind, had backed the Republicans. At first it looked as if the Republicans would easily retain control, for they seemed to have kept a grip on the situation in Barcelona and to have retaken those barracks where the soldiers were in revolt. But just as they appeared to be about to gain a crushing victory, they made an unforgivable political error: they gave orders for all the public prisons in the city to be opened up and for all those awaiting trial, be they political prisoners, convicted criminals or thieves, to be let out. This soulless, callous mob joined up with the paramilitary militias and roamed the city intent on plunder. The majority of these malcontents had no particular political convictions; all they wanted to do was steal. They burst into people's houses pretending to search for hidden reactionaries and counter-reactionaries. Terror spread throughout the city and thousands died.

The Nationalist rebels now declared that a fifth column or secret group of Franco sympathisers was hiding in the city, which brought about an even bloodier series of reprisals. This time the victims were not just the comfortably off but those who, while not going the whole hog in support of Republican doctrines, were too frightened to join the opposition. Such middle-of-the-roaders were known as Radishes, red (or Republican) on the outside but white on the inside. Many Radishes were Catholics who had seen their churches and cathedrals sacked and burnt, their priests and nuns mocked and ridiculed before being murdered. Now their only hope was to go into hiding. The violence and the lawlessness destroyed people's morale; it was no longer a matter of defending a cause or fighting for a belief, it was just a matter of defending oneself and one's family against extremists.

My younger sister Elena had been engaged to be married but, during one of the house searches, her fiancé was carted off in the name of the Republic by a self-appointed policing unit. No doubt he was charged with presumed membership of the fifth column. Later, Elena and my mother were themselves arrested as counter-revolutionaries, but thanks to a relative in the anarcho-syndicalist trade union, the CNT or Confederación Nacional del Trabajo, they were snatched from certain death and eventually released. When they were arrested it wasn't just they who felt fear: the whole family trembled.

The Republicans, who considered themselves to be the legitimate government, now called up all officers in the reserves in order to replace those soldiers who had joined the rebels. It was therefore my duty to report to my regiment, but I was loath to take sides in such a fratricidal fight; I had no desire to participate in a struggle whose passions and hatred were so far removed from my own ideals. But by not reporting, I became a deserter, absent without leave. I had to hide.

Hopes that hostilities would soon end faded by Christmas. I therefore decided to stay permanently with my girlfriend. I had always felt close to her mother and father, who were old friends of my own parents, our two families being bound together by ties of affection and friendship.

One evening, just before Christmas, I was making such a noise in their kitchen, cracking hazelnuts and walnuts with a hammer, that I failed to hear a knock at the door and so did not realise that a police patrol had arrived to inspect the premises. (Evidently, we had been reported by one of those many 'friends' one couldn't trust, though we never found out who it was.) The police made straight for the threshold of one of the doors and started levering up the wood with a chisel. They seemed to know the exact place where my girlfriend's father and brother had gouged out a secret hole for hiding jewellery and gold coins. The father was an agent for a large textile firm in Torrassa and had many contacts, so that as well as his own valuables, he had also hidden other people's. As a result, both father and son were arrested and so was I. For the police had continued searching the flat and had entered the kitchen only to find me with a raised hammer, my ear glued to the door leading to the dining room, trying to find out what was going on.

We were taken by car to the Metropolitan Police Station in Via Laietana, a great stroke of luck because it meant that we had fallen into the hands of one of the more popular militias, or I am sure I would not now be telling this tale.

I was kept in prison for a week, despite repeatedly protesting my innocence. I kept assuring the police that I had only been in the house because I was engaged to the eldest daughter, but they continued to question me remorselessly, for as far as they were concerned I was a deserter. I was petrified, fearing that I might have to pay with my life. 'Going for a walk' was a common experience in those days.

Meanwhile, my girlfriend had got in touch with one of the units of *Socorro Blanco*, a secret organisation which endeavoured to assist those who were being persecuted for idealistic or religious reasons. One of their girl helpers posed as a revolutionary and arranged for me to be let out of the prison at dead of night. Free, I joined the ever-growing number of those leading a clandestine existence. I went into hiding again.

Remembering my position then makes my hair stand on end. The only way I can view it calmly is if I look upon it as an old bill I discounted forty-five years ago. But at the time I was all too aware that I had, unwillingly and unwittingly, become a criminal. I had no papers and would be in even worse trouble if the police caught me again.

I spent the next year in one of those sordid, narrow streets in the sleazy working-class area of Barcelona down by the harbour. The rented flat I was hiding in belonged to a taxi driver who lived there with his wife and son, a shrewd boy of about nine. The taxi driver was away most of the time, ferrying recruits to the Aragon front. He told me that the shortage of arms was so great that newcomers had to get their guns from those who'd been killed or wounded. Men complained bitterly that everyone had a gun at the rear but up at the front line they were expected to fight for democracy without them.

Food was hard to get and there were long queues everywhere. One day, when the taxi driver's wife was out shopping, the police knocked at the door and demanded entry. In a split second, which seemed like a century, I signalled to the boy that I was going to hide under his bed. He then opened the door and with complete sangfroid began to tell the police that his mother was out hunting for food and his father was at the front, fighting the 'factious rebels'. The police asked him various questions as they searched through the different rooms. When they came to the one I was in the boy threw open the door with great aplomb, switched on the light and announced that this was his room. The police then left; the boy's studied casualness had convinced them he had nothing to hide.

I was so grateful for what he had done that I spent hours giving him lessons, for the schools had all been closed. He was a quick learner and I much enjoyed teaching him; the lessons added a new dimension to my life and left me less time for worrying.

A few months later the taxi driver took his wife and son to join her parents in Lleida. I was now entirely alone in the flat, but as the neighbours were under the impression that it was empty, I was unable to move around in case I gave myself away. Three times a week a girl brought me food; otherwise I just sat there tormented with fear of discovery. I became so depressed and withdrawn, so utterly miserable, that I lost over twenty kilos. I began to look like a decrepit old man of forty although I was only twenty-five.

As I grew weaker, I became desperate and knew I could not hold out much longer. The girl who brought me food finally managed to obtain some false identity papers from the *Socorro Blanco* making me out to be too old for the army.

An old friend, who was secretary to one of the many branches of the General Workers' Union, suggested that I go and see some people who were running poultry farms in the area. When I found them, I was delighted to discover that several were old friends from my Royal Poultry School days.

I asked if I could join their union and was duly enrolled without any problem. At first I hung around attending the endless meetings they were always calling, but I soon tired of these and asked for an assignment. They suggested that I become the manager of a farm they'd taken over at Sant Joan de les Abadesses in northern Catalonia. I accepted with alacrity for it was a long way from Barcelona and only about twenty-two miles from the French border.

My family had all been scattered by the civil war. Elena's fiancé had been taken away during a house search, Joaquin had had to join the Republican army, and my mother and Elena had gone with Buenaventura and her husband Frederic to Aiguafreda, so there was no one to whom to say goodbye.

Upon arrival at Sant Joan, I reported to the municipal council, who had requisitioned all the farms, factories and houses in the area when the civil war broke out, forcing the owners to flee. By the time I appeared on the scene none were working well, for they lacked technical expertise and direction. Everyone gave orders: no one wished to obey. There was much resentment and workers complained that, instead of one boss, they now had committees of seven or more.

Nobody seemed to mind that I had no proper identity papers; I was merely asked to report once a week to the municipal council, which consisted of representatives of most of the parties and unions in the area. It was a very easy life: I lived in the local hotel, I was paid regularly and found the work undemanding for there were less than a thousand beaks to look after. Every afternoon I walked to Ripoll and back, a round trip of about thirteen miles, in order to get fit, for I was planning to cross into France. One Sunday I went even further; rising at the crack of dawn, I climbed to the top of Mount Puigmal, from where I could see the 'promised land'. Then I set off at a brisk pace down to Ribes de Freser, on to Ripoll and back to Sant Joan by sunset, about forty miles.

But man proposes and God disposes. A few days after my mammoth walk, I heard that a fairly large expedition had been intercepted while trying to cross the border illegally with the help of some guides; some had been arrested, others wounded and several killed. As a result, the border guards had been strengthened.

I was now afraid to cross over by myself, nor did I know how the French authorities would react to my arrival. Would they hand me straight back to the Spanish authorities? If so, it would mean certain death, for orders about escapees were unequivocal.

It was now 1938 and, being a man of restless nature, I was becoming impatient. The civil war continued its macabre course. Every day each side claimed to have inflicted heavy losses on the other; they would give figures for the numbers killed, wounded and taken prisoner, issuing grandiloquent communiqués about towns, villages and hamlets destroyed. The price paid was immaterial so long as glory was achieved in action: the greater the havoc and the desolation, the more splendid the victory. How long, dear God, I wondered, could this continue? Was there to be no end to the sacrifice? The war seemed to rage with increasing intensity, which filled me with a deep depression compounded of fear and apathy. I was appalled that once-civilised men were now obsessed with spreading their obnoxious ideas by fire and the sword. Spaniards were destroying each other in their lust for power while the country's youth died unsung and unrecorded.

The poultry farm was not a success. To put it bluntly, its profits were non-existent. There were too few hens – a thousand was not an economic number – which were too old to

lay well, and my wages were too high, for I could have looked
after two or three times the number. Overhead, wages and capital investment divided by the number of hens led to negative
profit. I asked the local councillors if they would increase their
investment in the farm by expanding the premises and buying
more chickens of a higher quality so that I could achieve better
returns, but they just wanted more profits from the existing
set-up. I was not prepared to keep being told off while they did
nothing to put the business on a sounder economic footing.
Our consultations grew increasingly acrimonious.

I am not a man given to arguing and I dislike dubious deal-
ings so I decided to 'exit' from the stage, as they say in the
theatre. I handed in my resignation but offered to stay on for
a week to train an old farmer, whose lands had been expropri-
ated and who had been wandering around the place living off
the locals' generosity, to do my job. I never heard of farm nor
farmer again.

I was now determined to cross over to the other side, for
I naively thought that once among the Nationalists I would
be left alone to live my own life. I decided that the only way
of being able to do this was to volunteer for the infantry as a
veteran soldier and hope that I would be sent to the front, from
where I could desert. I therefore presented myself to a recruiting office in north Barcelona. My false identity papers made me
out to be older than I was, but the officer seemed delighted to
enrol me. All of us who had joined at the same time were then
sent to a training unit outside Les Borges Blanques, a pretty
little village in the province of Lleida, set in a torrid landscape
surrounded by olive trees.

The demand for fresh troops for the front was so great
that our training was brief. For a fortnight about a hundred
of us deployed, advanced, skirmished and practiced shooting
around the outskirts of the village, and then we were sent off
to Montblanc, some twenty miles to the east, where one of the
new International Brigade units was training. We were now in

the Tarragona area near the river Ebro and much closer to the front line.

We had been made ready for war in two weeks. But before joining the International Brigade itself, the sergeant asked whether any of us could drive, and fifteen or so recruits offered their services. He then asked for bricklayers, carpenters and blacksmiths; each time a handful more volunteered who were, or thought they were, experts. I realised that the infantry group was fast diminishing and, as I wasn't anxious to end up as cannon fodder, I decided to wait no longer. When the sergeant asked for those with a knowledge of telegraphy, I resolutely stepped forward.

I was convinced that this would keep me out of the firing line, for I was determined not to become involved in a struggle in which I did not believe and which went clean against my personal convictions. Years of hiding and persecution had made me bitter; my dreams had been shattered; my life seemed to have been nothing but disappointments and privations; I hated being a soldier and longed to escape to a new life. I blamed all my misfortunes on the older generation whose endless political wrangles had led us into civil war.

The signal corps soon realised my inadequacies. Finding my answers to questions about Morse code, telephone installations and flag signals extremely hazy, the sergeant jokingly inquired if I knew how to lay cables between the front line and the different commands. This time I was able to be positive, and so I came to join the signals unit attached to the International Brigade, which, owing to the lack of foreign volunteers, consisted mainly of Catalans.

My baptism of fire took place when our unit arrived at the northern bank of the Ebro at about noon. A very noisy plane flew in low from the south-west over the old destroyed Ebro Bridge and made straight for a temporary pontoon filled with troops and vehicles coming and going. Orders were shouted to disperse and, in a matter of seconds, we swarmed over the fields and sheltered under the olive trees. The rebel plane released its deadly load over the frail pontoon, smashing it to matchwood. The bombs hissed as they descended, thunderous explosions followed and the air was filled with millions of splinters as huge columns of water gushed upward. The violence of the impact made us rigid with fear. I don't remember whether any other bombings took place later or not. What I do remember is that as soon as the plane disappeared we made straight for the nearest undamaged pontoon and crossed the Ebro. Once on the opposite bank, we marched along the railway line, parallel to the river, until sunset.

We found the battalion we had come to relieve up in the Sierra de la Fatarella Mountains. Firmly dug into trenches which zigzagged along the contour line halfway up from the valley floor, they could see the enemy, who were only three hundred metres away and equally securely entrenched. The two fronts juxtaposed each other in an uneven straggling line; sometimes our land protruded into enemy territory, in other places their line jutted into ours.

The changeover occurred next day. Those we relieved were returning for a well-deserved rest, for they had seen heavy fighting and in many cases had lost over 50 per cent of their men from death, wounds or defections.

Conditions on the front line were bad. Morale was low, discipline slack, and my fellow soldiers were full of complaints about the way the war was being conducted and talked frequently about going over to the enemy. All we Republicans ever had to eat was a plate full of lentils seasoned with lard or a trace of pork, day in day out, for breakfast, lunch and dinner.

Every night as the sun went down, the rebels would yell, 'Hey Reds, what've they given you to eat today? Lentils again?' Then they would regale us with details about their varied diet, the three or four courses available to them every meal and the wide variety of different dishes which they had to choose from. This would make many on our side decide to desert during the night.

After the opening verbal salvo about lentils would come amusing debates about a particular shot or a specific meal. Party rivalry and doctrinaire disputes were forgotten in curses and argument, insults and counterclaim. The mutual dissensions and recriminations would have been very comical had the situation not been so tragic.

I would walk up and down the front line checking my telephone cables and would chat with those in the trenches. From our side we could see the enemy clearly, and as soon as evening mess time was over and the sun had set the shouting contests would start. My company captain, a carpenter by trade, was quite happy to participate in exchanging pleasantries, but whenever the enemy dwelt on the exquisiteness of their food, feeling ran high and the number of desertions increased. Then drastic measures were taken. Our company barber, caught trying to escape, was executed in front of the whole battalion, but the stream of deserters continued; our hunger was too great.

Starving, disenchanted with life and longing for more congenial company, I decided to try to cross over to the 'enemy'. Looking back now I would never take such a hazardous risk again. To cross from Republican to Nationalist lines was the craziest thing I ever did in my long and adventurous existence.

About seven o'clock on a clear, moonlit evening, three of us prepared to desert. I took two hand grenades for reassurance although I had no intention of using them, but before I could slip out of my trench, my two companions jumped clumsily out of theirs and started a landslide of small pebbles which clattered as they rolled down the rocky hillside. A sentry heard the noise and raised the alarm. I hesitated for a moment and then started off, hotly pursued by a patrol. Confused, I made for a patch of pine trees, where I tried to hide. In no time I had completely lost my sense of direction, but I carried on and began to climb up the hill. Unfortunately, I was climbing up the very hill I had just come down, straight back into my own lines.

When I realised my error, I turned and raced back down the hill again, dodging the bursts of gunfire; taking huge strides, half sliding, half leaping, I soon reached the bottom, where I went to ground in a reed bed. I could hear the voices of the patrol hunting for me, thrusting the butts of their rifles into the reeds, rightly guessing me to be close by. After about fifteen minutes I heard them change direction, so I crept out of the reeds as quietly as I could and dashed up the hill – the right one this time – into a belt of pines.

I found a shallow ditch about the width of my body and slid in, covering myself over with leaves and twigs. I could have thrown my two hand grenades at the Republican patrol who were only a few feet below me, but my conscience held me back: although I was desperate, I recoiled at the carnage. The patrol stopped for a smoke and, just before some rain clouds obscured the moon, I caught a glimpse of their silhouettes, they were so close. There were six of them. I lay there shaking with fear and covered in sweat, waiting for them to return to their lines.

As soon as I heard the Nationalists start their customary evening banter, 'Hey, Reds, what've they given you to eat today?', I decided to move, using their voices as a guide. I took off my boots, so as to get a better grip on the slippery gravel slope, and left them and my hand grenades in the ditch.

Slowly, taking great care, I began to clamber up the hill, across some terraced fields and over a couple of walls. Suddenly, I heard voices very close. I got such a fright, I must have passed out, for phrases seemed to echo through my head as if in a nightmare: 'Don't worry now, lad' and 'We're coming to you'. Recovering, I raced to the top where I found my two companion escapers. They'd made it across in a matter of minutes, while I was exhausted, hungry and bleeding.

They told me that when the Republicans started firing the rebels had asked them what was going on and they had said that there was a third person out there trying to escape. Whereupon the rebels had begun their nightly exchange of views while they sent out a patrol to search for me, presuming I had got lost.

For two days we slept in our new trenches and ate and ate. When another escapee joined us, he told us that the Republican patrol had eventually found the ditch where I'd been hiding and had discovered my boots and hand grenades. It had been a wild and suicidal idea to escape and I swore never to embark on anything so dangerous again '... world without end. Amen'.

My naive hopes that, after a few explanations, I would be sent to the rear were shallow fantasies. Endless hours of interrogation followed before we ex-Republicans were put in goods train wagons for Saragossa. Once there, we spent the night in the corridors of the military academy before being taken by passenger train to a concentration camp at Deusto in the Basque area of northern Spain.

We were imprisioned in the university and slept on the bare floorboards of the lecture halls. Every morning we would wake up to find ourselves covered in lice of every shape and size. There was a real plague of them: they would creep into the folds of our skin, burrow into private crevices and roam around inside our clothes. The only place we had to wash in was the ornamental fountain in the middle of the university campus and, given the number of people in the place, it was always packed to capacity. Every morning we would push and shove and struggle to get a little trickle of water. Lice races were a common pastime, some even betting their food on the results since Republican coins were not recognised currency to the Nationalist rebels.

I had been eating as much as I could get hold of since changing sides but, after such a long period of semi-starvation, my stomach reacted violently and I could hold nothing down. Wracked with pain, I took refuge in the infirmary where they fed me light broths and milk.

However, I didn't give up. I had managed to preserve my fountain pen throughout all my escapades and I now sold this to one of the camp guards at a slight loss. With the rebel currency he gave me I bought a cheap pen, paper, envelopes and stamps and began to write to all my friends and relatives, especially those on my mother's side who were living in Grenada. I asked them for financial help and if they would vouch for me so that I could be let out. Some wrote back with vague propositions, a few made equivocal promises, while fewer still enclosed money but never enough to be of much help.

But one person to whom I had written did respond positively: he was the Reverend Father Caledonio Ocen, Brother Superior of the Order of St John of God, a very old friend of my father's and head of the psychiatric hospital at Palencia, near Santander. He made the long journey to the camp and personally presented himself to the authorities, where he spoke on my behalf, making himself answerable for my actions and vouching on oath that I was honest, apolitical and a Christian.

You can imagine my joy at seeing him: it was an unforgettable moment. Although he died a fair number of years ago, I remain eternally grateful to him for what he did and always hold the fondest memories of his kindness toward me. On his way back to Palencia he called in at Burgos, the Nationalist capital, and stirred matters up to such an extent that three days later the order for my release arrived at the camp. At his request, I spent a week in his hospital at Palencia and was then sent to join the Nationalist troops at the St Marcial barracks in Burgos. This time I enlisted under my true age.

At my first medical examination they diagnosed acute bronchitis and sent me back to the hospital for twelve days. Then they allowed me to convalesce at a *Frente y Hospitales* rest centre in Burgos, where I sat about playing cards and gossiping. Many local girls of good standing contributed to the war effort by helping with the wounded there, and one in particular interested me greatly for she was good looking and played the piano extremely well. Although my knowledge of music was rudimentary, my ear was good, so I would sit beside her and we played duets. We soon became great friends and I would accompany her to mass each morning. Eventually, I asked her to become my 'war mother', which she accepted, and we saw even more of each other. I discovered that she worked as a clerk in the war ministry for General Dávila.

When I had enlisted at the St Marcial barracks in Burgos I had not only given my true age but I had also told them that I had originally been conscripted in 1933, had served six months and had ended up as a second lieutenant in the reserve. On learning this, my case was forwarded to the army's legal department and I was placed under the command of a lieutenant colonel in charge of investigating my anomalous position.

While I waited to take up my commission, I was temporarily awarded three stripes, but was only given a third of a full officer's pay, which was very little. So in order to cut down on my expenses, I decided to sleep in the St Marcial barracks, which meant that I had to report to the commanding officer, a martinet, every evening for roll call.

Somewhere around the beginning of November 1938, the people of Burgos decided to hold a demonstration in honour of Francisco Franco and his rebel Nationalist army to celebrate the opening of his attack on the Catalan front. I was asked to join a group from *Frente y Hospitales* and surged along with the throng. During all the excitement, an enthusiastic Catalan soldier exchanged his Carlist red beret for my military cap. It was strictly forbidden for a regular army soldier to wear any political insignia and such behaviour was always severely punished, even though the Carlists were one of the motley band of militia which made up the Nationalist army. I was well aware of the rule, but had not thought that it applied that day as it was not a military occasion. Unfortunately, however, the commanding officer of the St Marcial barracks had seen me exchanging headgear from the balcony of the Burgos military headquarters.

That evening, when I returned to the barracks for roll call, the duty Sergeant asked me to report to the arms hall, where an officer was waiting for me. He led me to the commander's room. I went in and stood at attention. The commander then asked me if I had been wearing a Carlist red beret during the demonstration earlier that afternoon. I replied that I had, and explained that a Catalan had swapped my cap for his beret. He asked me to hand over the beret and, when I told him I didn't have it, he gave me two vicious slaps to the face which nearly knocked me over. Shouting insults, he tore the stripes off my uniform and sent me to a prison cell for the night.

Admittedly, I was at fault, but I did not feel that I'd done anything heinous enough to deserve having my face slapped and the stripes torn off my uniform.

I was rudely awakened before dawn and taken to a dormitory where about fifty soldiers were putting on full battle kit. Without any explanation, I too was kitted out and issued with a rifle and ammunition. A corporal then marched us to the station. I asked the corporal where we were going, to which he replied that we were off to the front at Teruel. I couldn't believe my ears and didn't know what to do. I thought of telephoning my war mother, but she did not have a phone and, even if she had, I would never have dared ring her up at that early hour. Demoralised and frightened, I got on the train with the rest. They joked and laughed as we rumbled along, but I felt too miserable to join in; I just stood there, trying to think of a way out of my predicament. I kept badgering the corporal with questions. From him I gathered that we would change trains at Calatayud and continue on to a small village near Teruel, from where we would trek up the mountains by mule. I also tried to get some answers from some of the soldiers in my detachment. Although many were raw recruits, some were experienced veterans returning from leave. One of the latter told me that the part of the front line we were off to was cold and wild and overrun by rats. Any soldier who killed a hundred was automatically given a week's leave. He'd obviously become quite an expert: he'd kept reporting to the quartermaster with all the rodents he'd caught and so had managed to get two weeks' leave in less than a year.

We finally reached Calatayud late in the morning and the corporal gave us permission to stretch our legs. I quickly found a phone and called my war mother in Burgos to tell her what had happened. She had been worried when I had not turned up that morning for mass and was relieved to hear my voice. Telling me not to worry, she said she would try to find out what could be done to help me. I then dashed off a letter to her giving her all the details again just to make doubly sure, and posted it before we caught the next train.

We got out at a little wayside station near Sierra de Santa Cruz in south-west Saragossa, where four mules were waiting to be loaded up with the various sacks and boxes we had brought with us. As we walked up the mountain, I chatted to the mule-teer and asked him about conditions at the front; he told me that the captain was a young, well-educated man from a noble family, a monarchist who took a great interest in the welfare of his men.

It took us about five hours to reach the top in a biting wind. On an arid patch of bare, flat land we saw soldiers marching at the double in order to warm themselves up, for it was the end of November and an icy wind blew down the mountain ridge, lashing our faces and bringing the temperature during the night down to below zero. Later, I was to find out that sentries took shorter turns than was customary here, but even so some ended up with numb hands and feet and had to be given brandy on being relieved.

I went straight to the captain and, standing to attention, said: 'Juan Pujol García, second lieutenant in the reserve, sir.' Raising his head, he cut me short: 'I haven't asked for officers. Anyway, why do you call yourself that when your papers say you're just a raw recruit?'

Briefly and bluntly, I explained what had happened, adding that my case was being looked into in Burgos and that I expected to be recalled any day. Puzzled, the captain pointed out that there was nothing he could do for me; however, he was most sympathetic and suggested I sleep in the sergeant's quarters. He put me in charge of a section and told me to keep them occupied.

I wrote to my war mother, giving her my new address. Twelve days later I received a parcel containing a pullover, a religious book, some sweets and a cake which she'd baked herself. But best of all there was an affectionate letter full of hope, assuring me that it wouldn't be long before I received orders to return to Burgos.

Three weeks later the captain sent for me and handed me orders to report to the military judge in charge of my case in Burgos. The captain seemed pleased that what I'd told him initially had indeed been the truth and congratulated me on having got everything sorted out. Next day I accompanied the mules down the mountain by the same route I'd come up just over a month before, only this time I was alone with the muleteer and feeling much happier.

On arrival at Burgos, I reported to my lieutenant colonel, who told me that I could make an official complaint about the St Marcial barracks' incident if I wished and explained to me exactly what this would entail, but he stressed that I must not forget that I would be reporting a commander... He had no need to finish as I understood exactly what he meant. I chose to take no action, merely making sure that I never entered the St Marcial barracks again. Instead, I rented a poorly furnished, but cheap, room by the San Pablo Bridge near the Espolón Promenade. Several times, while walking up and down the promenade in the evenings, I came face to face with the commander taking his wife to Our Lady of Carmel Church. I really enjoyed those encounters now that I had regained my stripes; I would look him straight in the eye as I saluted and then give a cheerful grin, as much as to say: 'Here I am alive and kicking although you sent me to the front.'

I had managed not to fire a single bullet for either side by the time Madrid fell a few months later, bringing the war to an end.

Luck continued to protect me. The day of the victory parade found me on leave in Madrid. Three weeks later my lieutenant colonel also arrived, delighted to be working in the capital at the centre of influence. When we met as arranged, he said that he would continue to investigate my case, but meanwhile I could return to Barcelona.

Two months later I reported to him again in Madrid and he gave me back my graduation certificate, on which was written the rank I had been given when I left Barcelona's Seventh Light Artillery Regiment.

The civil war was over, reputedly leaving behind a million dead, innumerable cities destroyed, a ruined economy and a long trail of suffering and desolation. Larra's words, written a century before, seemed apposite: 'Here lies half of Spain, killed by the other half.' Life in Madrid that hot summer of 1939 was tough: food was scarce, the black market was booming, prices were extortionate and I did not have a job. However, I had got to know a woman of gypsy extraction called Señora Melero, owner of the Hotel Majestic in Calle Velázquez, who was advertising for a manager. Although the hotel had been taken over by the International Brigade during the Nationalists' siege of Madrid and was in a pitiable state as a result, with its central heating system completely shattered, I took the job. A young Spanish aristocrat, calling himself Enrique, Duke of La Torre, gave me a reference. He seemed to be on Christian-name terms with two ageing ladies whom he called aunts and pompously alluded to as princesses of Bourbon, but in truth I never discovered who he really was.

My life in Madrid as a hotel manager began peacefully enough, apart from the odd difficulty inevitable in such a job. But as the days wore on, the problems increased, particularly structural ones as there was no money for repairs, nor the necessary capital to bring the hotel up to even the most basic standard of comfort and elegance. Nor were there enough adequately trained staff because of the war: many were still in uniform, others were stranded far from their homes. All the responsible, skilled workers already seemed to have jobs; those who came my way were either irresponsible or lacked the qualities needed for working in a three-star hotel. The truth was it didn't even deserve one star, let alone the name Majestic, for the lack of central heating in the winter made the nights unbearable. All I could do was sort out daily problems as and when they arose, with varying degrees of success.

But there were greater problems than those posed by the hotel which made me far more upset. On 3 September 1939 England had declared war on Germany. The contest had been foreseen but, like the wavering flame of an oil lamp, there had been a glimmer of hope that peace might prevail. It was a tug of war between the democracies on one hand and the Axis on the other. The future for Spain looked gloomy; to sit around a table with either Hitler or Mussolini would be like trying to plough sand. Both dictators seemed to be driven by the spirit of revenge, especially the one ruling the Germany of his dreams. I could see another catastrophe looming over the horizon and thought more than once about leaving Spain where hatred, and thirst for vengeance between victor and vanquished, was rife. When the chance presented itself, I seized it avidly.

It was extremely difficult in those days to get hold of a passport unless one could produce an excellent reason. One day, the Duke of La Torre, whom I now called Enrique, told me that his aunts were upset because they were unable to buy any Scotch whisky in Madrid and they considered such a drink essential, given their social position and entertaining commitments. So I suggested to him that since these princesses must wield considerable influence, it was surely possible for them to purchase the whisky abroad. All they needed to do was to get hold of some passports and head for Portugal; if they crossed the border at Estremadura and continued to Évora, they would be able to buy as many bottles there as they liked. 'Rest assured,' I told him, 'if we accompany your aunts, there'll be no problems.'

And that is how I managed to lay my hands on a document which at the time was nearly impossible to obtain. Even if my new passport was only valid for Portugal, it had great possibilities for the future.

With four of these documents in our possession, we left for Portugal in their car, with me acting as chauffeur. When we got to the border I produced the two princesses' passports and the guards leapt to attention. They raised no objections to our crossing, especially when I told them that we were only going as far as Évora. We bought half a dozen bottles of good Scotch and put them in the boot; the customs police didn't even search the car at the frontier on the way back.

I was really pleased with my brand new passport, although I soon learned that it was one thing to have a passport and quite another to obtain an exit visa, which was only issued in exceptional circumstances.

The first months of the Second World War saw Poland overrun despite heroic resistance. But what could that country have done before the might of Germany and Russia when these two had signed a secret pact first and then proceeded to carve up Poland between them? In April 1940 Germany invaded Norway and Denmark, and in May unleashed a lightning offensive on Holland and Belgium. The impregnable Maginot line was then outflanked and taken from the rear. Over a quarter of a million members of the British Expeditionary Force were pushed back to Dunkirk, from where most managed to escape across the Channel. England accepted the defeat with fortitude and became temporarily passive before a seemingly invincible enemy spreading its Nazi doctrine right across Europe.

4

MADRID

Ever since the world began, the race of Cain has experienced first birth, then murder and dishonour and finally death...
Ramón de Campoamor, El Licenciado Torralba

If a Pythian oracle had foretold the chequered existence that lay before me, I would have sneered sarcastically at the soothsayer, so little intention did I have of behaving in the way I actually did.

When I was a boy, I had considered war to be an inexorable scourge, a cruel and severe punishment sent by a relentless and harsh providence for our sins. But I found it difficult to continue to hold this view after I had been through the vicissitudes of our civil war when some people, in the name of the fatherland and of freedom, had wilfully imposed their views on us; we had been forced to submit to the diabolical dogmas of the perpetrators, who were themselves devilish creatures, able instigators of a new apocalypse.

Now I began to hear words like 'aryan', 'race' and 'superior being' on the radio and also saw them printed in newspapers and magazines. Such words had meant nothing to me up till now but I soon learned that, under cover of notions such as these, ordinary citizens in Germany were being harassed, citizens whose only crime was either not being aryan or children of the race, or who refused to believe in the cult of a superior being. Now the Germans were being forced to submit to diabolical dogmas just as we had been during our civil war; only it seemed that in Germany these things were being done in order to furnish Germany with new and wider frontiers. The artful tricks devised by the German leaders to bamboozle their population never ceased to amaze me, lacking as they did any moral, ethical or even rational sense. Those Germans who were subject to such doctrinaire propaganda were obviously not as much to blame for what happened later as those who preached such a socialist policy. It was a brand of socialism where the owner did not have his cow requisitioned, just milked dry.

The people, the great masses, followed their idol in raptures of frenzy. Using a variety of arguments, he continued to harangue them and to demand their submission. What a farce!

The March 1933 elections had given Hitler power; the contest, his contest, his *Mein Kampf*, was inaugurated the day he masterminded the burning of the Reichstag, for which he blamed his enemies, especially the communists and other extreme Left groups. What started as a witch-hunt ended in the extermination of whole peoples. To confuse matters even more, Hitler decided to change Anton Drexler's German Workers' Party into the German Nationalist–Socialist Workers' Party, whose members went on to proclaim themselves Nazis. Here was a poisonous potion indeed.

Socialism is a word used too lightly today. The concept was first introduced by those who pioneered social reform; people nowadays classed as Utopian socialists. They attempted to outline the ideal society, appealing for justice, ethics and a rejection of capitalism in order to bring about their ideal. They were thinkers like Charles Fourier, Henri de Saint-Simon, Robert Owen and Pierre Leroux, who was the first one to use the word 'socialism' in 1832. But these idealists failed, ruining their financial backers. It wasn't until there was a break between the bourgeoisie and the proletariat, around 1848, that Marx and Engels propounded systematic modern socialism, the one we now call Marxist. Even since then, various socialist tenets have taken root in different countries. A great many people have yearned to make the word their own, hoping to attract the huge dispossessed masses who long for a better life which they feel they have been denied. Some call themselves social democrats, others Christian socialists, and those who are attached to the communists declare themselves to be Marxist socialists. Some just call themselves socialists, while there are those who borrow the name of the doctrine but succeed in distorting it to such a degree that only the name prevails. The Germans called it National Socialism; the Italian Fascist movement was defined as 'political, social, corporate and hierarchical'; Portugal's Corporativismo was described as a 'method of collegiate political and social unity where the body politic intervenes in a qualitative, but not quantitative, manner in the policy of the nation', a rule defended by António de Oliveira Salazar.

The Spaniards, not to be outdone, proclaimed themselves falangistas, from phalanx, thereby creating for themselves a party as full of long-winded words in its definition as it was devoid of coordinating principles. Its name was as allegorical as it was contradictory. It was a monster of a name: Falange Española Tradicionalista y de las Juntas de Ofensiva Nacional-Sindicalista, the last stretch being abbreviated by its followers to JONS. Some socialist winds even reached America, initiating such parties as Acción Democrática in Venezuela and APRA, the American Popular Revolutionary Alliance, founded by Haya de la Torre in Peru in 1924. In Argentina, Perón's followers too laid claim to socialism, underlining their claim by calling themselves 'The Ragged'. I could go on naming the various branches and twigs of what is a very old notion, but I won't; I will just point out the curious fact that all these systems have both very strong dictatorial and liberal connotations within their different theories. The term socialism has been borrowed by dictators and democrats alike, which has resulted in definitions as complex and various as the night is from the day.

Two dogmatic and important politicians of this century took up socialism and transformed it into Nazism and communism. Both systems were implanted at the expense of countless victims. The first ended with the death of its leader at the end of a war which he himself had brought about; the other still prevails, hovering over the whole world, still dreaming of an empire of submissive nations subject to its power and authority. I do not mean to offend anyone who might profess these ideas as, above all, I am a man who loves democracy, which makes me respect, even if I do not share, these doctrines of theirs. I have friends who are communists; others who are anarchist in their outlook; yet other friends of mine support right-wing dictatorships which are such common phenomena in South America. 'Each one to his own taste,' I say. It is their choice. I too have my own ideas, many of which people will not share. Am I the odd one out? Am I wrong or are they?

Let us return to history. Concentration camps for political prisoners started in Germany in 1933 when the Nazis came to power. At first they were meant to re-educate or eliminate anti-Nazi Germans, that is to say, they were for communists, social democrats, Jews, Catholics and Protestants. After the occupation of Poland, which sparked off the declaration of war in 1939, camps of this type proliferated. Thousands of Poles and people from other countries occupied by the Nazis began to fill these camps, creating a huge reserve of servile workers for the German war machine. To use an expression coined at the Nuremberg Trials, it was 'extermination through work', with inmates working shifts of up to twelve hours and more a day sustained by scant nourishment and little rest. Soon the Nazis systematically began to exterminate and eliminate the so-called inferior races: Jews, gypsies, Slavs and, to a lesser extent, Latins and Arabs. They became fuel for the camp crematoria.

In Spain few knew of these horrors. But, despite censorship, word eventually spread about the horrifying deeds perpetrated by those butchers who carried out the orders of their superior officers in Himmler's SS. Their monstrous behaviour was such that even those who had admired the German Kondor Legion in the civil war were stunned by the appalling information that was seeping through.

My humanist convictions would not allow me to turn a blind eye to the enormous suffering that was being unleashed by this psychopath Hitler and his band of acolytes, the very same people who had murdered Röhm and other political adversaries on the Night of the Long Knives in 1934.

But what could I do to arrest such excess? Little, very little, in fact practically nothing except to talk *sotto voce* about the terrible crisis already hanging over humanity. In my hours of loneliness I would be tormented by odd pieces of information and graphic details, which merged in my imagination into a confused and horrible nightmare. Unable to express my feelings, I yearned for justice. From the medley of tangled ideas and fantasies going around and around in my head, a plan slowly began to take shape. I must do something, something practical; I must make my contribution toward the good of humanity.

One January day in 1941 I presented myself without further ado at the British embassy in Madrid, Britain being the only European country to have preserved her independence and to be challenging the Germans in a war that was clearly going to be long and bloody. On arrival, I asked for an interview with one of the diplomatic attachés as I had something I wished to reveal. The man at the reception desk, a Spaniard, asked me exactly what it was I wanted to talk about. As my replies were somewhat vague, he handed me on to one of the secretaries in reception.

It is always difficult, not to say impossible, for a stranger to speak to a senior official in an embassy of an important country, but much more so when war is raging, as it was for the British, although Spain, of course, was neutral. And so I was sent from receptionist to secretary, from clerk to minor official, each one of whom expressed an interest in finding out or getting me to clarify exactly what it was I wanted to say in the confidential interview I sought. Finally, one of them said that the staff at the Foreign Office were far too busy to comply with requests for interviews like the one I was after. If I believed what I had to say was of crucial importance, then I could put it in writing, giving a detailed account of my motives.

Although a newcomer to these pursuits, I wasn't so naive as to think that it would be a good idea to put down my intentions in writing, even if they were none other than to put myself at the disposal of British Intelligence. I wanted to work for them, to supply them with confidential information which would be of interest to the Allied cause, politically or militarily, data which I hoped I would be able to obtain.

I must confess that my plans were fairly confused. I intended to go on living in Madrid while I made use of contacts and acquaintances who did not yet exist but were still just figments of my imagination. I was well aware that my ideas lacked clarity and that it would be difficult to make headway while my suggestions were so hazy, so I started to look around for helpful contacts and kept an eye open for any jobs which might eventually turn out to be useful, such as an opening in journalism or the chance of becoming one of those who kept watch on Nazi supporters.

No one at the British embassy seemed interested in me, so out of *amour-propre* I decided to prepare the ground more carefully before I approached them again; clearly, I must be much more specific about exactly what I was going to do and how it would adapt itself to the end I had in mind: helping the Allies.

I decided to attempt to sound out the opposite side, but using a different approach to the one I had tried with the British, which had ended in rejection. Bit by bit, I worked out my plan of attack until I thought it was good enough. I did not ask anyone else's advice.

In order to offer myself to the Nazis, I first studied their doctrines, then I telephoned the German embassy and asked if I could talk to the military attaché as I wanted to ask him to put someone in touch with me as soon as possible, because I was willing to offer my services to the Axis cause and to that of the 'New Europe'. They suggested I ring back the next day, when they would give me an answer. The person at the other end of the line spoke slowly in a firm, guttural voice, in far from perfect Spanish. However, he had sounded hopeful, so maybe I would be able to speak to someone who had the power to make decisions.

I rang back the next day at about the same time. After a pause, I heard that same guttural voice that had spoken to me before. The voice told me that a fair-haired gentleman with blue eyes, dressed in a light suit and carrying a raincoat over his arm, would be sitting waiting for me at one of the tables at the far end of the Café Lyon at 4.30 p.m. next day. He said that the man would be called Federico and asked for details of what I would be wearing for the rendezvous and for a brief description of what I looked like. He then asked my name, which I gave him, and rang off. My contact with the Germans had started.

I went to the café in Calle Alcalá at the appointed time and found a young German sitting alone at a table who identified himself as Federico. His Spanish was fluent, without a trace of a foreign accent. Harbouring real hopes that my plan would succeed, I began to make use of my gift of gab and ranted away as befitted a staunch Nazi and Francoist. At first I seemed to be holding the man's attention, although he did not show much interest in my fervour for the Führer and the Third Reich, even if he was glad to know I was enthusiastic. After a bit it dawned on me that I wasn't making such a good impression on him as I'd first imagined, for he kept asking me what exactly it was I thought I could contribute toward the success of the war. He was clearly proud of Germany's victorious advance, although every now and then he would stress that many hard and bloody days lay ahead. I tried to minimise the problems, repeatedly emphasising that what had already been achieved was extraordinarily magnificent and that victory lay inevitably with 'our' side. But he continued to try to pin me down, to make me explain exactly why I had requested the interview, so I told him that I was at the complete disposal of his superiors for anything they wanted – I could work in the embassy and make contacts for them with people with access to information. I told him a thousand foolish things, such as that I had friends in official and diplomatic circles, and then I poured out more empty verbiage about National Socialism. At the end, he told me that he would have to talk to his superiors and would come back with an answer in two days. He gave me a new rendezvous: next time it was to be the Cervecería de Correos beer house near Café Lyon, still in the Calle Alcalá but opposite the Ministry of Communications.

I spent the next two days dreaming up new rigmaroles about Nazism. But the second meeting was much easier because neither of us felt so tense; the awkwardness of our initial encounter had gone. After shaking my hand warmly, he told me in clear and forthright language that they were not in the least interested in any of my propositions; they just wanted material that would be of use to the Abwehr, the German semi-military intelligence and counter-intelligence service. To which I replied, somewhat rashly perhaps, that if they could get me a job as a foreign correspondent for a Spanish newspaper or magazine, I had what was necessary to travel to Britain, namely a passport. Once there, I'd be able to obtain information for them. Federico thought that a much more interesting alternative and asked for more time to think about it. I thought it best not to run for another interview too quickly, so told him that I was going to see my family in Barcelona – which in the end I never did – and that I would give him a call on my return.

After the civil war, General Franco's government was in dire need of foreign exchange. The Bank of Spain was heading for bankruptcy, for neither industry nor agriculture were in any position to earn money through exports. A big advertising campaign was launched requesting people to surrender their gold and jewellery to help the nation, but little was forthcoming. Then they asked if Spaniards with assets abroad – and those who had emigrated to America – would make their resources available to help the nation, but the results of this appeal only covered a few months' deficit. Finally, the Bank of Spain said that it would open all doors and offer every facility to anyone who could procure any foreign assets for the national coffers.

It occurred to me to pretend that my father had left funds and shares in Britain and that all the relevant documents were in a deposit box in a Portuguese bank. This story got me my exit visa in no time at all, with the additional help of a Basque-Cuban friend of mine, Zulueta, who held some honorary post with the Bank of Spain's currency police. Furnished with a passport and an exit visa for Portugal, I decided to leave Spain and to settle down in a country which offered better prospects for peace and security. Not that I had abandoned the possibilities opened up by my German contact in Madrid, but I had to earn a living and life at the Hotel Majestic was going from bad to worse.

To help me on my arrival in Portugal I had obtained a heavy gold chain from a relative, which I hid inside a wide belt in order to smuggle it through customs. I was careful not to arouse suspicion as there were stiff penalties for taking gold or jewellery out of the country. Once in Lisbon I stayed at the Hotel Suizo-Atlantico in Rua da Gloria, which was near both the Spanish consulate and the Spanish embassy. There was a large Spanish colony in Lisbon and I was determined to get to know as many of them as possible, beginning with the consular and embassy staffs.

I registered myself at the consulate as a Spanish resident abroad, alleging that I was a writer working in partnership with Luances, an Austrian poet living in Lisbon. Together we wrote two bilingual six-page pamphlets on what was happening in Europe, with Portuguese on one side and Spanish on the other, and sold about 10,000 copies of these to the various Allied embassies, who then gave them away free of charge as propaganda. I made sure that my signature was not on the pamphlets as I did not want my name spread around, least of all in foreign embassies.

I had thought that once in Portugal it would be easy for me to get a visa for Britain, which I would be able to show Federico when next we met, but when I went to the Spanish consulate to get one, they turned me down. The reason they gave was that as my passport had been issued by Madrid's General Police headquarters, I had to go there to get my visa. I replied that I didn't have enough money to return to Madrid before going on to England. I could only go if they would pay for my trip. 'I've only enough money to get to London. I am on Spanish territory in this consulate, so I think that in all fairness I have a right to have my case dealt with here.' But they were adamant, neither excuses nor reasonable explanations would move them; they stuck to their guns and would not budge.

But I too can be stubborn. I went to the Spanish embassy and asked to see the ambassador, Nicolás Franco, whose brother, General Francisco Franco, was dictator of Spain. I was dealt with by the ambassador's secretary, who, if my memory serves me right, was the Marquis of Merry del Val. I asked him if he would make my passport valid for a visit to Britain, as at the moment it could only be used for Portugal, but the interview turned sour. Several times I explained why I wanted to go to Britain and kept insisting on the right of any Spaniard to be provided by his embassy with the necessary documents in the country where he happened to be residing. But he claimed that there was nothing he could do to resolve this matter, only the consulate at the General Police headquarters in Madrid could do so. The more I talked, the more excited I got, until I threatened to destroy my present passport so that they would have to issue me with a new one, which they would then be empowered to extend.

Angrily, I pointed out that I was a Spaniard away from home, unloved and helpless, standing in my own embassy, which international law had established was territorially a piece of my own country, so why should I have to return to Spain for a visa? As my fury increased, my voice rose higher and higher until the ambassador himself appeared to ask what on earth was going on. Immediately, I reeled off all my arguments again. The ambassador assured me that he would try to solve my problem and courteously asked his secretary to take down my particulars; then he suggested that I leave.

I returned to my hotel a little happier, although my problems were by no means over, but I placed great hopes on the ambassador's assurances. But days went by and I heard nothing, which was very worrying for it was becoming increasingly urgent that I return to Madrid to renew my contact with my German friend Federico. Just as I was getting desperate, I met someone who influenced me to take an entirely different course of action.

The owner of the hotel where I was staying was a Galician who'd been living in Lisbon for some time and done very well for himself; he now introduced me to another Galician staying in the hotel, who showed me with great pride what he claimed was his special diplomatic visa. This was a sheet of paper headed Ministry of Foreign Affairs and embossed with the arms of Spain, underneath which was a typewritten text asking that every assistance be extended to Señor Jaime Souza, who wished to travel to Argentina; below the text was the ministry's rubber stamp and an indecipherable signature. This document was produced by the owner with a great flourish, for he thought himself very important because of it. He told me that he was waiting for a seat on the Pan American hydroplane to South America, but that there was such a demand for places that he did not know for sure when he would be leaving.

I resolved to become better acquainted with the owner of such a magnificent document and spent many evenings cultivating his friendship, visiting local amusement parks, night clubs and cabarets with him. He was older than I, a paunchy fellow who dressed well and gave the impression of a man of means, for he was always waving away my attempt to pay for tickets and meals. Being a Galician, his command of Portuguese was better than mine and he would translate jokes and repartees for my benefit, particularly when we went to some light review where the plot turned on a country yokel's visit to town. Jaime always had an excellent grasp of the intricacies and subtleties of the story and would make sure that I understood what was being said.

We spent many warm nights at terrace cinemas where we could sit drinking while we watched the film; other nights we would frequent cafés where *fados* were sung, those sorrowful Portuguese laments full of inconsolable woe which are not unlike Seville's *saetas* with their poetry, their love and their melancholic nostalgia. I have heard *fados* sung many times since, but none with the intensity they had in those Lisbon cafés, which were shrines of tradition.

In order to repay him for his generosity, I decided to ask Jaime to visit the casino at Estoril with me, although my finances were in a parlous state. I had sold the heavy gold chain brought from Spain, but had spent nearly all the money and now had no other source of income.

My invitation was not entirely without an ulterior motive. I wanted to take a photograph of Jaime's diplomatic visa without in any way hurting him; honour after all demands loyalty to friends. If I could make a copy of such a document, I could show it to Federico as proof that I was serious about my projected trip to England, so I proceeded to borrow a sophisticated camera.

We put up at the Monte-Estoril Hotel, which was near the Lisbon–Cascais coastal railway line and only about three streets away from the casino. We not only shared the same room but we each put 10,000 escudos into a common purse to gamble with and agreed to split our gains and losses evenly between us. We played with great caution, moderation was our motto, and ended the week slightly up on what we had started with.

One afternoon, while we were gambling at the casino, I began to complain of abdominal cramps and told Jaime that I'd have to go back to the hotel but I hoped it wouldn't be for too long; I suggested he continue to play as we seemed to be on a winning streak. Once back at the hotel, I quickly photographed his diplomatic visa and then returned to the casino.

At the end of the week I paid both our hotel bills and was able to leave Estoril with only a few escudos less than I'd had on arrival. Once back in Lisbon, I had two enlargements made of the photograph I'd taken. I then cut the Spanish coat of arms off one of the enlargements, took it to a firm of engravers and asked them to make me a plate. Armed with this plate and the other enlargement, I went to an old printing works – Bertrand Irmãos, 7 Rua Condessa do Rio – and, posing as someone from the Spanish Chancery staff, gave them the plate and the enlargement and ordered 200 copies. When these had been printed, I collected them without anyone asking any questions and then went elsewhere to order an identical rubber stamp to the one visible in the enlargement. Using the same false identity as before, I said nonchalantly that the previous stamp had deteriorated to such an extent that it was now useless. I never knew, nor indeed was interested in finding out, whether or not they believed my story: all I do know is that having been paid, they produced the stamp.

Jaime had been ringing Pan American Airways every day to see if there was any chance of him getting a seat; he was worried that a long delay might lead to his trip being cancelled altogether. To help him, I suggested that he sound out one of the airline staff about his chances or give someone there a tip so that he was offered the first seat that came up. I presume he did as I suggested, for a few days later he left for South America on what he called a 'political and cultural mission', without once having suspected any of my stratagems.

Although I still hadn't a very clear idea of exactly how I was going to make use of my newly printed visa forms, I did not think I'd need very many, so I got rid of all but ten or twelve; it was going to be difficult enough to smuggle even that number back into Spain as it was. If I was returning to Spain, you may well ask, why ever had I come to Portugal in the first place? Well, I had come with the sole aim of being classified as a Lisbon resident. This, you may argue, was not in itself of great value. But I always considered it exceptionally important, for it meant that I would never have to apply for an exit visa again, as I now qualified as permanently resident abroad, and this would enable me to move about much more freely.

I was fully aware of the risks I was running and always had a lurking fear that my whole operation would suddenly collapse, but as I seemed to have managed so far without raising any suspicions, I carried on with my plan to return to Madrid. I was just trying to decide how I would smuggle in the wad of visa forms with their official-looking seals when I received a summons to the Spanish consulate.

It was only three weeks since my contretemps there, so I was very surprised when one of the consular officials greeted me with: 'What influential people have you been stirring up, Señor Pujol? Who are your friends in high places?' As he said this, he handed me a telegram from Madrid, which asked that I be granted visas for Europe, excluding Russia, and the whole of America, except for Mexico. It was signed Colonel Beigbeder, Minister for Foreign Affairs. It was indeed a shock, for it was much more than I had ever dreamed of getting, and with this and my Lisbon residency permit I need no longer worry about a few sheets of embossed and rubber-stamped paper. However, I held on to them because, as the popular Spanish saying has it, a mouse is lost if he only has one means of escape, for if he fails to reach it, that's the end.

I returned to Madrid in the early spring of 1941 and put up at a small bed-and-breakfast lodging house on the Gran Via. More enthusiastic than ever, I was ready for action. I telephoned Federico and arranged to meet him at the Café Negresco near the Bank of Spain on the way to the Puerta del Sol.

The meeting was much longer and more fruitful than either of the others had been. I began by telling him that I had been to Portugal instead of Barcelona, and then invented a long, fictitious story about my friends the Zulueta brothers; through them, I said, I had been approached by the Bank of Spain's Foreign Exchange Police section and asked to go to Portugal on their behalf to contact a man who wished to buy pesetas in exchange for escudos. I said that I had monitored the transaction and brought the escudos into Spain, while the pesetas were to be handed over to the Portuguese man's trusted contact in Madrid. Interspersing lies with the truth, I explained to Federico that my main interest in the transaction had been to get to Lisbon in order to become a resident there and so gain a resident's visa, both of which I had accomplished. I hoped this proved to him that I was able to move both in and out of Spain.

We then started to talk about the possibility of my taking up residence in Britain and I told him how easy that would be for me now that I had a new passport with a valid visa; all I needed was a motive for being there, such as a job as correspondent for a Spanish newspaper or magazine. He agreed to study my suggestions in depth and we made a new appointment to meet at a later date. In the end we had more than five interviews.

However, it was clear from these interviews that I would have great difficulty in becoming the British correspondent of a Spanish newspaper: most papers already had people accredited to London as it was the nerve centre for Allied news. I decided I would have to think up some other idea.

Frederico seemed to be utterly convinced by my Portuguese stories, so I decided to explore this seam in greater depth. As I have already explained, many people at this time were involved in dubious currency deals which creamed off the escudo at the expense of the peseta, so I decided to tell Federico that, as I was already an old hand at catching such people, I had offered to go to Britain for the Zulueta brothers in order to hunt down those gullible and naive enough to carry out such deals. I said that I was waiting for their answer and asked him what mission the Abwehr would entrust me with if my deal with the Zuluetas came off and they sent me to England.

More meetings followed; I think I visited more cafés at this time than during the whole of the rest of my life. If I wasn't meeting Federico in the Aquarium, it was at Calatravas or the Maison Doré, or one of the many other cafés in the centre of town. He was becoming increasingly interested and spent hours advising and training me. After a month, however, it was clear that I was the one making the running.

As I was anxious to speed things up and finalise our deal, I told Federico that I had an important document to show him. We were sitting in a café so, feigning extreme caution, I slid a piece of paper out of my pocket and pushed it toward him under the table, making sure that no one else in the café saw it. It was one of the bits of paper I had had specially printed in Lisbon, now filled in with my name and giving me a diplomatic assignment to travel to London on a special mission for the commercial administrative department. I let Federico have a quick glance at it, then folded it up and put it back in my pocket. I asked him to keep my mission a secret as it was confidential and the government did not want anyone else to get involved. Finally, I told him that I was expecting to leave in about ten days' time. Federico swallowed the story, hook, line and sinker.

Looking back on this period of my life and analyzing the steps I took, I cannot but reflect that I was playing an extremely complicated and dangerous role. Either I was a great actor, as one of Ml5's officers, Cyril Mills (known to me as Mr Grey), later suggested, or Federico was exceptionally naive. But I don't think Federico was on his own; he must have had encouragement and support from people high up in the German Secret Service. I was personally convinced at the time that he had recruited me on the advice of his superiors; I am equally convinced that, intoxicated by my verbosity, he personally fought for all my suggestions, projects and plans and warmly recommended them to his superiors. But why he had such blind faith in me

I do not know. Whatever the truth of the matter, a few weeks after our first meeting, he brought me a bottle of invisible ink, some secret codes and the sum of $3,000, making sure that I had them in good time before I left for Britain. Then he briefed me about the kind of reports they expected me to send them.

Now that I had the invisible ink and the codes, I realised that it was dangerous for me to remain in Spain as any unexpected chance meeting could easily expose me. At first I thought of going to the British embassy in Madrid and showing them my new acquisitions to prove to them how wrong they'd been to brush me off, for I had no doubt whatsoever that these secret items would make it absolutely clear to the British that I had a valuable contribution to make to the democratic cause. But I was afraid of meeting someone I knew at the embassy, where so many of the staff were Spaniards. How could I be sure that the Germans had not planted an informer inside the British embassy?

In July 1941 I left Spain for Portugal, temporarily renting a room in Cascais from a poor fisherman and his wife. Later, I moved to a house in Estoril so that I could be more independent, but kept moving around so that I could not be traced, for it should not be forgotten that in those days Lisbon was the nerve centre for European espionage and counter-espionage: British, French, American, Italian and, of course, German intelligence agents were everywhere. Taking the most careful precautions, I now tried to contact the British again through their Lisbon embassy.

What follows may seem unbelievable but it is true. All my attempts to hand over my valuable new acquisitions, my ink and my codes, failed; I was quite unable to reach anyone of importance whom I felt I could trust at the British embassy. After all that I had done, all that I had gone through, all the subterfuges I'd invented, the deceptions and the chicanery, the tension and the strain, let alone all the time I had spent, I was no further forward than I had been when I made my first attempt.

It seemed utterly incredible and was the most bitter disappointment to me. I just could not understand why the British were so difficult when the Germans were so understanding and cooperative. Why, I kept on asking myself, was the enemy proving to be so helpful, while those whom I wanted to be my friends were being so implacable? However, I've always had a stubborn streak: I was determined not to give up but to continue my own bizarre form of espionage on my own; perhaps things would eventually change for the better.

5

LISBON

Juan Pujol's rejection by the British embassy in Madrid was not, as he suspected, an instinctive, bureaucratic refusal to get involved in espionage. In fact, the refusal had been motivated by altogether more complicated considerations.

In January 1941, when Juan approached the embassy, the British ambassador was Sir Samuel Hoare, formerly the home secretary in Chamberlain's government. His principal mission was to keep Spain out of the war, and he was so determined to avoid any diplomatic incident in the capital or elsewhere that he imposed severe restrictions on the work of the local British Secret Intelligence Service representative, Captain Hamilton-Stokes. Hamilton-Stokes was allowed very little discretion by Hoare, who made it perfectly clear that he strongly disapproved of SIS's activities and would not hesitate to send anyone home who breached his injunction. It was in these circumstances that Juan Pujol's offer to help the Allies had been turned down. No doubt Hamilton-Stokes had labelled the Spaniard a probable agent provocateur. Certainly, the primary function of the Nazi embassy, under Baron Eberhard von Stohrer, was to accommodate a substantial German intelligence presence. In contrast, the British contingent was tiny.

This is not to say, of course, that British Intelligence was inactive in Spain and Portugal. On the contrary, both of Britain's intelligence gathering agencies took a close interest in everything that went on in the Peninsula. The Security Service, known as MI5, maintained a Spanish counter-espionage section which identified enemy agents visiting the United Kingdom and the colonies, while SIS, its overseas counterpart, operated from a series of stations around the world. Most of these stations gave their staff cover as passport control officers, a manoeuvre which sometimes afforded them a measure of diplomatic protection and gave an opportunity to examine the credentials of those wishing to visit England. Although Sir Samuel Hoare had put an embargo on any potentially embarrassing secret service work in Madrid, the SIS station in Lisbon was able to conduct their affairs with the blessing of the ambassador, Sir Ronald Campbell. There the SIS head of station was Commander Philip Johns, a Royal Naval officer who, before the war, had served at the SIS station in Brussels. Johns's office was located on the second floor of the British embassy in the Rua do Sacramento à Lapa, and he operated under the cover title of the financial attaché, with the rank of second secretary.

Before returning to Juan Pujol's narrative, we should briefly examine the work of the wartime British intelligence apparatus and, in particular, the background of its ring of double agents. The fact that the British had gained experience in running such a system in the First World War had become known publicly in March 1920, when Captain Ferdinand Tuohy, a former British Intelligence officer, gave an account of a double agent operation in *The Secret Corps*. He described the case of a German spy named Carl Muller and revealed that 'after we had shot Muller we continued for three whole months to draw funds from Muller's German employer'. Tuohy's indiscretion was widely circulated, but it seems to have had little impact on the Germans. In any case, the Security Service, perhaps a little optimistically, had prepared the foundations of a repeat performance.

The first spy to join MI5's stable of double agents was Arthur Owens, a Welshman who had professed nationalist sympathies to the Abwehr while on a pre-war business trip to Germany. Owens subsequently reported his illicit contacts to the Naval Intelligence Division in London and was passed on to the Secret Intelligence Service. Codenamed SNOW by SIS, Owens was considered to be of doubtful reliability, even after he had surrendered a German wireless transmitter. The Security Service responded by adding Owens's name to a list of suspects who were to be detained upon the outbreak of hostilities in 1939. Owens was highly indignant at his arrest and suggested to his MI5 case officer, Major T. A. Robertson, that he be allowed to transmit messages, under supervision, to Hamburg.

This timely offer was MI5's first chance to lay the foundations of what was to become a massive deception campaign. Four months before the German invasion of Poland a French expert from the Deuxième Bureau had lectured a selected group of MI5 officers about the advantages to be gained from the development of a ring of plausibly run double agents. The audience had been suitably intrigued, but to date no suitable candidate had presented himself for recruitment; and the entire proposition rested on the 'turning' of an agent who had already established himself as a trusted source with his Abwehr masters. Arthur Owens qualified on every count and, under the supervision of a prison warder who happened to hold an amateur radio licence, made contact with an Abwehr station in Hamburg.

The Abwehr welcomed the dialogue with Owens, whom they had code-named JOHNNY, and the radio exchanges that followed seemed so promising that MI5 collaborated in the recruitment of two assistants to help Owens gather information. Both G.W. and CHARLIE were accepted by the Abwehr as members of JOHNNY's network, although both were Ml5's nominees. Gwilym Williams, whose initials made up his Security Service code name, was in reality a retired police inspector from Swansea who had proved useful to MI5 while serving in his retirement as a court official in London. Owens introduced him as a trusted member of the Welsh Nationalist Party and, late in October 1939, the deception was completed when SNOW and G.W. kept a rendezvous with their Abwehr controllers in Antwerp. One of the first results of this historic collaboration was the identification of the Abwehr paymaster in Britain, Mathilde Krafft, a German woman who had been living near Bournemouth. No time was wasted in arranging her arrest, although MI5 subtly ensured that the Germans could not blame SNOW for her detention.

In the months that followed, SNOW's spy ring expanded and more double agents were added to MI5's growing pack, although in reality most of them were entirely 'notional'. Instead of trying to find enough suitable nominees, a task hard enough in peacetime but fraught with extra difficulties during a war, MI5 opted for the more convenient arrangement of simply inventing plausible but non-existent personalities. This expedient gave MI5 total control over their reported activities, and would work so long as the enemy continued to trust SNOW and never demanded to meet their newly recruited spies. The Abwehr seemed delighted with SNOW's progress, and MI5 were equally pleased. Robertson's B1(a) section also grew, and a number of new MI5 officers were let into the secret of the double agents. Among them was a solicitor, John Marriott, and Cyril Mills, member of the famous Bertram Mills circus family. Both were to play important roles in the development of the GARBO case. In spite of the scale of their achievements, B1(a) operated with a relatively small staff, numbering some eight case officers (including one woman, Gisela Ashley, to handle any difficult female double agents) with a similar number of secretaries.

During the late summer of 1940, when a German invasion seemed imminent, the Abwehr stepped up their infiltration of agents into the British Isles and gave MI5 plenty of opportunities to capture the spies and 'turn' them. A special detention centre was discreetly established in an old nursing home in south-west London, where recent acquisitions could undergo the 'turning' process with the minimum of bureaucratic interference from the Home Office or military authorities. Designated Camp 020, Latchmere House provided a secure environment in which espionage suspects could be interrogated in complete isolation.

Among the first Nazi spies to be dealt with by the Camp 020 staff were SUMMER and TATE, two Abwehr volunteers who parachuted into England in September 1940, equipped with wireless sets, and were arrested almost immediately. After a brief period of resistance, both were persuaded to join the double-cross system, and TATE continued to deceive his controllers in Hamburg until the end of hostilities. Precise details of their cases are not relevant here and their full story can be found in *MI5: British Security Service Operations 1909–1945*.

In recent accounts of the double-cross system insufficient distinction has been made between those agents who volunteered their services, and were therefore trusted entirely, and those who had operated after a measure of duress, and were therefore kept in secure accommodation under constant surveillance. Considerable attention has been given to the latter variety – such as SUMMER and TATE, who were offered an unpleasant (and conclusive) alternative – because of the challenge they had initially presented to their interrogators. Of the four most successful MI5 double agents, BRUTUS, MUTT, TATE and GARBO, only TATE possessed the motivation to resist. All the others were already ideologically suited to the turning process and had never intended to genuinely complete their mission for the Abwehr. GARBO's case was to be unique because he had specifically set out to become a double agent. None of the others nurtured such a dangerous ambition and only stumbled into the espionage arena unintentionally.

The identification and arrest of the enemy's spies was one of the double-cross system's chief objectives, but gradually it became clear that MI5 had actually scooped up every Abwehr source in Britain. Because there were no independent agents left at liberty there was little chance of the enemy checking the information channelled to them from either the remaining spies who were operating under MI5's control or the non-existent notional agents. This unexpected result presented plenty of opportunities for perpetrating elaborate deceptions on the enemy, and the Germans unwittingly assisted the scheme by giving advance warning to what they supposed was their extensive espionage network of forthcoming additions in the form of parachute agents. In due course, dozens of schemes were devised and executed with considerable success, and a special committee drawn from all the main Allied armed services, known as the Wireless Board, was created to coordinate the activities of the double agents. There was, however, one further, crucial windfall, which was to prove extraordinarily valuable. It too was delivered by these early double agents, and was in the field of radio communications.

The one disadvantage of the W-Board was the seniority of its membership, which included SIS Chief Colonel Stewart Menzies, Director of Military Intelligence Major-General Beaumont-Nesbitt and Director of Naval Intelligence Admiral Godfrey. These officers were ideally suited to drawing up policy, but they were too far removed from the field to contribute much to the prosecution of B1(a)'s campaign, despite the efforts of Guy Liddell, the imaginative director of Ml5's counter-espionage B Division.

By Christmas 1940 MI5 had been able to analyse the wireless traffic of SNOW, SUMMER and TATE. All were transmitting on a regular schedule, and the Security Service was in the enviable position of being able to construct a message itself, and then watch and intercept its receipt and acknowledgment in Hamburg, followed by its recipherment for further transmission to Berlin. Because the exact wording of the original signal was known to Ml5's wireless branch, known as the Radio Security Service, it was a relatively straightforward matter to work backward and decrypt the Abwehr's own interim communications. In the absence of any local illicit traffic, a secret wireless interception station was constructed at Hanslope Park, some ten miles to the north of Bletchley, where huge radio masts were erected to pick up the Abwehr's signals. The ciphers given to SNOW and his companions provided the RSS with a head start in solving the Abwehr's most secret messages. And because MI5 had taken every German agent into harness, the RSS were able to focus their resources on the interception and decryption of the Abwehr's wireless communications. One experienced cryptanalyst, Oliver Strachey, led a team of scholars and academics who concentrated solely on this traffic and gradually succeeded in breaking into many of the signals passing between the Abwehr outposts in Lisbon and Madrid and its headquarters in Berlin. This profitable source, which ran in parallel to other, more famous cryptographic work by the 'Government Communications HQ' experts at Bletchley Park, gave Ml5's case officers a unique insight into the standing in Berlin of each individual double agent. Whenever an Abwehr message was solved, it was translated and then passed to the appropriate MI5 section under the code name ISOS, which had been formed from the initials of 'Intelligence Service Oliver Strachey'.

ISOS proved itself to be better than the information from any single Allied agent. The Germans transmitted huge volumes of signals between their various outposts and evidently believed their ciphers to be inviolate. Much of the traffic was of an administrative nature, but there was also plenty of material relating to future plans and, astonishingly, the movements and activities of individual agents. Naturally, the Germans took the precaution of referring to their sources of information by code names, but there were still useful clues in some of the texts. For example, one message might state that agent number 317 had just arrived in Cádiz and had checked into a named hotel. A quick look at the hotel register would betray the agent.

SIS developed a special organisation, designated Section V, to exploit ISOS and follow up any of its leads. For security reasons, Section V led a semi-independent existence and was headquartered in a country mansion near St Albans in Hertfordshire. By the end of 1941 SIS had posted specially briefed Section V officers to both Spain and Portugal. Kenneth

Benton was sent to Madrid (in spite of the ambassador's protests) and Ralph Jarvis, a merchant banker in peacetime and formerly a member of General Templer's intelligence staff with the ill-fated British Expeditionary Force in France, went to Lisbon. There he established an office in the British Repatriation Office, so as to avoid being too closely associated with Johns's passport control office.

MI5 quickly realised that every care had to be taken to protect both the double-cross system and Bletchley's 'most secret source'. Accordingly, the circulation of the ISOS decrypts was rigidly controlled. Measures to conceal the existence of the system itself were rather more complex. In January 1941, with the appearance of TRICYCLE, yet another German spy – of the real variety, equipped with a transmitter – the Wireless Board authorised the formation of a subgroup of specialist intelligence officers to develop the double-cross system further and coordinate the real and notional activities of their charges.

One problem associated with B1(a)'s work was the necessity to supply the enemy with a convincing volume of plausible intelligence. If MI5's double agents only communicated banalities while working in harness the Germans might understandably lose interest, and a valuable conduit would be lost to the Allies. But spicing the harmless information with more attractive tidbits required considerable skill and judgment, and a precise knowledge of future plans. It would be entirely counterproductive to guess at proposed operations and hope that coincidence did not bring the notional idea into conflict with reality. In such circumstances a well-meaning case officer might invent what he believed to be a non-existent military operation, perhaps a raid on a particular target in France, and then discover later that his chosen target had indeed been selected for attack. It would be equally embarrassing to suggest the location of a heavily camouflaged ammunition dump, and then learn that there was indeed some sensitive site located in the neighbourhood. If such an incident ever occurred, the military authorities would justifiably cease cooperating and the informal flow exchange of information, upon which B1(a) relied, would be jeopardised.

During the months of late 1940 B1(a)'s eight double agents were being serviced with a satisfactory amount of intelligence, but the routing required much more refinement. The Wireless Board itself met infrequently, owing to the elevated status of its members, who had many other demands on their time. The business of acquiring and collating information for the enemy was a trifle haphazard and was left largely to the initiative of the individual case officers. They would travel the country, acting out the role of their charges, and would note various items of interest. Before inserting such material into the texts of messages for delivery to the Abwehr, the case officers would secure an unofficial consent from the intelligence division of the interested authority. If, for example, TATE had been asked to confirm the location of a particular aerodrome in East Anglia, his case officer, Bill Luke, would ask Major Robertson to clear the information with the director of intelligence at the Air Ministry, Air Commodore Archie Boyle. As it happened, Boyle was one of Robertson's most enthusiastic supporters and probably would have given every assistance, but his views were not always shared by other senior intelligence bureaucrats who were doubtful about the advantages of giving the enemy our secrets. Less constructive colleagues opted for the altogether safer choice of substituting entirely innocuous or erroneous information. Such manoeuvres were less controversial and therefore easier to defend at a later date, but they also weakened the credibility of the agent in whose name it would be transmitted. In the interests of watertight security, only a few officers in the service intelligence departments could be advised about B1(a)'s work, and those who had not been indoctrinated were reluctant to disclose operational details without formal sanction. The ideal solution to the continuing dilemma was the introduction of a new coordinating body, staffed at a lower level than the Wireless Board and chaired by a non-partisan figure who could command everyone's respect. That man was J. C. Masterman, then a don at Christ Church, Oxford.

The son of a naval officer, Masterman had been educated at Osborne and Dartmouth before going on to graduate from Worcester College, Oxford, and Freiburg University. He was an accomplished athlete and played cricket, hockey and tennis for England. During the Great War he had been interned at Ruhleben, the notorious civilian prison camp constructed on a racecourse near Berlin, where he gave memorable history lectures and captained the camp's cricket team. His well attended courses were only interrupted by his brief absence early in August 1918, when he escaped. His four years in captivity made a lasting impression on Masterman who, along with many of his Oxford contemporaries, joined the intelligence corps in 1940. On 2 January 1941 Masterman took the chair of the Twenty Committee, so-called because of the two Roman numerals of double-cross.

Although Masterman was a newcomer to B1(a)'s work, his agile intellect soon grasped the intricacies of the operation. He was also assisted by a permanent committee secretary, John Marriott, who was also Robertson's deputy. The creation of the Twenty Committee, which coincided with the welcome arrival of TRICYCLE, marked a turning point for the Security Service. From this stage onward, the progress of each agent was monitored by the committee, with responsibility for the day-to-day running of each remaining in the hands of the individual MI5 case officer. The new scheme freed the case officers from the sometimes dangerous chore of collecting information. Instead, the Twenty Committee was required to obtain the cooperation of the services and supply the case officers with suitable material for the enemy's consumption. To cut red tape and expedite B1(a)'s plans, each service intelligence department was invited to second a representative to the committee. These liaison officers were thus able to serve the committee's interests and simultaneously allay the fears and suspicions of their masters.

The Twenty Committee met on a weekly basis during the course of the following four and a half years (until 10 May 1945) – a total of 226 times, usually on Wednesday afternoons. Although its composition was to vary, the longest serving members were Robertson, Bill Luke (who succeeded John Marriott as committee secretary), Martin Lloyd (the SIS representative), John Drew from the Home Defence Executive and Ewen Montague from the Naval Intelligence Division. Whenever necessity demanded it, individual B1(a) case officers attended the committee's meetings, and from the spring of 1942, Tomás Harris frequently dominated the proceedings on behalf of GARBO. From 1943 onward, when the American Office of Strategic Services created a counter-espionage branch, Norman Holmes Pearson was delegated from their London office to liaise with MI5. This crippled academic, then professor of literature at Yale University, was granted the unique privilege of sharing Masterman's office in St James's Street, and was therefore privy to all the Twenty Committee's secrets.

As the double-cross system grew more sophisticated, and the ISOS decoders gained in experience, so the demand increased for some plausible 'covers' to mislead the enemy. One vital objective was to convince the enemy that British Intelligence was no match for the Abwehr, and in September 1941 an opportunity presented itself for MI5 to demonstrate some deliberate ineptitude. The purpose of the exercise, which bore a close resemblance to the wretched experience of Carl Muller in the Great War, was to persuade the enemy that MI5 were novices in the art of running double agents, and an uncooperative double agent code-named SCRUFFY was the chosen vehicle.

SCRUFFY was a genuine German spy and his real name was Alphons Timmerman; he was a twenty-eight-year-old Belgian ship's steward. He had presented himself at the frontier at Gibraltar, claiming to have trekked across Europe. He had been given a passage to Holland, but by the time his ship had docked he had been betrayed by an ISOS text from Spain reporting the successful conclusion of the first part of his mission. The reference to Timmerman had been linked to a further ISOS message reporting that a Belgian recently recruited by the Abwehr was to have his pay sent straight to his mother, whose address was provided. Having landed at Glasgow, Timmerman underwent a routine examination at the Royal Victorian Patriotic School, the reception centre where all new arrivals were accommodated before being cleared for official entry into the United Kingdom. Headed by Major Ronald Hayler of Ml5's B1(d), this huge establishment in Battersea processed many thousands of genuine refugees, and a small number of enemy agents. During his RVPS examination Timmerman was found to be carrying an unusually large sum of money and the ingredients for making secret ink. He was promptly transferred to the harsher regime at Camp 020, where skilled interrogators extracted an admission that his mother was living in the same Belgian village that had been mentioned in the ISOS decrypt. A confession soon followed, and Timmerman was removed to Wandsworth Prison for trial and eventual execution. In the meantime, an MI5 officer corresponded, somewhat ineptly, with Timmerman's German controller, using his secret ink and his post office box number in a neutral country. The idea was to persuade the Germans that their agent was still at liberty. As soon as the details of his arrest were made public, it was hoped that the Abwehr would realise that Timmerman's correspondence had been faked by MI5. According to the theory, the Abwehr would then congratulate themselves on MI5's incompetence, demonstrated by their poor choice of agent. The Belgian was found guilty under the Treachery Act and sentenced to death, and the execution was duly carried out on 7 July 1942. As was customary in those days, a brief public statement was released the following day and carried in most newspapers. MI5 had calculated that immediately the official announcement had been spotted the Abwehr would realise that all the letters purporting to have been written by their agent had been forgeries. A detailed review of the Timmerman letters would have confirmed the deception and revealed a number of deliberate errors. All had been thoughtfully constructed by B1(a) and then inserted into the covert texts but, much to MI5's chagrin, the Abwehr appeared to ignore Timmerman's death notice and the deliberate mistakes. Instead of suddenly breaking off contact, as had been expected, the Abwehr continued the traffic as if nothing was amiss, and the Twenty Committee decided to abandon the exercise before it got completely out of hand. The Abwehr could hardly have failed to spot Timmerman's death notice, yet they seemed willing to continue with the bogus correspondence. Evidently, the Abwehr considered MI5 to be even less sophisticated than MI5 had anticipated or wanted!

Although this particular ploy failed, it is an illustration of the extraordinary lengths MI5 were prepared to go to in order to develop the double-cross system. On this occasion, a real German spy, SCRUFFY, had been hanged simply to promote MI5's interests. As it turned out, the execution had failed in its prime intelligence purpose, to demonstrate MI5's inefficiency. If anything, the episode, and certainly the Abwehr's apparent willingness to remain in contact with an agent they knew to be dead, illustrated how easily the enemy could be taken in.

By the time Pujol emerged on the scene the Allied intelligence Machine had accommodated the Twenty Committee and had given due recognition to its achievements. The double-cross system now embraced the entire Abwehr effort in Britain, and was poised on the brink of much greater successes. B1(a)'s ever-expanding stable of real and notional agents had completely eliminated every independent German spy and had enabled the port security staff to prepare reception committees for new arrivals. RSS cryptanalysts were supplying GCHQ with valuable clues to the construction of the enemy's latest ciphers, and their study of the opposition personalities had enabled them to build an accurate order-of-battle for both the Abwehr and the Sicherheitsdienst (SD). The B1(d) investigators at the Royal Victoria Patriotic School also benefited from the system because they frequently received advance warning of suspects. Clues from B1(a) also helped the B1(e) interrogators at Camp 020 to extract damaging admissions from even the most well-trained of spies. Most were genuinely astonished at the extraordinary depth of MI5's knowledge about the Abwehr's operations and intentions which, of course, had been obtained from the invaluable ISOS.

By the spring of 1942 the British intelligence machine had gained sufficient experience to carry the double-cross system into the dangerous area of large-scale strategic deception. The necessary foundation had been laid; all that was needed was a suitable agent.

6

GIBRALTAR

No one can be perfectly happy till all are happy.

Herbert Spencer

I had smuggled the $3,000 that Federico had given me in Madrid into Portugal without any trouble. I had rolled the money up tightly and slid it into a rubber sheath, then I had cut a tube of toothpaste open at the bottom end, emptied out all the toothpaste, inserted the notes and rolled the bottom of the tube up to look as if it were half empty. I couldn't get all the money in one tube, so I had put the rest of the 100-denomination notes into a tube of shaving cream using the same method. It was perfect camouflage and I had no problems at the Fuentes de Oñoro checkpoint at the border.

With this money I now bought a Baedeker tourist guide to England, Bradshaw's railway timetable and a large map of Great Britain, and retired to Cascais to study them in detail. Then, in October 1941, I sent my first message to the Germans from Cascais, although, as far as Federico was concerned, I was already in England; it was quite a long message.

In invisible ink, I told them that before leaving Portugal I had posted the key to a safety box in the Espírito Santo bank to the German embassy in Lisbon, with instructions that they should send it to Federico at the German embassy in Madrid. I went on to explain that on arriving in Britain, I had got talking to the KLM pilot who flew us in to London and had become very friendly with him, introducing myself as a Catalan political exile who had had to flee because of my political views. I had then persuaded the KLM pilot to take my Spanish mail to the

Espírito Santo bank in Lisbon on a regular basis. In my letter I also said that he had not at first been too keen to help, perhaps because he suspected something, but that I had assured him that none of my envelopes would be stuck down so he could always see for himself what the contents were; my letters were meant, I had explained to him, to give my fellow Catalan patriots information about other Catalans in exile in England. I had also told the pilot, I said to the Germans, that this, my first letter, would merely be informing my fellow Catalans in Spain of my arrival in the British Isles. Finally, I suggested to the Germans that I was thinking of going to live near Lake Windermere in the centre of Britain because I had heard that there were a fairly large number of troops stationed up there.

I had had to devise this ploy about the KLM pilot because, as I was still living in Portugal, there was absolutely no possibility of my letters being franked by the British Post Office. So this, my first letter, consisted, on the surface in ordinary visible ink, of an enthusiastic account of England by a passionate Catalan democrat with all the information for the Germans written in between the lines in invisible ink.

I had become a real German spy.

I sent three messages to the Germans from inside Portugal (purporting to come from England), all of which were worded with the care and attention worthy of the most adroit German field agent. I tried hard to introduce new information gradually and to be cautious when I mentioned the new contacts I had recruited to help me. In my first message I told them that I had found three people who would continue to supply me with further information, whom I had made my subagents: one in Glasgow, one in Liverpool and one from the West Country. The naivety with which I told them the facts I had discovered probably contributed to the conviction that I really was in London.

In the second message I said that I'd been offered a job at the BBC and was about to accept. I also said that I'd heard that the navy was carrying out landing-craft manoeuvres on Lake

Windermere and described in detail how I had grappled with a whole string of obstacles.

The third message, which as always was a complete invention, had a unique impact, although it was not until much later that I learned of the stir it caused in the British Secret Service. In this third message I said that a convoy of five ships had left Liverpool for Malta, although neither the date nor the number of ships actually tallied exactly with my message. But the coincidence was sufficiently close for the British to think that a German agent was loose in England.

This worried the British enormously, especially when they were able to confirm that the Germans had carried out an aerial reconnaissance of the projected route and of Malta's Valletta Harbour. Who was this agent? Where was he getting all this information from which endangered British security?

The British were going crazy looking for me as they had no idea where I was and, indeed, whether I existed at all. Cyril Mills told me later that he was in Portugal at the time and that he had mentioned to the intelligence gatherers in Lisbon and to those in Madrid that the German agent ARABEL could have come from either of those cities. If so, how had he got into Britain? Everyone in Britain was hunting for me and trying to discover how I was getting information through to Madrid.

So much of this reads like a fairy story that it will not come as a surprise to readers to learn that it was this third message which led to the British accepting me, and which eventually enabled me to become both the German's top spy ARABEL and MI5's counterspy GARBO.

While I was in Portugal I received only one message from the Abwehr; this asked for more detailed and weightier reports on troop sightings and movements. From this I gathered that my coded messages were neither as good nor as consistent as had been expected. The farce was coming to an end. Apart from the risks that my continued presence in Lisbon posed, I was extremely worried because I did not know what to do or say in order to keep my operation running efficiently. I had never been to England and my knowledge of English was confined to a fleeting study of the language during my schooldays. And what of my military knowledge? I didn't have any idea about the composition of a foreign army, let alone the British military set-up. Given my inability to obtain direct British contacts, I therefore decided to abandon the whole operation and disappear from Europe altogether. But before doing so I thought I'd have one last try and risk all on the play of a card.

I went to the American embassy in Lisbon. The United States, it must be remembered, had just come into the war as a new belligerent against Germany, Italy and Japan. It must have been during one of the first days of February 1942 when I walked in and asked to speak to either the military or the naval attaché.

This time around my luck held. I was met by an official who, after I had been frisked by the marine on duty, ushered me into the naval attaché's office to meet Lieutenant Demorest. I cannot tell you what a relief it was to be able to sit opposite someone who was in a position to make decisions, even though I was aware that his powers were limited. I began to unburden myself by telling him about my attempt to contact the British in Madrid, my rejection and then my resolution, fired by *amour-propre*, to obtain some practical and useful information that would capture their imagination, vindicate my humiliation and enhance myself in their estimation so that they would believe that I was motivated by a desire to defend democracy.

I briefly outlined my contacts with the Germans and mentioned that they had given me invisible ink, a code book and money; I told him about my trip to Portugal, my second attempt to contact the British through their Lisbon embassy, my second rebuff, my resolution to press on with work begun and, finally, my last desperate move of coming to see him; I said that if that too failed, then all the work I had done so far would come to nought.

Demorest showed keen interest right from the very beginning and seemed amazed by my story. He asked me for proof, which I proceeded to give him. For the first time there seemed to be a distinct possibility that I had found the right person; at last, someone was going to help me to complete the mission I had set myself. It was precisely while I was telling him my story that its full implication struck me: I started to realise the potential value of the trick I had begun to play on the Third Reich.

Demorest asked for two days in which to follow up my story, confer with his British colleagues and convince them that they must get in touch with me. He gave me his phone number and urged me to be very careful and to avoid going out unless I had to.

Then Demorest evidently tried to make his British counterpart, Captain Benson, see that he had nothing to lose by telling his superiors that this alleged agent wanted to hand over some invisible ink and a code book, and he advised Benson that he must act swiftly as I had either to continue with the game or stop altogether.

Someone in England had already had the perception to suspect that the spy they were hunting for was probably the same person as the freelance agent at large in Portugal, so some days later Captain Benson asked Demorest to give me his phone number. I then telephoned Benson, who arranged for me to meet Gene Risso-Gill, an MI6 officer in Lisbon, on the terrace of a refreshments shop overlooking the beach at Estoril. Three days later Risso-Gill telephoned me to say that he had received instructions that I should be taken to London.

Old Risso-Gill was a most polite and elegant gentleman with a dark complexion and a short thick beard, who overwhelmed me with his affability. He seemed delighted to hear about my adventures, laughed heartily and immediately began to plan how I could leave Lisbon in secret, without alerting German informers in the aliens department or the border police. Sometime later he came around to my place to tell me that a four-ship convoy that was heading for Gibraltar lay in the Tagus and that he had arranged for me to leave on one of the ships the following evening. I was not to take any luggage but to give him the invisible ink and the code book and he would see that they reached London. It was my one chance to travel in safety, so I had better be quick about sorting out my Portuguese affairs.

I left Estoril at five o'clock the next afternoon for an unknown destination; I had to trust that the British would indeed get me to London from Gibraltar, but did not know how, when or in what capacity I would travel there and couldn't help wondering what treatment the British would have in store for me on arrival. Risso-Gill seemed to read my thoughts, for he kept reassuring me during the short walk down to the harbour. It will only be a short journey, he said, no need to worry. All I had to do was to board the ship right behind him and then go straight to the crew's dining room when he gave the signal; the captain had precise instructions what to do with me when we reached Gibraltar: he was to hand me over to two officers, who would provide me with money and find me somewhere to stay.

My legs were shaking as I walked up the gangway past the Portuguese policeman at the top. Risso-Gill said something to him, then led me down to the captain's cabin. The captain told Risso-Gill to warn me not to talk to any of the crew, but to have dinner with them and then go straight to my bunk, which the quartermaster would find for me as he knew of my arrival.

After Risso-Gill had left the ship, I went down to the crew's mess; so far all the arrangements for my departure from Portugal had been faultless, which increased my confidence. Sometime after supper, when I was lying on my bunk, I heard the bang and rattle of the engines as the ship slipped her moorings. Early next morning one of the crew tapped me on the shoulder and made signs for me to follow him to the mess for breakfast. Afterwards he signalled for me to follow him up on deck for a breath of fresh air.

It was a beautiful day; we seemed to be sailing twelve miles or so off the Portuguese coast, gently cruising along in convoy with three other merchantmen. The fresh air did me good, for I had found it rather claustrophobic shut up down below and had not much cared for the smell, which made me feel sick. At about ten o'clock an alarm went off, everybody raced to action stations and a sailor threw a life jacket at my feet, indicating that I should put it on. Were we in danger? Had they spotted an enemy submarine or a plane? Then I realised that this was not a genuine emergency, just a practice drill.

We coasted along the shore for twenty-four hours and then, very early the next morning, I heard the ship's engines stop. When I went on deck I found the Rock of Gibraltar towering overhead. At about 8 a.m. a small boat approached and two officers stepped on board. The captain sent a sailor to bring me to his cabin and there introduced me to the two officers, who both spoke Spanish: one said he was a port official and the other that he had been instructed by London to look after me. I took leave of the captain and followed them into the small boat; we landed and walked unchallenged through the passport police check and customs and headed straight for a restaurant. Over a large English breakfast, I was informed by one of the officers that there was a room at my disposal for my own exclusive use and that I could come and go as I pleased. He then handed me a wad of sterling notes and suggested that I buy some clothes as he knew I had brought no luggage whatsoever with me, not even a change of clothes. He ended by telling me that I might have to wait for two or three days before getting a plane for London, as I would be travelling on an unscheduled flight.

He then took me to my room, gave me his telephone number in case I needed it and said that he would call as soon as he knew when I was leaving.

I spent the whole morning exploring Gibraltar, which I found to be a huddle of small shops, restaurants and hotels all along one main street, the adjoining small alleys leading to the harbour being of little import. I bought some underclothes and a Spanish newspaper and sat in a café. After lunch in a restaurant, I spent most of the afternoon watching some people play tennis who seemed to be naval officers and their wives. The truth is that there wasn't much to see in Gibraltar; it is not endowed with many tourist attractions and most people only go there to buy things because they are cheap and duty free. I visited a large nightclub cum coffee house filled to the brim with soldiers listening to a Spanish all-girl band, but the din was so great that I couldn't hear the music. I didn't see any fights, but was told that scuffles frequently broke out between the soldiers and the sailors.

Two days later I left Gibraltar in an extremely uncomfortable military plane that had no seats, just long benches, which made me think that it was meant for transporting paratroopers. There were two other passengers, but we were never introduced, nor did we speak to each other throughout the long eight-hour journey. They were carrying mail so were probably diplomats or special couriers.

In order to avoid German fighter planes, we headed far out into the Atlantic and so did not reach Plymouth until late afternoon, when we arrived tired and hungry as all we had had during the flight was tea. I don't think I've ever drunk so much tea in all my life as I did during that long, cold journey, not even during the London Blitz when we used to spend hours on end in underground shelters. I must have had more than twenty cups in a desperate attempt to keep myself warm.

I caught a glimpse of Plymouth from the plane and was suddenly acutely aware that I was away from home and about to enter an alien land. Would the English be friendly toward me? Would they believe my story about the tussles I had had with their embassies in Lisbon and Madrid, which showed how inefficiently these places were being run? Would they understand my motives for all that I had done and honestly believe that I wished to work for the good of mankind?

I thought about the city states of ancient Greece, of Cleisthenes's Athens, or Pericles and of the beginnings of democracy. I reiterated to myself my firm belief that individuals should have a say in their own government and knew that I had been right to put all my efforts into upholding such a doctrine. I entered England full of restless anticipation. What would my future hold?

My first recollection of England on that calm, clear day in April 1942, as I walked down the steps of the plane, was of the terrible cold – cold outside and icy fear inside. At the bottom of the steps stood two officers from MI5, who would shape my destiny. The one who introduced himself as Mr Grey didn't speak a word of Spanish; I didn't say anything to him in my faltering English. The other, Tomás Harris, whom everyone called Tommy, spoke perfect Spanish.

7

LONDON

What Juan Pujol could never have anticipated was the British reaction to his three messages to Madrid, which were included in routine Abwehr transmissions to Berlin. Nor could he have guessed that the British were intercepting and decrypting a substantial part of the Abwehr's wireless traffic to and from Madrid.

The German intelligence organisation in Madrid was impressive: some eighty-seven Abwehr personnel were directly attached to the German embassy, along with a further 228 other assorted intelligence staff. The full total of 315 greatly outnumbered the genuine foreign ministry diplomats, of whom there were only 171. The Abwehr contingent was believed to control no less than 1,500 senior agents spread throughout Spain. Headed by Commander Gustav Leisner, this remarkable network produced such a volume of information that some thirty-four wireless operators and ten female cipher clerks were required to handle the radio traffic. Madrid was a sufficiently important cog in the German intelligence machine to keep up an hourly wireless schedule with an Abwehr relay station near Wiesbaden. As well as intercepting this radio traffic, the Allies were also monitoring the signals passing between the Abwehr representatives in Lisbon and Madrid.

Literally translated as 'defence', the Abwehr was centred in a four-story office block in Berlin's elegant, tree-lined Tirpitzufer Street, overlooking the Landwehr Canal. The organisation was divided into three main branches, dealing with espionage, sabotage and counter-intelligence. Within those three divisions there were numerous subsections, but most of the

Abwehr's work was conducted by twenty-three overt suboffices spread throughout Germany's military districts. Each of these 'Abstelles' (usually abbreviated simply to 'Ast') had responsibility for particular foreign countries. Abstelle V, located in Hamburg's residential Sophienstrasse, was the headquarters of those groups targeted against Britain and the United States. Although the work of the Abstelles was secret, their physical presence in each German military district was not concealed. However, in neutral and allied countries the Abstelles were known as Kriegsorganisationen (literally, war organisations, and invariably abbreviated to KO). By 1942 the Abwehr had established ten KOs, each with an internal structure divided into three branches, mirroring the headquarters in Berlin. They were located in Lisbon, Berne, Stockholm, Helsinki, Zagreb, Ankara, Casablanca, Bucharest and Shanghai, the first and largest being in Madrid.

The Madrid KO or Abstelle had been established in 1937 by Leisner, who had been recruited into the Abwehr the previous year by his former brother officer in the navy, Wilhelm Canaris. Soon after the First World War, Leisner had emigrated to Nicaragua to open a small publishing house, but on the outbreak of the Spanish Civil War, Canaris had persuaded him to go to Spain as his personal representative. With the blessing of General Campos Martínez, the head of Franco's intelligence service, Leisner the publisher was transformed into 'Gustav Lenz', an apparently respectable businessman operating from the offices of the Excelsior Import and Export Company, a commodity brokerage firm dealing in strategic metals, which, in reality, was a front for the Abwehr's undercover operations. On the outbreak of war, Leisner transferred his activities to the German embassy, situated at 4 Castellana, and eventually built a huge network, incorporating some thirty suboffices spread throughout Spain. Where possible, these field sections were housed in German consulates, thus giving a measure of diplomatic protection to the Abwehr's personnel. By detailed analysis of the wireless signals passing between the suboffices and Madrid, the British succeeded in identifying all the permanent members of the Madrid Abstelle and all their duties. They also knew all about the officers who came into contact with ARABEL.

Leisner himself was assisted by his secretary, Fraulein Haeupel, who handled his mail, and Frau Obermuller, who arranged his appointments and maintained a card index of the Abstelle's agents. His administrative secretariat was run by Senior Staff Paymaster Max Franzbach, with Staff Paymaster Zimmer and Private Pfau (who supervised the car pool). Leisner's principal aide was Lieutenant Colonel Eberhardt Kieckebusche, who headed the Abwehr I group, which supervised the Abstelle's general espionage operations. His adjutant was Reserve Lieutenant Wilhelm Oberbeil, who handled any special plans, and Fraulein Meyer-Quittlingen, who maintained the registry and discharged the unit's secretarial duties.

Under Kieckebusche's command were seven departments, each with their own clearly delineated responsibilities. The most important of these was the Vertrauensmann section, run by Karl-Erich Kühlenthal. Kühlenthal held the rank of specialist captain and had a personal staff of five: Corporal Gustav Knittel, the office manager, Private Zierath, the interpreter, Private Knappe, agent-controller, Fraulein Heinsohn, the secretary, and Fraulein Mann, the confidential clerk who corresponded with the agents and developed any secret ink messages. All of these individuals handled ARABEL's traffic at one time or another, although much of the burden fell on Fraulein Mann and the special documents section headed by a scientist, Dr Kuenkele. This section operated from its own sophisticated laboratory and manufactured all kinds of secret inks, which were later used by ARABEL.

The six remaining sections were devoted to particular aspects of intelligence gathering and consisted of Army, Navy, technical and Luftwaffe, air, radio communications, and documents. All eventually received information from ARABEL.

As we have seen, the British presence in the Spanish capital was almost insignificant by comparison, and was inhibited by official Spanish surveillance and an ambassador who was entirely unsympathetic to the small group of intelligence officers attached to his stall. Hoare was determined not to provoke the Generalissimo or give even the slightest excuse for a diplomatic incident, but in spite of his restrictions, Section V of the British Secret Intelligence Service was able to reconstruct a complete order-of-battle for the enemy's local intelligence establishment. Very little of this would have been possible without ISOS, which enabled British Intelligence to monitor all the enemy's activities in the Iberian peninsula from long distance.

In addition to Section V's team, there was also a small MI5 section known as special research, and designated B1(b), which analysed the ISOS decrypts relevant to German espionage in England. Headed by Herbert Hart, a future professor of jurisprudence at Oxford University, its staff included the art historian Anthony Blunt, Patrick Day, the Oxford philosopher Edward Blanshard Stamp (later a lord justice of appeal) and a peacetime solicitor, John Gwyer. Together they attempted to build a profile of the mysterious ARABEL and trace his movements. Meanwhile, B1(a) case officers watched their own agents' traffic for any references to the newly established ring. However, the total burden fell on B1(g), the Iberian section responsible for countering Spanish, Portuguese and South American espionage, headed by a 28-year-old journalist, Dick Brooman-White. Who was ARABEL, and how had he got into the country? Answers to these questions were urgently sought by Brooman-White and his three B1(g) case officers, Paul Matthews, Alicia Pitt and Tomás Harris.

Dick Brooman-White was a product of Eton and Trinity College, Cambridge, and, in 1938, had been selected as Tory candidate for Bridgeton, Glasgow. In the same year he had been appointed public relations officer of the Territorial Army and, soon after the outbreak of war, he had been transferred to the Security Service, then housed in Wormwood Scrubs. The other B1(g) officer destined to play an official role in the GARBO case was Tomás Harris.

Harris was a gifted artist, born in 1908, who had transferred to MI5 from Special Operations Executive (SOE), the sabotage organisation created in July 1940 following the fall of France. Harris had joined SOE on the recommendation of Guy Burgess, one of SOE's earliest recruits, and had been posted to SOE's first special training school, which had been established at Brickendonbury Hall, a large country house set in woodland near Hertford. Harris and his wife Hilda remained at Brickendonbury for six months, and then, in the words of Kim Philby, he 'was soon snapped up by MI5, where he was to conceive and guide one of the most creative intelligence operations of all time.'

Harris possessed great imagination combined with a very practical talent. He had won the Trevelyan Goodall Scholarship to the Slade School of Fine Art at London University. His achievement was all the more remarkable because he had gained the award when he was just fifteen years old, which, in theory at least, disqualified him from receiving it. Having been educated in Spain, where his mother had been born, Tomás knew the country well and spoke Spanish virtually as a first language. After attending the Slade, he had spent a year at the British Academy in Rome studying painting and sculpture. His father, Lionel, was an English Jew and a renowned Mayfair art dealer. His Spanish Art Gallery concentrated on the sale of the work of Velázquez, Goya and El Greco, and in 1930 Tomás joined his father's business and scored several saleroom coups. Tomás was highly regarded by critics, and his expertise extended quite beyond painting and etching. He was also a sculptor of some merit and occasionally worked in ceramics, stained glass, tapestry and engraving.

As well as Tomás, Lionel Harris had three daughters, Conchita, Enriqueta and Violetta, who followed Tomás into

MI5 as a Spanish-speaking officer serving in B1(a). The Harris home, 6 Chesterfield Gardens, which Tomás subsequently inherited from his father, was a magnificent house, rich with oriental carpets and medieval tapestries. It also doubled as Lionel's place of business, and eventually became a favourite meeting place for Ml5's and SIS's few Bohemian employees. Both Tommy and his wife Hilda were lavish entertainers and acquired a well-deserved reputation for producing fine wine and gourmet meals for their friends, in spite of wartime rationing.

Later in the war they moved away from Mayfair into an even bigger property, Garden House, Logan Place, but their home still retained the easygoing atmosphere of an informal intelligence officer's club, with youthful MI5 and SIS men drifting in and out. The Harris *galère* of wealthy, university-educated young men included Guy Burgess, David Liddell, Victor Rothschild and Anthony Blunt from MI5, and Dick Brooman-White, Kim Philby, Tim Milne and Peter Wilson from SIS. Most of these individuals (with the exception of Philby and his successor as head of Section V's Iberian unit, Tim Milne) distinguished themselves in various other fields after the war. Burgess went from the BBC into the Foreign Office, and later defected to Russia; David Liddell became a successful artist; Victor Rothschild became a scientist; Anthony Blunt returned to the Courtauld Institute; Brooman-White was elected Conservative Member of Parliament for Rutherglen; Peter Wilson became chairman of Sotheby's.

Late in 1941 Brooman-White transferred to SIS to run Section V's Iberian unit, known as V(d), and Tomás Harris was appointed to succeed him as head of B1(g). By this date B1(g) had undergone some expansion because of its increasing responsibilities. Initially, the subsection had operated a couple of agents inside the Spanish embassy in London, had interrogated espionage suspects wishing to enter Britain and had investigated suspected breaches of censorship to Spain and South America. B1(g)'s workload was escalating daily, and

Paul Matthews was not in good health. In addition, there was too much for just three secretaries to cope with. Accordingly, Harris began looking for an extra member for his section. One morning he met Sarah Bishop, whom he knew spoke fluent Spanish, on the stairs of St James's Street, so he asked her to join them.

Sarah Bishop had started her secretarial duties in the Cabinet office, but had asked to move elsewhere when her immediate superior had switched from political work to the preparation of economic statistics. Thanks to the intervention of friendly MI5 officer (and future high court judge) Toby Caulfield, Sarah Bishop was offered a post in Ml5's French section, which was then headed by a youthful Peter Ramsbotham (who was subsequently knighted and became Britain's ambassador in Washington). After a brief spell learning about the role of the Security Service, Sarah now moved on to join Tomás Harris in B1(g). Here she was told that the ISOS analysts had spotted a new Abwehr personality, whom the Germans thought was reporting from England under his code name ARABEL but whom Herbert Hart's analysts believed was a Spaniard still in Portugal.

As the pieces of the ARABEL jigsaw were put together, it seemed likely that the man who had come to the British embassy in Madrid and later in Lisbon to offer his services to the Allied cause, Juan Pujol García, and ARABEL were one and the same person. It was also evident to MI5 that ARABEL's information was fictitious, although ISOS monitored a distinct increase in the Abwehr's estimation of him. Incredibly, the Germans seemed to swallow every one of his lies, and even approved the bizarre expenses demanded on behalf of his obviously notional agents. ARABEL had been unable to master the predecimal English currency of £ s.d. and therefore submitted some very unusual accounts, which were always listed in shillings. ARABEL also seemed to believe that the Portuguese legation, with the rest of London's diplomatic missions, moved to the coast at Brighton in order to escape the intolerably hot summers in the capital. On one occasion he reported that dockers in Liverpool became usefully in discreet about shipping movements when brought a litre of wine. In spite of these glaring errors, ARABEL's fraudulent messages sometimes prompted considerable military undertakings by the Germans, and it was also true that ARABEL sometimes hit on the truth or came uncomfortably close to it.

A lengthy debate followed Juan Pujol's approach to the British embassy in Lisbon: should ARABEL be accepted and taken into MI5's fold of double agents or not? Was he genuine or a plant by the Germans? Would it be best to leave him alone?

The head of Section V, Felix Cowgill, pointed out that very little was known about Pujol apart from information that he had volunteered himself in Madrid and Lisbon, and his ISOS dossier, which contained copies of his three decrypted messages and several appreciations of him as a reliable source that had been intercepted between Madrid and Berlin. Having once been deputy commissioner of the Calcutta Special Branch (before his recruitment into the Secret Intelligence Service in February 1939), Cowgill was acutely anxious to preserve security and, in particular, to protect the integrity of ISOS. In the realm of intelligence gathering there will inevitably arise a conflict between the desire to avoid compromising existing sources and the need to develop new ones. Such conflicts had hampered Section V's operations because Cowgill had been reluctant to exploit new channels of information if there was any risk to the mother lode, the flow of signals intelligence from GCHQ. The debate over Pujol simply reopened many of the old disputes. Did he represent a genuine offer, which should be taken up before he changed his mind, or was he something more sinister? The Abwehr's internal communications, which had also been intercepted, revealed ARABEL to be highly regarded by the Abstelle in Madrid and Abwehr headquarters in Berlin. Such opinions might, in some circumstances, have counted against him, but there would have been little logic in 'turning' an agent who did not enjoy the enemy's full confidence. Indeed, counter-intelligence officers argued for his recruitment, pointing out that Pujol's recruitment would enhance B1(a)'s existing double agents and provide an unrivalled conduit for misinformation. After all, they insisted, Pujol had got over the first hurdle, that of establishing himself with the enemy as a credible source. The controversy over the advisability of accepting Pujol raged on, with the more experienced members of Section V taking the safer line. Some of V(d)'s younger staff, such as Kim Philby and Desmond Bristow, were determined to seize an opportunity which, they felt, might never be repeated.

The stakes were certainly very high. If Pujol was exactly as he appeared, then MI5's total domination over the Abwehr would be confirmed and could be exploited further. If, on the other hand, he turned out to be a deliberate plant, the entire double-cross system might be placed in danger. As Cowgill had pointed out, even the integrity of ISOS might be jeopardised. There were also a number of other possibilities. Pujol's offer might be part of an elaborate trap to identify or kidnap a British Intelligence officer on neutral territory – an event that was not entirely unknown. A similar incident in November 1939 in Holland had resulted in the loss of two experienced SIS men. Another alternative scenario had the Abwehr anxious to promote a 'triple agent' so they could learn the fate of all the rest of their spies. If Pujol gained the confidence of the British, he might be able to judge the reliability of the Abwehr's other sources.

Pujol's approaches were debated in London, St Albans and all the meeting places where Britain's counter-intelligence experts gathered. On the whole, the opinions divided along organisational lines. Section V was against taking on a relatively unknown agent in a neutral environment where no physical control could be exercised over him; MI5 advocated his being brought to England so he could complete his mission before the Abwehr tripped him up and discovered how easily they had been duped. The concluding factor in the decision to recruit

Pujol was a series of decrypts from Bletchley which showed
that the Germans were planning to ambush an Allied convoy
in the Mediterranean that had apparently left Liverpool bound
for Malta. Although plenty of convoys had attempted the perilous journey to relieve the siege of Malta, then at its height,
none sailed from England. Most of the ill-fated supply ships
had come from Alexandria and had been sunk by German
and Italian bombers. The hard-pressed island was enduring
constant air bombardment and, during the first thirty days of
1942, Malta endured more than two thousand attacks from
enemy aircraft. During February 1942 more than one thousand
tons of bombs were dropped on the island. On 7 February
Malta underwent a record thirteen hours of air raids, involving
sixteen separate enemy sorties. The RAF had only a handful
of fighters to defend Malta, so even a few hours' respite was
welcomed by those on the ground.

ARABEL's non-existent convoy offered just a pause in the
Axis onslaught. According to his messages, he had recruited a
spy who worked in Liverpool. This notional agent, who later
took the identity of a certain William Gerbers, eventually was
to succumb to a convenient illness when his continued presence in the area was considered too dangerous. But, in the
meantime, Gerbers reported regularly to ARABEL and described
the tempting convoy apparently bound for Malta. This news
was relayed to the Abwehr, causing elaborate plans to be
made in the Mediterranean. Subsequent decrypts confirmed
that the German admiralty had prepared their attack on the
basis of information received from ARABEL via the Abwehr.
U-boats were diverted to an ambush site just east of Gibraltar
and Italian planes armed with torpedoes were transferred to
Sardinia. The Axis amassed an impressive force with which
to sink the British shipping, but they achieved precisely nothing. Even when the long-awaited convoy failed to materialise,
having wasted thousands of man-hours and tons of valuable
fuel, the blame for the operations failure was left with the

Italians and not the Abwehr. Indeed, the intercepts proved that no one had actually doubted the veracity of ARABEL's messages. The entire exercise, which resembled a fiasco from the German viewpoint, was an eloquent demonstration of ARABEL's standing with the enemy. In Malta the brief respite was an opportunity to regroup the defences and provide a well-deserved breathing space.

If it was within Pujol's power to cause such mischief unwittingly, what might be the result if his efforts were directed in concert with other weapons of deception? This was the carrot dangled by MI5, although Section V of SIS seemed reluctant to grasp the opportunity. When the idea was originally proposed by MI5 it was formally rejected on security grounds, and MI5 concluded that SIS was reluctant to cope with the logistics of giving Pujol a means of surreptitious exit from Portugal, perhaps thereby compromising their secret fishing-boat ferry service. Throughout the war SIS ran a very useful, very illicit shuttle between Lisbon and Gibraltar. Did their refusal to deal with Pujol conceal an unwillingness to provide valuable covert transport facilities for an untried agent? Did they still fear penetration by an enemy agent provocateur who might denounce the boat service to the PVDE (Polícia de Vigilância e de Defesa do Estado)? Was the possible prize of a direct line into the enemy's intelligence and decision-making structure not a worthwhile risk? Might Pujol, who was, after all, already well established, deliver an invaluable insight into the Abwehr? Such tempting imponderables won the day and it was agreed that Pujol should be invited to travel to London and continue under MI5's supervision. The Secret Intelligence Service eventually agreed to this idea and nominated a Spanish-speaking Section V(d) officer, Desmond Bristow, to supervise the case for SIS and liaise with MI5 and the Twenty Committee. He, more than any other Section V officer, had been in favour of pursuing Pujol's offer, and he accepted the task with enthusiasm. SIS also agreed to convey the invitation to Pujol, so a coded message was sent by courier to the SIS station in Lisbon. Delivering the message was one thing; executing it under the watchful eyes of the Germans and the Portuguese was quite another.

At this time, in March 1942, the situation was extraordinarily complicated. Although Portugal was Britain's oldest ally, the president of the council of ministers, Dr António Salazar, showed a distinct reluctance to honour his obligations and oppose the Axis. The 500-year-old mutual defence treaty of 1373 required Portugal to support the Allies and declare war on Germany, and a somewhat half-hearted offer to this effect had been made in 1941, although the War Cabinet in London had decided that it would be more advantageous not to invoke the ancient treaty and let Portugal retain its neutrality. However, it was suggested that the Portuguese government might grant the RAF permission to base aircraft in the Azores so the Atlantic convoys could be protected. (In August 1943, after many lengthy negotiations, Dr Salazar secretly gave his consent to the plan and allowed the RAF facilities on the strategically located islands.)

It did not pass unnoticed in London that little progress was made in the diplomatic exchanges until the military balance began to alter in favour of the Allies. Victory in North Africa cemented Portugal's cooperation, but in the meantime the Nazis never missed an opportunity to woo Salazar. The principal German suitor was Baron von Hoyningen-Huene, an aristocrat who had been born in Switzerland to an English mother and Baltic German father. He was Ribbentrop's long-serving ambassador in Lisbon, who had deftly courted influential friends among those close to Salazar. And von Hoyningen-Huene's embassy also housed a very substantial Abwehr presence headed by Major Albrecht von Auenrode, a colourful Viennese intelligence officer who invariably masqueraded as 'Ludovico von Karsthof' and kept a pet monkey named Simon in his office. According to rumour, von Auenrode's secretary, Mausi, was also his mistress.

Responsibility for maintaining surveillance on all the suspect personnel of all the belligerents' diplomatic missions was left to the dreaded international police, the PVDE. This internal security force, which had acquired a particularly grim reputation during the Spanish Civil War, was headed by Captain Agostinho Lourenço and, in theory, was under the direction of the interior minister. In practice, Lourenço answered only to the premier, Dr Salazar, and was generally considered to be one of the country's most powerful (and ruthless) men.

Lourenço was a professional army officer and had fought with the Portuguese contingent in France with the Allies during the Great War. He also held a British decoration, having been made an honorary Companion of the Royal Victorian Order for services performed while head of the Lisbon division of the security police during the brief visit in April 1931 of the Prince of Wales. In spite of these apparent qualifications as an Anglophile, Lourenço and his formidable organisation were regarded by the British as thoroughly hostile. According to a secret assessment made of Lourenço by the British embassy shortly before the war, he was

> an extremely energetic and efficient officer, in whom far greater trust is placed than is suggested by his rank. His practical control of the service connected with the suppression of communism, which is regarded as the country's greatest menace, is smart in appearance, but blunt in manner. At one time threatened to resign because many of the persons he arrested were liberated by the minister of the interior, and only consented to continue in office when it was decided that he should be supported.

One of Lourenço's senior lieutenants, Captain Paulo Cumano, was believed to be very pro-German, having been trained in police procedures in Berlin before the war. He had also been to a German engineering college, where he attended a mining course with Erich Emil Schroeder who, by coincidence, happened to be posted to the German legation in March 1941 as a scientific aide. In reality, he was the Gestapo's local representative, with special responsibility for liaising with Lourenço's PVDE. Another senior PVDE official with close German links was Lourenço's deputy, Captain Jose Catela, who also headed the security department.

In addition to the dreaded PVDE, there was another, unofficial, intelligence service known as the Legião, or Portuguese legion. This was a powerful paramilitary group run by well-known Fascists who based it on similar blackshirt organisations. By far the most important branch of the Legião was the intelligence section, which was generally regarded as enjoying a fraternal relationship with the German embassy. There was hardly an area of Portuguese life that had not been thoroughly penetrated by the Legião.

Section V's representative in Lisbon was Ralph Jarvis. London's order in March 1942 to find ARABEL placed Ralph Jarvis in considerable difficulty. He and his staff at the British Repatriation Office (located on the other side of town from the embassy) were constantly followed by none-too-subtle PVDE agents. It was equally difficult for the head of station to undertake the mission as all the diplomatic personnel were watched and Ambassador Sir Ronald Campbell had already warned Commander Johns not to engage in any activities which might compromise the rest of the embassy. The building itself, in the heart of Lisbon's old quarter, was surrounded by narrow streets and was quite unsuitable for exotic, clandestine manoeuvres. The PVDE had no difficulty in keeping tabs on everyone, including the Americans who, since December the previous year, had lost their neutral status and were therefore equally vulnerable to Lourenço's attentions.

However, Section V had a couple of people working for them who had considerable freedom of movement: Jarvis's most trusted aide, Graham Maingot, and Maingot's contact, Risso-Gill.

Maingot was a veteran British agent with film star good looks who had spent the pre-war years in Rome under commercial cover. He had been obliged to leave Italy when Mussolini declared war in 1940, and since that date he had been operating within the expatriate community in Portugal, recruiting informants and running the occasional double agent. By far his best catch was Eugene Risso-Gill, a Briton of Gibraltarian extraction who worked in the oil division of the Seconi Vacuum Corporation.

Risso-Gill's father had been an engineer who had married into an old Portuguese family and settled in Lisbon at the turn of the century, when British companies were modernising the country. Lisbon's tram system had been built by a British company, and forty years later even the telephone company remained, under license, in British ownership. Eugene Risso-Gill, known to all his friends as Gene, had been born in Tangier in 1910 and was sent to school in England, where he attended Prior Park in Bath. He was a natural linguist and became completely fluent in French, German, English, Spanish and Portuguese. When his education had been completed he returned to Portugal, where he acquired rather a dashing reputation as a sportsman, gambler and womaniser, and eventually married his childhood sweetheart, Guilhermina Soares de Oliveira, whose family owned an apartment in the same building as his parents. At the time of their wedding, in October 1934, Guilhermina's father had been president of Portugal's Council of Ministers for four years. Before that, General Domingos de Oliveira had been military governor of Lisbon and the minister with special responsibility for internal justice. The general was his country's strongman for more than a decade, until his retirement in 1938 when he became head of the Supreme Military Justice Tribunal. He was a committed Anglophile and had represented his country in London at the coronation of King George VI. He was also on very good terms with Dr Salazar, whom he originally brought into his administration as minister of finance. In other words, Gene Risso-Gill was superbly well connected. In addition, his wife had no less than four brothers, who all achieved high rank in the military (the general's eldest son was appointed governor of Macao) and two of her three sisters married senior Portuguese army officers. To cap it all, Risso-Gill was very friendly with Captain Lourenço of the PVDE and enjoyed a close relationship with Selgado, the head of the Legião's intelligence branch.

In view of these influential family ties, it is not entirely surprising that when Risso-Gill approached the British embassy in 1940 with an offer to join up he was given an interview with the ambassador, Sir Walford Selby. Selby asked him to remain in Portugal, where he believed he might be more useful to the British government, and then discreetly passed his name to Commander Johns's predecessor at the SIS station, Commander Austin Walsh RN. Armed with an introduction from Selby, Walsh approached Risso-Gill and asked if he was prepared to undertake 'work of a secret and dangerous nature'. Risso-Gill agreed, and in due course Graham Maingot contacted him with the proposal of a wartime career in espionage: Risso-Gill would spy for Britain, and in return he would be seconded to the embassy with the rank of an assistant attaché, a cover which would offer him some diplomatic immunity. But instead of working from the main Chancery building, he would operate from accommodation at the consulate in the Rua da Emenda which, coincidentally, housed the passport control office. Later in the war he was to use an office on the first floor at 178 Rua de S. Bento as a cover address and safe house where he could meet agents.

Risso-Gill's recruitment was a brilliant coup for SIS, and he became a valuable go-between with the Portuguese Ministry of Foreign Affairs, especially during the delicate negotiations for the Azores. Risso-Gill continued to operate as Maingot's chief agent until he was involved in a post-war scandal and cited as a correspondent by Sir Donald Campbell in his much-publicised divorce case.

Risso-Gill's large, modern apartment, at 34 Avenida Álvares Cabral, in Lisbon's smart residential district of Estrela, made an ideal safe house and was used as a convenient rendezvous for covert meetings. Although he came into contact with numerous wartime agents, including many fleeing from occupied France, by far his most important contribution was his role as ARABEL's first British case officer.

When Ralph Jarvis therefore received London's request to find Juan Pujol García, code-named ARABEL, he got in touch with Gene Risso-Gill and asked him to track down the man, win his confidence and persuade him to travel to England. Coincidental with this happening, Pujol made an approach to the American legation, where he met the assistant naval attaché Captain Arthur Benson RN. Benson had his own channels to London and, having bypassed the local SIS station, got a message through to Section V(d) describing Pujol's offer to help the Allied cause. Although Benson's route took some time, it arrived at the right moment: just as Risso-Gill was starting to look for ARABEL, he had identified himself to the very people who were anxious to trace him and transform him into a controlled double agent.

Lieutenant Demorest and Benson gave Risso-Gill Pujol's address at his new rented house just a matter of yards from the Estoril casino. Fortunately, Gene Risso-Gill's family kept a seaside villa, the Chalet Rola, at Oeiras, halfway between Lisbon and Estoril, and this made an ideal location for the two men to rendezvous away from the watchful eyes of the PVDE. The exact details of Risso-Gill's meetings with Pujol are unknown, but more than forty years later the double agent still kept a record of Risso-Gill's home and office telephone numbers: Lisbon 61089 and Lisbon 60402.

Pujol was delighted to accept the British invitation, but there was a major obstacle in the way. Travel to and from Portugal was strictly controlled by the authorities, and the PVDE were known to sell the list of arriving and departing passengers

to the German legation. In addition, Corte Real, the principal PVDE supervising officer at the Cabo Ruivo flying boat
terminal on the river Tagus, was definitely in the pay of the
Gestapo. How could Pujol leave Portugal without the PVDE
reporting the matter to Germans? If he left the country by
any ordinary route his name would certainly be spotted by the
Abwehr who, of course, had been led to believe that ARABEL
had been living safely in England since the previous July. No
amount of explaining would be likely to regain the Germans'
confidence once they realised they had been deceived for the
best part of nine months. Nor could he be allowed to use SIS's
secret shuttle to Gibraltar in case he was an enemy plant and
under Abwehr surveillance.

Jarvis and Risso-Gill overcame this obstacle by arranging a rendezvous at sea with a British steamer heading for
the Mediterranean. Captain Benson, the shipping attaché,
persuaded the skipper of a merchant vessel to smuggle Pujol
aboard and give him a berth as far as the Rock. The following
morning the steamer rejoined its convoy, and two days later
Pujol was met in Gibraltar by Donald Darling, representing
the local SIS station. Darling, who had recently been transferred to the Rock from Lisbon, had the job of a glorified
transport officer, welcoming escaped Allied servicemen and
other resisters onto the only territory on the continent of
Europe left in British hands. For unexpected arrivals there
were days of inevitable, frustrating delays awaiting confirmation of their bona fides. Other agents, who had been able to
send an advance warning, were luckier and given places on the
next ship returning to England. In very special cases much-
prized seats were found on transport aircraft and seaplanes
which flew the 1,500-mile trip entirely over the sea. Naturally,
Pujol fell into this latter category, and he was accommodated
in Darling's spare room, which doubled as a safe house for
evaders, while space was found for him. Darling also provided
him with some temporary travel documents and confided that,

because SIS had failed to inform him of Pujol's code name, he had taken the liberty of selecting one himself. He had chosen the name of his favourite hot drink: BOVRIL.

8

GARBO'S NETWORK

Juan Pujol's arrival in England on Saturday 25 April 1942 concluded SIS's contribution to operation BOVRIL and marked the opening of a new career for Pujol with MI5. He was met at the flying boat terminal at Mount Batten, Plymouth, by a B1(a) representative, Cyril Mills (calling himself 'Mr Grey'), and Tommy Harris from B1(g), who acted as interpreter. Also present was MI5's senior driver, Jock Horsfall. After welcoming Pujol to England and clearing him through the port security formalities, they drove him to a hotel in Plymouth, before setting out early the next morning for London and a safe house at 35 Crespigny Road, Hendon, NW4. This discreet, semi-detached family home in north London was similar to many hundreds of others in the area and boasted just three bedrooms upstairs and a sitting room, dining room and kitchen on the ground floor. It was a modest, typically late Victorian, middle-class property, which had been rented by the Security Service for the duration of the war from a young Jewish army officer. Before BOVRIL took up residence it had already accommodated a number of other double agents, including two Norwegians code-named MUTT and JEFF. But by April 1942 both MUTT and JEFF had moved on, and Pujol shared the entire house with a trusted MI5 housekeeper named Miss Titoff, and, a week later, with his wife and son, whom MI5 had had brought over to England.

The day after Pujol's arrival he was visited by Cyril Mills and Tommy Harris who, on this occasion, were accompanied by Desmond Bristow, the Section V officer who had been monitoring ARABEL's progress for some months. Bristow had been brought up in the south of Spain and, like Tommy Harris, spoke fluent, idiomatic Spanish. This was the first of many debriefing sessions at which Mills, Bristow and Harris examined BOVRIL's bizarre story. They continued from 26 April, with a one-day break on 5 May, until Monday 11 May. When they were all convinced of Juan's bona fides, Harris collaborated with the double agent on the construction of his first genuine message from London to his German controllers. At subsequent meetings, Juan was collected by Cyril Mills and Tommy Harris, and driven by Jock Horsfall to a small office located in Regent Street, close to the Café Royal. This office was used by several MI5 case officers as a convenient place to hold the occasional meeting with an agent, but it soon became evident that Harris and Juan would have to spend many hours together, piecing together the many complicated strands of his non-existent organisation.

It was also vital that Juan's personal security be preserved, and it was agreed that he should only meet the minimum necessary number of MI5 officers. Accordingly, new premises near the Jermyn Street shopping arcade were hastily acquired by Tommy Harris in order to brief BOVRIL in detail and develop the case further. Security considerations prevented the use of his own office in MI5's headquarters, and the arcade office was conveniently close to St James's Street and just a matter of yards from Section V's London branch in Ryder Street. The debriefings that followed must have been truly extraordinary. Pujol had no idea that his activities had been watched so closely, and Harris had yet to realise that he was destined to spend much of the next three years in the company of the young Catalan. Gradually, they fell into a routine of office work in their small office, with occasional meals at the Martinez restaurant in Swallow Street and the Garibaldi restaurant in Jermyn Street. As cover, MI5 equipped Pujol with documents identifying him as Juan García, a translator working for the BBC. During these prolonged discussions, Juan revealed a secret that he had not even disclosed to the Nazis: after the Spanish Civil War he had got married and had one baby son, Juan Fernando. His wife, Araceli, and their son were still in Portugal, so MI5 promptly arranged for them both to be spirited to London. When they arrived they joined Juan at Hendon, and the security service hired a nanny to help Araceli.

BOVRIL's debriefing quickly established his credentials once and for all. As well as ARABEL, Pujol had, in effect, delivered a ready-made espionage network, even though it existed only in his head. The fact that the Germans had taken it seriously was sufficient justification for MI5 to play along. He boasted two civilians who flew regularly between England and Portugal and willingly acted as couriers for his messages, and Agents ONE, TWO and THREE, who were scattered around the country and were apparently able to report their own independent observations. Later on, some wrote their own messages and reported directly to the Germans, but they all received their instructions via ARABEL. This administrative bonus enabled Pujol to exercise total control over his subagents, answer for all of them and ensure consistency. It also had the advantage of giving him a unique insight into the Abwehr's handling of a group of agents. Naturally, he received each reply (and acknowledged it on behalf of his agent) and then compared the questionnaires to similar requests sent to his other agents. His comprehensive knowledge of every detail concerning his spy ring demonstrated BOVRIL's incredible powers of invention. The particulars of each non-existent agent were duly recorded into a logbook by Tommy Harris, who marvelled at Pujol's remarkable talent for duplicity. Indeed, Cyril Mills was so impressed that he suggested that BOVRIL's British code name should be altered to reflect his status as 'the best actor in the world'. Harris concurred, and the code name GARBO was agreed upon. The choice reflected MI5's high regard for their agent and also offered some cover. If the Germans ever discovered that MI5 were operating a double agent with the name of a famous actress, they might assume the agent to be a woman.

BOVRIL (or GARBO, as he had become) was unaware of these developments and concentrated on describing his notional subagents for the benefit of his MI5 audience.

His first recruit, designated 'J(1)' by MI5 (an abbreviation of Juan's Agent ONE), was the air steward who had assumed the role of courier. It had been his job, since his first appearance on 15 July 1941, to fill and empty the bank deposit box at the Espírito Santo bank in Lisbon, which ARABEL had established in the 'typically English name' of 'Mr Smith-Jones', and Harris therefore made arrangements with Section V for Gene Risso-Gill to continue these duties. In the future, Pujol and Harris would prepare and encipher the test of ARABEL's messages and deliver them to Section V in London. Thereafter, they would be passed to Risso-Gill via the regular king's messenger service to Lisbon. He continued this routine, without mishap, until the end of hostilities. The Germans, of course, had no reason to suspect any alteration had been made in ARABEL's system. Each of Juan's notional agents was designated his own individual code name, and a complete organisational chart of them appears at the beginning of the book. Although MI5 referred to each by their numerical name (Agent THREE etc.), the Abwehr personalised Juan's sources and usually mentioned them by their code names. Thus, in the Abwehr's signals Agent THREE was always BENEDICT.

Pujol's choice of a KLM pilot as a regular courier to England was an inspired one, because the chief KLM pilot on the route was indeed a spy, although Pujol never knew it. The civil air lanes between Portugal and England were maintained throughout the war, although the unarmed aircraft were certainly not entirely immune from enemy attack. Nevertheless, the British Overseas Airways Corporation kept a regular seaplane schedule with Empire flying boats of the Clare and Clyde class on the route between Poole Harbour and Cabo Ruivo on the river Tagus. They also offered an alternative service with four twin-engined DC-3 aircraft, the forerunner of the famous Dakota, leased from KLM and operated between Sintra (later Portela) and Whitchurch aerodrome, just south of Bristol. In spite of the wartime conditions, complete secrecy concerning arrivals and departures was virtually impossible, and security at the Portuguese end of the flight was, inevitably, extremely poor. In fact, the KLM pilots were often obliged to park their machines next to Lufthansa planes at Sintra. German ground staff were frequently spotted running to a telephone to report an arrival and aircrews of all nationalities mixed together in the transit quarters. At the British end security was a little better, with passengers instructed to report to the Grand Spa Hotel in Bristol rather than the aerodrome at Whitchurch. It is worth recalling that for much of the war this was the chief civilian air link with Europe. A more hazardous and irregular, night-time-only service also operated between Scotland and Stockholm. The Luftwaffe largely dominated the rest of Europe's skies, thus barring them from Allied civil aircraft. It was in these circumstances that Lisbon had become known as the crossroads of Europe.

At the beginning of hostilities the four Dutch airliners had been stripped of their original markings and flown to Heston, where they had been camouflaged and reregistered as British aircraft. Each carried a crew of pilot, co-pilot, engineer and radio operator, and could seat twenty-one passengers. The flight took a very indirect route to avoid encountering hostile fighters, involving a detour of some 1,000 miles, and lasted over ten hours. Under normal conditions the luxury airliner cruised at 165 mph (with a top speed of 210 mph) but in order to cover some 1,500 miles the planes were generally flown at a lower speed and a reduced payload of just thirteen passengers. This circuitous route also demanded a refuelling stop at Oporto.

The four Dutch planes, *King Falcon*, *Buzzard*, *Aigrette* and *Ibis*, were flown by a team of KLM aircrew, headed by Koene Dirk Parmentier, a long-distance pilot who had won the handicap leg of the 1934 London to Melbourne air race. In the spring of 1939 he had won the Batavia–Sydney prize. As well as being a renowned aviator, Parmentier was also an occasional employee of the British Secret Intelligence Service and had performed various secret missions. These included the dramatic rescue of a German diplomat, Wolfgang zu Putlitz, who had defected from the Nazis in 1934 while serving in London and subsequently had been transferred to The Hague, where he continued to provide valuable information from inside the German legation. Late in 1939, the Gestapo had been tipped off to zu Putlitz's duplicity and he had been forced to flee. The British had used Parmentier to fly zu Putlitz out of Holland from Schiphol just hours before he was due to be arrested.

By the time Pujol had landed in England in April 1942, BOAC's KLM charter planes had flown more than 4,000 passengers to and from Lisbon and a twice-weekly run to Gibraltar had been introduced. The airliners were attacked by the enemy on only three occasions. The *Ibis*, the first of the all-metal DC-3s in Europe, sustained only superficial damage on 15 November 1942 when a Messerschmitt 110 made a short, strafing attack, and on 16 April 1943 the incident was repeated. Apart from a few bullet holes, including one in a hat belonging to a Swiss diplomatic courier, no serious harm was suffered. But less than two months later, on 1 June 1943, the *Ibis*, piloted by Captain Quirinius Tepas, was shot down, with the loss of all the passengers and the Dutch crew.

The destruction of BOAC flight 777a from Lisbon made headline news around the world because the film star Leslie Howard was among the seventeen people killed. Another victim was Tyrrel Shervington, a Shell Oil executive and a valued member of the British Secret Intelligence Service station in Lisbon. He had been returning to London for some well-earned leave. Others aboard included Leslie Howard's manager, the Washington correspondent of Reuters, a representative of the Jewish Agency, some elderly businessmen, three women and two children.

When news of the loss was announced, GARBO complained bitterly to the Germans. Their behaviour had jeopardised the lives of members of his network and had threatened to destroy his valuable line of communication with the Espírito Santo bank. The Luftwaffe subsequently held an investigation into the incident and it was established that the unarmed plane had been shot down by a Junkers 88 from the mixed fighter wing Kampfgruppe KG 40 based at Kerhouin-Bastard airfield, near Lorient, piloted by a Luftwaffe flight lieutenant named Bellstedt. Bellstedt and his staff had been on routine patrol across the Bay of Biscay when they had encountered the DC-3 shortly after midday. Both he and his crew were described as young and inexperienced, and they made two cannon passes at the defenceless transport before it crashed into the sea in flames. No action was taken against Bellstedt, and he was later killed in combat over Germany, but his radio operator and navigator survived the war. According to one account, they were subsequently forced to ditch in the North Sea and were rescued by an RAF air-sea rescue launch. But when the two Germans had been hauled out of the sea they had inadvisedly boasted of having shot down the airliner 'for target practice'. Before being put ashore both had been badly beaten up. It is worth recording that although the Luftwaffe did not officially discipline Bellstedt, there were no further attacks on civilian aircraft flying between Portugal and England.

Pujol's second notional agent was J(2), the KLM airline pilot who fulfilled a back-up function as a courier for J(1). He was soon considered superfluous by MI5, bearing in mind the new method of communication offered by Risso-Gill, and he was therefore allowed to slip quietly into the background.

Pujol's most experienced agent, and future deputy, was designated Agent THREE, a wealthy Venezuelan student named Carlos. In order to protect his identity, the Abwehr always referred to him in their secret communications by the code name BENEDICT. These, of course, were routinely intercepted at Hanslope Park and decrypted. BENEDICT allegedly lived in Glasgow and had promised to recruit his own subagents in the north of England. According to Pujol (and this was subsequently confirmed by ISOS decrypts), BENEDICT had first materialised in a message from Lisbon dated 7 October 1941. His brother, Agent FIVE, was also a student and was supposedly based in Aberdeen. He was reported as having joined his brother on 14 June 1942, was sent on a special intelligence-gathering mission to the Isle of Wight, and then on another to the West Country, but was then forced to travel to Ottawa later in the summer. In reality, this involved Cyril Mills's moving to Canada, and will be described in detail later.

The KLM steward (Agent ONE) and William Maximilian Gerbers (Agent TWO) proved less satisfactory, and in due course each had to be dispensed with. Agent ONE eventually resigned in November 1942 after having been caught up in a disastrous deception plan, code-named COCKADE, which will be covered shortly. William Gerbers, who lived in Bootle, was obliged to contract a serious illness during the preparations for TORCH, the Allied invasion of North Africa in November 1942. He had been credited with reporting ARABEL's infamous Maltese convoy, which had never existed and had caused the German admiralty so much difficulty. Gerbers's failure to notice or comment on the unmistakable military build-up in the Liverpool docks prior to embarkation would be stretching German credibility. It was reluctantly agreed that his absence could only be plausibly explained by his transfer into a hospital, and he eventually succumbed, after a lengthy illness, on 19 November 1942. A suitable obituary notice was placed in the *Liverpool Daily Post* on Tuesday 4 November 1942:

GERBERS – Nov. 19 at Bootle, after a long illness, aged fifty-nine years, WILLIAM MAXIMILIAN. Private funeral. (No flowers please.)

The newspaper cutting was promptly sent to Lisbon. MI5 subsequently took advantage of the tragedy to arrange for TWO's widow to continue her late husband's good work in London.

Having heard much of Pujol's story, Harris recognised that the first priority was to allow ARABEL to find some truly important sources who were sufficiently well placed to supply some information of better quality. MI5 feared that unless ARABEL developed some useful contacts the Germans might be prompted to review the material they had so far received. Harris was convinced that an analysis of any depth would inevitably conclude that ARABEL was manufacturing his own intelligence and probably had never visited England. After consulting with the Twenty Committee, he obtained permission for GARBO to recruit his best source yet, a non-existent character, designated J(3), who occupied a senior position in the Ministry of Information. This news was sent to Lisbon, buried in the text of a typically long-winded report from ARABEL, on 16 May 1942.

J(3) was ARABEL's first source of any significance, and was entirely the product of the Harris/Pujol collaboration. He was generally rated very highly, although he never suspected (or so claimed ARABEL) that he was collaborating with a Nazi spy ring. When J(3) came to be described by Harris in a secret, internal report, he commented that J(3)

> could possibly be identified as the head of the Spanish section of the Ministry of Information. For a time, GARBO was employed by him on translation work for the MOI. He is suited for the passing of high-grade information of a political or strategic nature. He has frequently been quoted by GARBO as one of his best sources. He believes GARBO to be a Spanish Republican refugee and treats him as a close personal friend. He is an unconscious collaborator.

J(3) was quickly followed the next month by CHAMILLUS (Agent FOUR), who was portrayed as a Gibraltarian waiter working in the NAAFI (Navy, Army and Air Force Institutes) at a secret, underground establishment in the famous caves at Chislehurst. Pujol described how the agent had become increasingly anti-

British, having been forcibly evacuated from the Rock along with the rest of Gibraltar's civilian population. He apparently found the climate in Kent very disagreeable and was a willing recruit. CHAMILLUS was to prove an exceptional spy, not so much because of his access to the secret work being undertaken in the caves or his observation of army units passing through the depot, but because of his many useful contacts. In fact, soon after the introduction of Agent FIVE, the Gibraltarian master-minded the recruitment of Pujol's wireless operator.

The necessity of wireless communication had become apparent to Harris and MI5 after Pujol had been in harness for just three months. The decision to develop GARBO's network so dramatically was only taken after ISOS decrypts had been examined and had been found to indicate that the improvement in ARABEL's information had not gone unnoticed in Madrid and Lisbon. The escalation was well-justified, and also allowed MI5 to exploit the network more effectively. Pujol's letters to Lisbon usually took a minimum of a week for delivery, and often took longer if a king's messenger was not scheduled to visit Lisbon or Gene Risso-Gill was otherwise occupied. A swifter means of communication offered more opportunities, not the least of which was the acquisition of some valuable signals intelligence.

Once the Twenty Committee had given their consent, Pujol informed Madrid that CHAMILLUS, the Gibraltarian waiter, had befriended an enthusiastic supporter of the Spanish Republican Party who, before the war, had held an amateur radio opera-tor's licence. Apparently, he had served as an ambulance driver during the Spanish Civil War and was now a convinced pacifist. He was classified as a conscientious objector who lived alone on a farm, and therefore presented an ideal candidate for the post of ARABEL's wireless operator. Pujol explained that his new recruit, designated Agent 4(1), had retained his wireless illegally and was perfectly willing to transmit messages to Spain. Pujol had neglected to tell Agent 4(1) that he was a German spy, and had instead fed him a story about a group of Spanish

Republicans in London, led by Dr Juan Negrín, who supposedly wished to keep in touch with the communist underground
movement in Spain. As GARBO pointed out, the advantage of
this ploy was in the extra protection it offered. Even if the
British traced the transmitter and closed it down, none of
the rest of Pujol's ring would be endangered, and the likelihood was that the police would accept the cover story at face
value. In any event, the agent would never learn the text of his
signals as Pujol proposed only to supply him with enciphered
messages. As expected, the Abwehr was delighted with Pujol's
proposal and quickly gave its approval to the plan. It also
provided a transmitting schedule, a set of variable transmitting frequencies and, perhaps most importantly of all, a newly
introduced cipher, which was received with delight by the Radio
Security Service.

In practice, the new wireless operator was Charles Haines, a
French-speaking field security NCO who had indeed taken an
interest in becoming a 'radio ham' before the war. He was not,
however, a communist sympathiser. In reality, he had worked as
a clerk in Lloyds Bank, an occupation he was to return to after
the war. Since Juan's English was still rudimentary, and MI5 had
no radio operators fluent in Spanish, the two men conversed
in French. The Radio Security Service gave him a crash course
in Morse and a transmitter was set up in the back garden of
Crespigny Road. Once the link between Hendon and Madrid
had been opened on a regular basis, the RSS was provided with
a veritable flood of valuable intelligence. Continuous monitoring of the Abwehr channels revealed that ARABEL had risen in
the Germans' esteem, and also betrayed some of the Abwehr's
internal code names. ARABEL, for example, was sometimes
referred to as V-man (for 'Vertrauensmann' or confidential
agent) 319. The Venezuelans were referred to as V.373 and
V.374, while Haines was given the code name ALMURA. His principal contact in Madrid signed off the wireless net as CENTRO.
All this information was registered on card indices at Section

V headquarters, while MI5 authorised Tommy Harris to separate the GARBO operation from the rest of the Iberian section.
Accordingly, Harris and Sarah Bishop moved into a tiny new
office in Ml5's headquarters and set to work developing the
network further.

By the end of 1942 GARBO had only lost Agent TWO (William
Gerbers), but had gained its ninth source, code-named DAGOB-
ERT. DAGOBERT was an ex-seaman living in Swansea, and was
described by GARBO as 'a thoroughly undesirable character' who
worked only for money. Nevertheless, he was later to acquire
a further seven subagents and thus became GARBO's link with
an important, self-contained, network. When seeking Madrid's
permission to go ahead with DAGOHERT's recruitment, GARBO
pointed out that his addition would give the network greater
geographical coverage. He also suggested that, as a seaman
who occasionally visited neutral ports, DAGOBERT was in a position to smuggle documents and other items of espionage para-
phernalia which were too bulky for his regular K LM couriers
to handle. As predicted, the Abwehr responded positively, and
the scene was now set for large-scale exploitation of a widely
spread spy ring. GARBO had achieved everything hoped for and
was now basking in the praise of no less than two contented
and opposing intelligence organisations.

Having established GARBO as a reliable source for the Abwehr,
the Allies were anxious to flex their muscles and demonstrate
the scope of their powers. Unfortunately, the first opportunity to participate in a major deception campaign proved less
than satisfactory.

The major military preoccupation of 1943 was defensive in
nature, in anticipation of the two huge, long-term Allied operations planned for the future: the invasions of Italy and France.
The chiefs of staff were agreed that despite demands from
Moscow there was no likelihood of marshalling the necessary
forces before 1944, so the deception planners were instructed
to make the enemy believe that the Allies were planning no less

than three amphibious landings during the summer of 1943: STARKEY was to be across the channel in the Pas-de-Calais region, WADHAM was an American attack on Brittany, and TINDALL was a supposed invasion of Norway. All three deception plans, known collectively as COCKADE, were designed to bottle up German troops in Norway and keep the enemy guessing about the exact target of the landings in France. The basic objective was to keep the enemy contained in northern and western Europe and the Mediterranean, in the hope of easing the burden of the hard-pressed Red Army. In addition to STARKEY and WADHAM, fourteen raids were to be conducted along the coast to capture prisoners. Code-named FORFAR, these brief incursions were supposed to unnerve the defenders and convince them that their kidnapped sentries had been taken prisoner so they could be interrogated about the local troop strengths.

Another of COCKADE's optimistic objectives was to lure the Luftwaffe into a series of air battles over the Channel. The idea was to promote belief in an invasion, thus forcing the Germans to deploy their aircraft at particular moments when the RAF could press home their advantage. In the event these aerial ambushes failed to materialise.

COCKADE was approved by the chiefs of staff on 10 February 1943 and the Twenty Committee enthusiastically committed GARBO and his network to playing their part. No time was wasted, as can be seen by the claimed recruitment by BENEDICT, just three days later, of a source reported to be an airman. He was followed on 10 April by GARBO's introduction to a censor in the Ministry of Information, designated J(4). Finally, the NAAFI waiter at Chislehurst announced on 25 April 1943 that one of the soldiers on guard duty at his depot had started to provide some useful information. These were the individuals chosen by the Twenty Committee to perpetrate the most ambitious deception yet on the enemy's intelligence service. It was to be the forerunner of many more successful schemes.

The mechanics of channelling bogus information to the Axis has already been described, as has the elaborate system developed to coordinate the activities of the various parties involved in the manipulation of the double agents. It now remains to sketch how, at the planning level, the overall cover operations were formulated. As it progressed, it became clear that deception had become a weapon of strategic importance, but the essence of an effective deception policy was good coordination, with all the services playing their parts. Acting in concert, it was perfectly possible to mount a truly ambitious scheme and convey it to the enemy. Experience indicated that such operations could not be mounted piecemeal if they were to have any hope of success. More specialised, influential bodies were required to supervise deception policy, so in June a new, highly secret unit, the London Controlling Section (LCS), was created under the auspices of the chief of staff to the supreme allied commander (COS SAC) and, in the autumn, General Eisenhower established SHAEF Ops B, of which more will be heard later, to concentrate on preparing for D-Day.

After the Allied chiefs of staff had agreed on their objectives for the future, their staffs proposed a number of alternative cover plans. Some of these were of sufficient merit to be of possible use when the real invasion took place; these were shelved in case they might be needed and become a reality. Others were considered suitable for the feints of COCKADE and FORFAR. Once the chiefs of staff had made their minds up and decided the priorities, the issue of cover plans was passed to the London Controlling Section for implementation. Basically, LCS had three weapons at its disposal: physical deception (with camouflage and dummy equipment); signals (to imitate the presence of a large body of troops); and the conduit discreetly referred to as 'special means.' In fact, this last category (which, incidentally, proved the most potent) consisted of controlled leakages of information, either to 'neutral' diplomats in London (who would promptly report the latest rumours in the capital) or via MI5's stable of double agents. And among MI5's double agents GARBO had quickly established a formidable reputation. It was therefore to him and his network that the LCS turned in February 1943. The head of LCS was Colonel John Bevan, and it was one of his senior assistants, Colonel Harold Peteval, who presented the COCKADE project to the Twenty Committee at one of their regular Wednesday afternoon meetings. A plan had been drawn up involving a number of imaginary troop formations. Would GARBO's network report a few plausible sightings to persuade the Germans that the south coast of England was teeming with men from a non-existent Sixth Army, formerly based in Luton, which was about to cross the Channel? Although he may have regretted his decision later, Tommy Harris committed GARBO's network to relaying the deception to the Abwehr.

By later standards, COCKADE was far from sophisticated, and got off to a bad start. Of the fourteen FORFAR raids planned, only eight were mounted, and only one actually made contact with the enemy. The combined operations team was spotted by a German trawler on his way ashore so the entire plan was abandoned. Of the forty-two aerial operations planned in support of STARKEY, only fifteen were completed in full, mainly thanks to the vile weather, which also delayed the actual mock invasion twenty-four hours. This was eventually carried out on 9 September 1943, and although no less than twenty-one ships congregated ten miles off Boulogne, the Germans appeared not to notice. Even at the sight of such a tempting target the German coastal batteries remained quiet. When no enemy aircraft ventured over the fleet to investigate it turned around and steamed back to port.

STARKEY's failure was mirrored by the enemy's lack of interest in either TINDALL or WADHAM. Some half-hearted efforts had been made in Scotland to simulate the preparations of an airborne raid on Stavanger but the RAF could only spare a few dummy gliders. Such measures that were taken – for example, the creation of a notional Fourth Army at Edinburgh – failed to provoke the expected German reconnaissance flights. The only consolation from these two failures was the knowledge that the Germans had been told that WADHAM, the American assault in Brittany, was only scheduled to go ahead if STAR-KEY had succeeded in achieving a beachhead. Since STARKEY's puny invasion force had not even been fired on it was agreed that WADHAM, which had been intended for the Bay of Biscay, could be abandoned without further ado. Instead, a couple of Canadian wireless vans cruised along the south coast, simulating the signals traffic of convoys of landing craft returning to their dispersal areas, which the Germans monitored through their high-frequency direction-finding apparatus.

The COCKADE fiasco taught the deception planners many lessons, not the least of which was the importance of involving the three services at an early stage in a campaign. STARKEY had collapsed because the navy had refused to use any major ships as decoys, and the RAF had condemned TINDALL as 'play-acting'. Nevertheless, the whole deception plan had had some useful repercussions. A short newsreel had been made of American personnel practising amphibious landings 'somewhere in England' and had been released to certain neutral distributors. The film depicted an exercise with what were claimed to be combat-trained units, and apparently demonstrated that the Allies were really far further advanced in their preparations than they actually were. The film was only completed in August 1943 but, according to a calendar carelessly left in sight on an office wall, the exercise had taken place months before, in the early spring of 1943. Trees in the film were carefully pruned to give the impression that they had not yet come into leaf. These somewhat amateur ploys were to be the basis of the ambitious fabrications that were to follow.

COCKADE's failure created one major problem for GARBO. His network had been responsible for transmitting most of

STARKEY, and the caves at Chislehurst had been transformed (according to the NAAFI waiter and his friendly guard) into a huge depot for small arms and a communications centre. If the Germans believed for one moment that Chislehurst was to control the invasion they gave no sign of it. The chief victims were Agents ONE and SIX: ONE was required to resign in November and was heard no more of; Agent SIX, an NCO in the Field Security Police, was reported transferred and then killed in North Africa. By making these two subagents take the blame for STARKEY, GARBO himself survived intact, ready to take a more important role. While the Twenty Committee and the LCS had been wrestling with the problems of COCKADE, the chiefs of staff had been adding the finishing touches to a new plan, code-named OVERLORD.

The COCKADE post-mortem identified any number of short-comings which had served to undermine the operation's cred-ibility. Analysis of the ULTRA decrypts showed that the Germans had never been taken in, and had even reduced their strengths in Brittany, the target area for WADHAM. One armoured panzer division and two infantry divisions had actually been withdrawn in the period leading up to the alleged 'invasion'. Perhaps, more seriously, the expectations of many underground Resistance fighters in occupied France had been heightened, and it was feared that some lives might have been jeopdised. Another concern was the reputation of the BBC, which had speculated about the STARKEY invasion in several broadcasts.

The conclusion reached by Tommy Harris was simply this: there was no point in exaggerating the Allies' strength unless there was some genuine military build-up. He was convinced that GARBO still had an important role to play, provided the deception planners could persuade the service chiefs to take deception seriously and recognise its advantages. Fortunately, the creation of SHAEF Ops B heralded new opportunity and apparently offered a guarantee of cooperation from the depart-ments that had so effectively undermined COCKADE. SHAEF (the Supreme Headquarters Allied Expeditionary Force) was also to benefit from the transfer of a number of experienced deception specialists from the Middle East, who had achieved some notable successes in the desert campaign. They were optimistic about their chances of building a workable system to exploit GARBO's network which, in spite of the loss of Agents ONE, TWO and SIX, had acquired several new sources.

Agent TWO had been the Bootle man who had been eliminated to safeguard the embarkation of the Allied force destined for TORCH, the invasion of North Africa. On 10 March 1943 GARBO reported that his widow, Mrs Gerbers, had volunteered to take his place.

Another, more important source was the woman designated J(5), whose existence was first revealed on 4 September 1943. GARBO reported that she

> is far from beautiful and rather dowdy in her dress. Although in her early thirties she is clearly unaccustomed to attentions from the opposite sex. This makes her all the more accessible to mine. Already she is delightfully indiscreet.

In an internal Security Service memo dated February 1944, J(5) was described by Tommy Harris as

> a secretary in the Ministry of War, probably working in the office of the War Cabinet. She is carrying on an affair with GARBO, who she believes to be a Spanish Republican. Unconscious collaborator who has already been very indiscreet and could pass on very high grade political information. This source has been quoted by Madrid, when reporting to Berlin, as 'the Secretariat of the Ministry of War'.

It is possible that GARBO and Harris may have had Sarah Bishop in mind when they invented J(5), since she had indeed once worked as a secretary in the office of the War Cabinet. But there the resemblance ends, for Sarah Bishop was neither dowdy nor in her thirties. Apparently playing the 'sex card' was sufficiently controversial to provoke a discussion on the merits of such Mata Hari tactics. The American representative on the Twenty Committee, Norman Holmes Pearson, actually warned Harris that he was straying into dangerous territory and might even force the Abwehr to make unwarranted demands on her, which would lead to her demise, like Agent TWO. Pearson was a delegate from the American Office of Strategic Services; a professor of literature at Yale, he had been granted the unique privilege of sharing Masterman's office in St James's Street and was, therefore, privy to all the Twenty Committee's secrets.

Another important unconscious source, who was reported on in a message from the Welsh seaman DAGOBERT, dated 16 September 1943, just a week after the STARKEY fiasco, was 7(1), a soldier in the notional British 9th Armoured Division. This particular unit had been disbanded, but for deception purposes it was kept 'alive' with the aid of an ingenious device which enabled a single wireless set to simulate the transmissions of six. As we shall see, this project gradually turned the imaginary 9th Armoured Division into the entire Fourth Army, notionally stationed at Currie, near Edinburgh, which created enough wireless traffic for it and two army corps, the 7th British Corps at Dundee and the 2nd British Corps at Stirling, all apparently under the control of Scottish Command. The 2nd British Corps had actually once existed and had participated in the evacuation from Dunkirk. The Germans had taken so many prisoners from these corps that it was bound to be well known to them. The SHAEF planners had simply resurrected it on the assumption that the enemy were unlikely to have discovered that it had actually been disbanded in 1940. In reality, there were only a handful of signallers moving round the Scottish Highlands in radio vans to give life to the 'ghost' units.

According to BENEDICT, GARBO's deputy, he had made a useful contact while travelling on the same train as a young army lieutenant. This officer, who was serving in the 49th British Infantry Division in Scotland, apparently had no idea that BENEDICT was an enemy agent and was somewhat indiscreet about the assault training he had undergone. The purpose behind this exercise was the development of specialist unit which might be expected to take part in any major amphibious landing. If the lieutenant and his division was still reported in Scotland after D-Day, the Germans might reasonably deduce that a further attack was scheduled. MI5 designated the officer as 3(2).

Early the following month, the network was expanded further by CHAMILLUS, the NAAFI waiter. On 4 November 1943, he reported having met a garrulous American sergeant, GARBO described the sergeant as

> anti-communist and, to a lesser degree, anti-English Imperialist, following in part the ideas of Randolph Hearst, sustaining an admiration for Franco as Catholic crusader and first leader in the struggle against the Bolshevik.

As well as being 'sociable, jocular and fairly talkative', the sergeant worked as a clerk in some unspecified United States army headquarters in London and, therefore, had access to important military documents that someone of this rank would not normally see. Both GARBO and CHAMILLUS were sure that this imprudent serviceman would prove a useful, if unconscious, source of valuable intelligence. Harris designated him 4(3) and assigned to him the role of building up the American contribution to SHAEF's deception campaign.

The last two notional agents to be recruited in 1943 were both seamen, in an attempt to improve GARBO's marine observations. The first was a Greek deserter, who materialised on 19 December. The rich Venezuelan, BENEDICT, described how he had met the Greek, who had turned out to be a communist. Ever resourceful, GARBO's deputy had told him that he was a

Soviet spy on the lookout for new, trustworthy members of his ring. The Greek had promptly offered his services and had promised to submit regular reports from Scottish ports. The Germans were delighted by this, so Harris entered him in GARBO's growing logbook as 3(3).

The second former seaman came via DAGOBERT, the Welsh mercenary from Swansea, who had joined up with the leader of a small group of political dissidents. GARBO reported to Madrid:

> A friend of DAGOBERT has been a member of the 'Welsh Nationalist Party', but he had advanced ideas and he was not pleased with the liberal sentiment of the party, maintaining that the emancipation of his country would depend entirely on the establishment of what he calls the 'Aryan World Order Movement' to collaborate with all the Aryans all over the world. On account of this, he left the party more than two years ago and joined an Indian, a friend of his, who has lived for many years in this country, forming a group which he calls 'Brothers in the Aryan World Order'. As its position, owing to being clandestine, is very dangerous, they have had very little success, as only about twelve revolutionary members are affiliated, and their activities are very limited and rather ridiculous.

DAGOBERT claimed that the brothers in the Aryan World Order occupied themselves by compiling lists of political and racial undesirables (mainly Jews and communists) who were to be assassinated when they seized power. After receiving Madrid's approval, the ex-seaman was code-named DONNY and taken onto DAGOBERT's strength. Tommy Harris marked him down as 7(2) and arranged for him to take up residence in Dover. After further consultation early in the new year of 1944, the Indian fanatic was code-named DICK. MI5 designated him 7(4) and sent him to Brighton.

The Abwehr seemed so pleased with DAGOBERT's progress that GARBO and Harris decided to take full advantage of the situation and suggested the recruitment of the rest of the brothers. Because DAGOBERT himself was being paid a salary, this expansion would inevitably require further expenditure and, therefore, a greater commitment from Madrid. As well as the financial motive for the proposal, which might have seemed a little overambitious so soon after COCKADE, there was also a further, equally important, motive. By the end of 1943 the Twenty Committee was fully aware of the implications of OVERLORD and had been given advance warning of a ban which was to be imposed on people visiting certain coastal areas. The whole point of DAGOBERT's self-contained spy ring was its access to shipping. But if the entire network remained bottled up in South Wales there would be little chance of presenting a comprehensive deception plan. A good geographical spread was essential to any campaign, so DAGOBERT's sources had to be accepted into the network and dispersed to their chosen observation points before the ban was officially announced. If their recruitment was handled quickly, each could execute the move without delay and obtain the necessary residential qualification before applying for the much-valued permit to live in a coastal area. Naturally, none of this was spelt out to the Abwehr, and luckily it did not take long before the German consent arrived. As a result, four more brothers were promptly enrolled. One alleged dissident, designated 7(3), was DICK's secretary and mistress, who had recently been called up for the Women's Royal Naval Service. She had been ordered to report for war duty at a Wren depot at Mill Hill and, after her preliminary training, was to be posted to a camp near Newbury to sit a language examination. DAGOBERT was later to explain that she spoke fluent Hindustani, and this had led to her eventual transfer to South-East Asia Command's headquarters in Ceylon. In reality, her role was taken on by Peter Fleming, the deception expert on Lord Louis Mountbatten's staff, who proceeded to fabricate a series of letters which GARBO forwarded to Lisbon. ISOS decrypts later showed that these letters eventually ended up with the Japanese military attaché in Berlin, who had them transmitted to Tokyo. This 'barium meal' gave the code breakers at Bletchley Park valuable clues to the Japanese diplomatic cipher.

The other brothers brought into DAGOBERT's ring in December 1943 were three Welsh fascists: DRAKE, who was portrayed as one of DONNY's relations and instructed to go and live in Southampton; 7(6), who was due to move to Exeter; and DORICK, who was notionally placed in Harwich. These arrangements were later changed early in 1944 when the Twenty Committee decreed that it was too dangerous to allow DRAKE to go to Southampton as there were too many sensitive military and naval installations for him to observe. So GARBO remarked on 18 February 1944, in his sixteenth letter to Lisbon (which, incidentally, was deposited at the Espírito Santo bank concealed in a tin of curry powder), that DRAKE had gone to Exeter and that 7(6), who had originally intended to go there, had stayed in South Wales instead.

Before describing how MI5 mobilised all these characters into the most successful deception campaign ever, it would be well to retrace our steps briefly and catch up with BENEDICT's brother, MOONBEAM, who had been obliged to beat a hasty retreat to Canada in the summer of 1943 and had started GARBO's North American network.

The 'Canadian connection' really dated back to 10 December 1942, when the Royal Canadian Mounted Police (RCMP) had arrested their first important, genuine German spy of the war. The agent, who carried clumsily forged papers identifying himself as 'Mr Braunter', a radio salesman from Toronto, had been spotted in the small town of New Carlisle passing out-of-date Canadian currency. Virtually everyone in Quebec's Gaspé Peninsula had been warned about possible landings by Nazi spies, and this particular stranger could hardly have been more conspicuous, arriving in a tourist area out of season. The RCMP had been alerted swiftly and a local constable had challenged him on a train bound for Montreal. He had quickly admitted his true identity – that of a German naval officer named Janowsky attached to the Abwehr – and had claimed to have been landed the previous evening by a submarine in Chaleur Bay; he was then allowed to show the RCMP the spot on the beach where he had buried his captain's uniform. After a brief interrogation he volunteered to be a double-agent and work his transmitter back to Hamburg under the RCMP's control.

Although, at that time, intelligence work was relatively unknown to the RCMP, which boasted just one full-time intelligence officer whose main function was liaison with London, they did have the use of an experienced former British Secret Intelligence Service agent named Gottfried Treviranus, who was then living in Montreal. Treviranus had been a veteran spy who had been obliged to flee Germany before the war when the Gestapo had discovered some of his covert activities. SIS had given him a new identity and had smuggled him to Mount Royal, Montreal, where he had lived quietly under the RCMP's protection. Treviranus had served in U-boats during the First World War and gradually built up a rapport with the spy, so much so that he persuaded the RCMP officer in charge of the case, Cliff Harvison, to contact MI5. Was the Security Service interested in running a double agent? After some discussion by the Twenty Committee, it was agreed that Cyril Mills, accompanied by a B1(a) secretary, Pixie Verrall, should travel to Ottawa to investigate further, and while he was there he would represent GARBO's MOONBEAM, who was becoming a liability in England.

Mills was met in Canada by the RCMP commissioner, Stuart Wood, and invited to run the spy. Once Mills was satisfied that the agent had truly turned (which was established when he disclosed his wireless security check: his secret signal that he had been caught and was operating under the enemy's control), he was dubbed WATCHDOG and was placed under guard in a three-roomed basement apartment under Treviranus's home. The RCMP built a fifty-foot aerial in the back garden and, with the aid of a powerful Canadian army transmitter (which proved more reliable than the ineffective radio provided by the Abwehr), successfully opened communications with Hamburg.

Meanwhile, MOONBEAM reported his own safe arrival and, with the collaboration of the Federal Bureau of Investigation, recruited a cousin who was resident just over the American border in Buffalo. MOONBEAM's messages, which were relayed to the Abwehr via GARBO, caused some amusement in London and Berlin because of the agent's mercenary nature. Every tiny item of expenditure was carefully recorded and claimed for. On one occasion, the Germans queried a small sum spent from petty cash for paying a labourer to clear snow from the path to his home, MOONBEAM responded by demanding to know how he could be expected to collect information if he couldn't get out of the house! The Abwehr promptly radioed their approval.

WATCHDOG himself came to an end late in the summer of 1943, when he ran out of funds, and he was transferred to Ml5's custody in England. Nevertheless, Mills continued with MOONBEAM and his cousin in upstate New York, and offered a safe refuge to those of GARBO's network who suddenly had to flee Britain. CHAMILLUS, for example, the wretched Gibraltarian, eventually deserted from his post in the NAAFI in October 1944 and made his way to Canada, where he was employed as MOONBEAM's wireless operator. This final act proved to be extremely useful because CHAMILLUS was entrusted with a new, high-grade cipher, a copy of which was delivered by MI5 straight to GHQ at Bletchley.

By February 1944 GARBO and Tommy Harris had completed the final sector of DAGOBERT's ring and had laid the foundations for a truly integrated deception operation. Twenty-four subagents and sources were spread evenly throughout the country and the entire machine had been cranked up ready for action. Early

in the month GARBO himself went on a tour of the south and
south-west of the country and handed Charles Haines a brief
message, which was transmitted from Crespigny Road at 8.10
in the evening of 17 February:

> An observation to which I give importance is that the distribu-
> tion of forces to date is all along the length of the coast and
> there is no concentration at special points.

This typically bland appraisal was to mark the beginning of
GARBO's active involvement in OVERLORD's cover plan, code-
named FORTITUDE. The only unforeseen hitch, which meant
little at the time of its receipt, was a curious signal, dated 15
December 1943, warning GARBO to leave London as soon as
possible. It was only six months later, after the first buzz bombs
had fallen on the capital, that the significance of the message
was fully realised. But by that time FORTITUDE was in full swing.

9

OPERATION FORTITUDE

While Operation OVERLORD was being planned, the Allied chiefs of staff became increasingly aware of two crucial problems: that establishing a beachhead in the midst of the enemy's defence was one thing; maintaining it in the face of a swift counter-attack would be quite another. Three separate needs were therefore identified. Firstly, a requirement to persuade the enemy to position his forces as far away as possible from the intended target area. This was done in the large scale by formulating a scheme to keep Axis troops committed in non-essential regions, such as the Balkans and the Mediterranean. In Europe itself the requirement was translated into providing plausible evidence that the coming invasion, which was recognised as virtually impossible to disguise, would be headed by a two-pronged attack on Norway and the Pas-de-Calais area. Secondly, the enemy had to be misled about the exact timing of the assault; and thirdly, the Germans had to be convinced that any landings along the French coast, apart from those in the Pas-de-Calais, were diversionary in nature. In other words, even after troops had begun to move ashore in Normandy, the Germans must be made to believe that this initial operation was but a feint designed to draw their forces away from the real target area, which was further north. To bring off this last trick was the tall order presented to the deception planners at the Supreme Headquarters Allied Expeditionary Force (SHAEF). Their eventual solution, known as FORTITUDE, was described by the historian Charles Cruikshank in his history of *Deception in World War II* (Oxford University Press, 1979, p. 170) as 'the largest, most elaborate, most carefully planned, most vital and most successful of all the Allied deceptive operations'.

Assembling the largest invasion fleet in history could not be achieved overnight, and the concentrations of landing craft and other essential equipment would be difficult to hide from German reconnaissance aircraft, quite apart from the 5,000 ships estimated to be involved, so the decision was taken to execute a variety of reasonable security measures to prevent unauthorised leakages. As GARBO had anticipated (and circumvented), a ban on visitors was placed on a zone ten miles deep along the coast from Cornwall to Lincolnshire and, in an unprecedented proposal, the Foreign Office discussed the imposition of a total ban on all uncensored communications to and from neutral diplomats in London, from a date yet to be decided in mid-April 1944.

The SHAEF planners, huddled over their maps in Norfolk House, St James's Square, knew they had two useful advantages they could exploit. The Allied chiefs of staff had decided not to try and capture a Channel port intact, which was the most straightforward answer to the logistical problem of supplying such a huge body of men and armour. Instead, they had opted for prefabricated harbours, consisting of huge concrete caissons, which were to be floated into position off the beaches. Once the caissons had been constructed, they were to be left submerged in the Solent and elsewhere until the moment came for them to be towed across the Channel. Provided the Germans remained ignorant of the true purpose of the floating harbours, code-named MULBERRY, there was a good chance that the Abwehr would recommend a concentration of defences around the Channel ports between Ostend and Brest. The second advantage lay in the Twenty Committee's confidence that every enemy agent in Britain was working under MI5's control. Although other double agents were to be employed in FORTITUDE, much of the burden would fall on GARBO and his network because the ISOS intercepts had demonstrated that he enjoyed the highest standing in Berlin.

The Twenty Committee, therefore, resolved to convey the elements deemed essential to OVERLORD's success: that the invasion could not be launched until at least July 1944; that it would be preceded by an attack on Norway; and that the eventual thrust into France would centre on the Pas-de-Calais, after some initial feints elsewhere. It was learned after the war that this strategy fitted neatly into current German thinking, which took a characteristically rational approach to their dilemma. Field Marshal von Rundstedt, for example, took four major factors into consideration when he decided that the Allies would opt for the shortest route across the Channel: the Allies would need at least one major port; they would require constant protection from the air, so the nearer the beachhead the better; Calais offered the most direct path to Germany; and the capture of the V-weapon launch sites would become an important political consideration once the bombardment of London had begun. In fact, the projected V-1 offensive did not occur until after D-Day, so SHAEF was never in a position to waste time debating the last factor. SHAEF never knew that FORTITUDE was actually confirming the conclusions that German high command had already reached, albeit tentatively.

The cover deception plan itself was divided into FORTITUDE NORTH, which concentrated on the notional build-up of troops in Scotland for the attack on Norway, and FORTITUDE SOUTH, which promoted the 'shortest route' assault. Just as the fictitious British Fourth Army was to play a vital part in FORTITUDE NORTH, it was Roger Hesketh's creation of an entirely bogus First United States Army Group (FUSAG) which was to be the key to FORTITUDE SOUTH. But in February 1944, just when SHAEF and the Twenty Committee had settled the final details of the operation, Tommy Harris suddenly stepped in with a bombshell: GARBO and his network should be withdrawn immediately.

The last-minute crisis was precipitated by another double agent code-named ARTIST. In fact, ARTIST was a young Abwehr officer stationed in Lisbon named Johann Jebsen who, since the summer of 1943, had been actively collaborating with a network of Yugoslav double agents. Jebsen, who was supposed to be virulently anti-Nazi, cut a colourful figure in wartime Portugal, driving between Lisbon and his villa in Estoril in a Rolls-Royce. He claimed to be an Anglophile, and his first link with the British came via two Yugoslav brothers, Dusko and Ivo Popov, who were code-named TRICYCLE and DREADNOUGHT respectively by MI5. Jebsen's excuse for his contact with the Popovs was that he was negotiating an underground escape route through Europe for evading Yugoslav airmen. At the end of January Dusko Popov returned to London, after a two-month stay in Portugal where he had held several meetings with Jebsen, and gave the Twenty Committee a lengthy summary of his conversations. Popov had known Jebsen for some years and trusted him implicitly, but Tommy Harris was aghast by one particular section of Popov's report, in which Jebsen attempted to prove his bona fides to the Allies by naming some of the Abwehr's chief agents run from Lisbon. Heading the list was the name of Juan Pujol, code-named ARABEL.

Harris accepted that Popov's judgement of Jebsen was probably the correct one and that he could be trusted, but he pointed out that the implication of not taking action against any of the spies on Jebsen's list was the equivalent of providing him with confirmation that they were all being run by the Allies. If Jebsen came to this conclusion, which was inescapable, he would inevitably realise that most of the intelligence they were supplying was nothing more than a clever fabrication. This information might indeed be safe with Jebsen, but supposing his circumstances changed: would his loyalties also change again? Another cause for concern was Jebsen's admission that his contacts with the Allies had the approval of the Abwehr controller in Lisbon, who had told him to develop some cover as a discontented German out of favour with the regime. On the present showing, argued Harris, OVERLORD's fate was held in the hands of a single man who happened to be an enemy intelligence officer. If Jebsen knew GARBO was controlled by MI5, he would guess that FORTITUDE was a fake and so jeopardise OVERLORD. It was not the kind of news any self-respecting security official cared to tell an Allied supreme commander.

The Twenty Committee deliberated over the ARTIST crisis and considered all the alternatives. The easiest option, which was to pull Jebsen out of Portugal, thus isolating him from the Abwehr, was ruled out because if the Germans learned that he had defected, they would automatically assume that all the agents that Jebsen had had access to would be compromised. Another possibility was asking the Secret Intelligence Station in Lisbon to assassinate Jebsen, but it was pointed out that such a move would be bound to attract a major German investigation into all the circumstances surrounding the incident, and that too might uncover Jebsen's illicit contacts with the British. Eventually, the Twenty Committee reached the only possible decision: they would do nothing, but ask SIS to keep an eye on him.

Understandably, Tommy Harris was greatly agitated about this decision, and it later seemed that his worst fears were about to be realised. But before describing the dramatic events of May 1944, we should return to the first stages of FORTI-TUDE, which were proceeding with GARBO's help in spite of Harris's objections.

The initial part was the pretence that the Allies were not yet in a position to launch a major offensive across the Channel and had, therefore, postponed their original invasion plans until much later in the year.

In the middle of February 1944 GARBO pretended to have undertaken a tour of the south coast of England. On 19 February, from Portland in Dorset, GARBO posted his fifteenth letter and mentioned having spotted some American soldiers in the neighbourhood of the town. He also described their shoulder flashes: 'the number "1" in red on a khaki ground'. This was a calculated reference to a genuine unit, the 1st US Infantry Division, which had in fact been brought back to England from the Italian front some months earlier, but SHAEF was anxious to conceal the return of these battle-seasoned troops until the last possible moment before the real invasion. GARBO's intervention was designed to win him credit for passing on some legitimate news. It had been argued that so many Africa Star campaign medals were being worn on uniforms in England, with its distinctive red and yellow ribbon, that it would be impossible to keep the division's arrival secret for much longer. Other agents supported GARBO's observation by stating that these hardened troops were engaged in training other troops, thereby promoting the idea that Allied preparations for the invasion were not particularly advanced.

GARBO explained that 'balanced forces are being held in readiness in England to occupy any part of north-west Europe against the contingency of a German withdrawal or collapse'. In his first message concerning SHAEF's strategy, which effectively marked the opening of Operation FORTITUDE, GARBO remarked that 'it does not require a very wise man to deduce that should the way be left free they would not hesitate to take advantage of it'. As additional evidence of the Allies' plan, he described how he had seen a pile of newly printed leaflets in the office of his contact in the Ministry of Information and had purloined a copy. Entitled *Avis à la Population*, it was despatched to Lisbon. The forgery, the only one of its kind ever printed, was marked for distribution to French civilians following a German withdrawal and urged them to cooperate with their new occupiers. As a foundation for FORTITUDE NORTH, GARBO reported that he had ordered his Glasgow-based deputy, BENEDICT, to monitor the growing number of naval exercises in the Clyde, and the Greek deserter had been instructed to find lodgings at Methil, on the east coast of Scotland. This he did on 1 April 1944, booking a room for the next six weeks. As confirmation that the British Fourth Army was still operational (and, indeed, the key to the northern campaign), BENEDICT reported to GARBO on 28 March 1944 that he had just returned from a trip to Dundee, where he had spotted the 52nd Lowland Division and a unit bearing shoulder flashes of a shell on a dark background. When relaying this message in a four-minute wireless transmission at 1920 hours that evening, GARBO commented: 'This insignia is completely unknown to me.' This was not entirely surprising, considering that Roger Hesketh had only just invented it!

Meanwhile, GARBO himself had been on a tour to check on some of DAGOBERT's informants. During a transmission at six in the evening of 7 March, he reported:

> I was able to confirm last Sunday the accuracy of the recent report sent by DONNY from Dover. I am, therefore, able to classify him in future as a good reporter.

In the same message he also authenticated messages received from DAGOBERT's other agents, including DICK the Indian fanatic: 'With regard to the military report, it is completely accurate so that we can catalogue this collaborator as being good.'

On 13 April he sent a radio message giving a good opinion of DORICK, one of the Welsh Fascists, who had reported seeing 'a lot of troops and vehicles of the ninth Division' passing through Norwich: 'I consider this first report of this collaborator fairly good as he tries to get details, from which one is able to appreciate the interest he takes in explaining what he has seen.'

On 22 April GARBO received a long letter from the Abwehr, dated 3 April 1944, Lisbon, which showed that they were particularly impressed with DAGOBERT's subagents:

> I have taken note with great interest of what you have told me in your letters about the amplification of your network, and the numerous messages which you have sent during the last few weeks have demonstrated to me that you have been absolutely right in your idea of nominating the old collaborators as subagents of their networks. In particular, the network

of DAGOBERT appears to be the one which is giving the
best results.

This message caused some celebration at Crespigny Road and St
James's Street, for it was the first real proof that FORTITUDE was
off to a good start. GARBO responded by relaying a message on
30 April from CHAMILLUS, the NAAFI waiter, who, on 27 April,
had volunteered to leave the depot at Chislehurst for a secret
invasion embarkation point. On 29 April CHAMILLUS telephoned
GARBO to arrange a rendezvous the following day at Winchester
railway station. At their meeting CHAMILLUS had disclosed that
his new base was Hiltingbury Camp, near Otterbourne in
Hampshire. GARBO reported that, according to CHAMILLUS,

all the 3rd Infantry Division are concentrated here ready to
embark. There are other camps full of troops ready for attack.
Have identified the 47th London Division in a camp to the
south of mine ... it is extremely difficult to leave the camp.
They are preparing cold rations for two days, also vomit bags
and lifebelts for troops' sea voyage.

The purpose of this particular scheme was to place CHAMILLUS in
a position where he might reasonably be expected to let GARBO
know when the invasion fleet had put to sea. Both GARBO and
Harris were adamant that advance notice of the invasion of
just one hour would be enough to enhance his reputation with
the Abwehr. The Twenty Committee accepted this idea, with
some dissent, but unfortunately the atmosphere soured early
the next month and the committee's attention was temporarily diverted. News arrived from Portugal which suggested that
ARTIST's (Jebsen) case had taken a turn for the worse. On 28 April
Jebsen had kept a rendezvous with Graham Maingot in Lisbon,
at which Jebsen had disclosed that the Abwehr had become
suspicious of TRICYCLE (Dusko Popov) and were convinced that
even if he was not now operating as a controlled agent for the

British he probably had been in touch with them at some stage. The relevant part of the Secret Intelligence Service's summary of Jebsen's debriefing is reproduced here as it sheds important light on the kind of agonising a case officer had to endure:

> Abteilung III has announced that in their opinion TRICYCLE's material is not controlled by the British. This judgment is entirely on the basis of TRICYCLE's latest report, and the Abteilung hold to their opinion that in one period of his career TRICYCLE was under Allied control. They explain the change as follows: the Allies provided poor material; ARTIST complained to TRICYCLE that he was not earning his keep; TRICYCLE then decided to collect material himself, and the result has been his last report – so good that Abteilung III is in entire agreement with the general staff that it is inconceivable that the British should have deliberately fed it. From ARTIST's point of view the outcome is a complete triumph, and he is sure that whatever happens now, these two departments whose confidence it is hardest to win will never reverse decisions so categorically expressed. To crown it all, ARTIST has been awarded the 'Kriegsverdienstkreuz, 1st Class', an honour shared by no one in Lisbon.

Although Jebsen had given SIS an optimistic account of his handling of Dusko Popov, he did admit that a week earlier, on 21 April, he had ducked out of a meeting he had been ordered to attend at Biarritz with Dr Aloys Schreiber, a senior Abwehr official also based in Lisbon, and a certain Major von Bohhlen. Jebsen had suspected that the location of the meeting, which had been to discuss various sums claimed by Popov, was conveniently close to the French frontier if the Gestapo wished to arrest him. Jebsen had excused himself, saying that he was anxious not to compromise his own cover as a German malcontent.

The day after Jebsen had reported to SIS he went to the German embassy in Lisbon to receive his decoration. As soon as he stepped through the door of Schreiber's office, he was knocked to the floor and interrogated. On 1 April he was bundled, unconscious, into the trunk of a limousine carrying diplomatic plates and driven straight to France, where he received an official escort for the remainder of his journey to Berlin. After a brief spell in a Wermacht prison, he was transferred into the custody of the Gestapo, who are believed to have executed him in the Oranienburg concentration camp on an unknown date in April 1945.

The first news of this catastrophe reached Bletchley on 2 May 1944, when a signal was intercepted from Schreiber to Berlin announcing the successful completion of Operation DORA. The message confirmed that Jebsen had crossed into France at Biarritz at 1500 hours the previous day. It was subsequently established that DORA was the code name for Jebsen's abduction.

An analysis of Lisbon's ISOS traffic showed that DORA had been a last-minute affair, and that Schreiber had been recalled from Madrid on 24 April to prevent Jebsen's rendezvous with the SIS, which the Abwehr believed had been arranged for the following day. It seems likely that either Jebsen's determination to discover the real identities of the Lisbon Abstelle's agents had led to his exposure or that his investigation of a particular spy on the German payroll had caused his downfall. All these possibilities were discussed at length by the Twenty Committee, which had no alternative but to hope that Jebsen resisted his interrogators at least until the end of D-Day. In order to reassure Tommy Harris, an MI5 officer who had not been let in on the secrets of OVERLORD was asked to review GARBO's correspondence to date to see if he could detect a bias in favour of a particular target area on the French coast. The officer concluded that there was only the slightest of imbalance in favour of the Pas-de-Calais.

Nevertheless, undeterred by these events, GARBO and his case officer continued their work as if nothing had happened. On 1 May GARBO relayed a routine message from DONNY, who had seen officers of the 28th American Infantry Division in Tenterden and Dover. At Folkestone he had spotted the American VIII Corps; GARBO commented that these (real) units were evidently on the move. The 28th Infantry Division had been portrayed elsewhere as an assault group unit and had also been reported recently in Tenby by DORICK, shortly before he had left South Wales. As D-Day got closer, the FUSAG forces (of which the 28th Infantry Division and the US VIII Corps were constituents) were to move slowly eastward toward Kent and East Anglia, adding support to the proposition that the expected attack would be spearheaded from the Dover area.

The following day, on 2 May, GARBO described an indiscreet chat with his mistress (who was working in the war ministry), who said that there was no chance of an immediate invasion, thus contradicting the view expressed by CHAMILLUS just three days earlier.

'I am disconcerted by what CHAMILLUS said and cannot under any circumstances advise or give information,' radioed GARBO.

The Abwehr, clearly preferring CHAMILLUS's version of events, replied the following evening:

> I do not consider that you should attribute too much importance to the opinion of J(5) in the present situation, since it is very probable that the ministerial personnel have received very severe orders with regard to the confidential handling of all military matters at the present moment. It is also possible that subordinates of ministries are being falsely misled intentionally.

For good measure, GARBO added a report from DORICK, who had seen armoured cars and tanks of the 6th US Division at Ipswich railway station.

The next day, 4 May, CHAMILLUS vouchsafed that the 3rd Canadian Division had just left Hiltingbury with orders to embark at Southampton. GARBO transmitted the message the same night and sent a longer text the next evening:

> CHAMILLUS communicates that orders have been given to clean and prepare the camp to receive troops once more. Agent supposes that these will be second-line units. This proves J(5)'s lie because she suggested, naively, today that troops in the southern area were on manoeuvres, information which has been disproved, as in this case troops would have returned. My opinion is that, assuming they have not landed on the Channel coast, the troops which embark must at this moment be moving toward their far-off objective or to join the fleet reported by BENEDICT in the Clyde.

In his next transmission, on 7 May, GARBO laid into CHAMILIUS who, he said, had

> displayed the ability of a simpleton. I am very disgusted with him, though I have not let him know this. He has, today, communicated with the troops he was awaiting, which he thought would be second-line troops, who have arrived, but they are the same as previously left, which is to say the 3rd Canadian Division. The troops at the other camps have like-wise returned. Though too late, he tells me that they have been in one of the many rehearsals which Churchill announced would be carried out before the second front was opened. My last comments about J(5) should be disregarded. I see that her information was true and that the fault has been partly mine through being impressed with my agent. I see that I could get more accurate information through my ministe-rial friends. CHAMILLUS, in excuse, says that his beliefs were confirmed by concrete military events, which I am unable to deny. In future he will make no further comments to influence

me or my chiefs. I am afraid he is a little discouraged by his great stupidity.

Madrid wasted no time in replying to this skilfully woven item of psychological arm twisting. GARBO received the following at 1959 hours, 8 May 1944:

I do not consider that we should reproach CHAMILLUS at all since the troops and the majority of the officers left the camps convinced that it was to be the invasion and only a few high officers knew the real objectives. If CHAMILLUS is disillusioned through his mistake, which he could not avoid, you should give him encouragement, as, if not, it might happen that when the real invasion is about to take place he will not notify this owing to over precaution.

Just half an hour later it was business as usual, with GARBO sending a report of troops from the 61st and 45th Divisions, and Nos 3 and 16 Commandos, seen by DICK between Brighton and Newhaven.

On the evening of 10 May GARBO transmitted a message in which he recounted a conversation he had had with CHAMILLUS's American acquaintance, the sergeant known as 4(3), who had said that

the second front would open as soon as the two army groups destined for operation were ready. One of these, the 21 Army Group, is under Montgomery. The other, the First Army Group, is provisionally under the orders of Bradley. The American troops which are expected here will enter the latter army group. He assured me that Eisenhower would give a very important task to the American army group.

BENEDICT also continued to keep the shipping movements on the Clyde under surveillance and supplied GARBO with a regular flow of intelligence. On 10 and 11 May he kept watch from Greenock and later spotted a big naval assault group exercising in Loch Fyne, and mentioned having noticed troops kitted out with arctic clothing. He was convinced that this was the prelude to an important attack on Norway, and this news was reported by GARBO's wireless on the evenings of 14 and 15 May. A similar picture was drawn by BENEDICT's Greek agent, who noted a gradual build-up of cargo ships in Methil. Apparently, they were to supply an operation in which a large number of troops were to take part. They had already been assembled in some other ports along the Scottish east coast.

The pace was now hotting up, with a strong implication in GARBO's messages that perhaps a two-pronged attack across the North Sea and the Strait of Dover was being planned. The ever reliable DAGOBERT was producing some useful intelligence from the south of England. Each sounded eminently plausible, and the ISOS decrypts from Bletchley confirmed that the Germans believed them to be authentic.

On the main Romsey–Ringwood road I saw 125 military vehicles of all types, including Bren gun carriers, with the insignia of the 54th Division. I also saw vehicles with the insignia of the 47th London Division.

Meanwhile, it was realised that CHAMILLUS's reported conversation with the American sergeant, 4(3), had made the necessary impact, for GARBO received the following questionnaire from Madrid by radio on the evening of 17 May:

With reference to the latest reports of 4(3), I send the following questionnaire, the reply to which would be of much interest. Where is the headquarters of the 21 Army Group, English? The numbering of the armies within the said army group, and their headquarters. How many and which divisions are within each of the armies of the said army group, indicating, where possible, which divisions are armoured and which are infantry.

Ten days later GARBO described a further exchange he had had with the American:

> I questioned him on the 21 Army Group, but it seems that he does not know much about this formation. He was only able to say that there are a few American troops in it, but that the Americans are mainly in the First US Army Group.

Heavy emphasis was being placed on the obvious build-up of Allied forces in the south-east and eastern counties. On 25 May DAGOBERT saw 'the sign of the panda several times' around Ipswich, a reference to the divisional identification of the 9th British Armoured Division, which was evidently moving into East Anglia. GARBO himself made a contribution the following day by sighting 'many troops with sign of a knight with lance' at Lewes. This was further evidence that the 8th English Army Corps Headquarters had moved into eastern Sussex. A week later, on 1 June, DAGOBERT noticed the 9th Armoured Division outside Tilbury. The entire division had been transferred right across the country, surely more proof that the invasion was imminent and heading for the Pas-de-Calais?

While the German high command absorbed these reports, GARBO had other, more mundane, developments to report. Agent DRAKE's behaviour, for example, had been giving cause for concern. He was supposed to have set himself up in the West Country, but on 19 April he had reported from Taunton that he had failed to get into the local prohibited zone. A month later he had sent an anxious letter from Exeter:

> I entered this prohibited area where vigilance is extremely strict. I do not see any possibility of remaining here owing to

the continual demands for documentation, which up to the moment I have been able to evade.

His luck had only lasted another fortnight. On 2 June 7(6) reported from Swansea that DRAKE had been arrested and sentenced to a month's imprisonment:

Apparently, there is no indication that any suspicion exists regarding the mission with which he was entrusted by me and that it was only a routine case for not having complied with the present restrictions.

This effectively eliminated DRAKE from FORTITUDE and ensured that he did not have to experience any awkward lapses during the invasion. Having removed DRAKE, it was decided to silence 7(6) by portraying him as another of DAGOBERT's failures. Accordingly, GARBO told Madrid:

I have received a long letter from 7(6) with reports, the majority of which were stupid. We can therefore discount the ability of this agent as an informant in spite of the repeated instructions given. His usefulness to the military information service is nil.

This ploy was designed to add some authenticity to GARBO's work. After all, however brilliant an organiser he might be, not all his agents could plausibly be presented as excellent performers. DRAKE and 7(6) proved that occasionally GARBO experienced a setback. Nevertheless, GARBO's network was maturing well, and the letter and wireless traffic to Madrid was gradually being built up. In fact, the volume got so great that Harris became concerned that it was probably too much for a single person, so GARBO sought permission to bring BENEDICT the Venezuelan down from Glasgow to act as his deputy. He also asked for Mrs Gerbers, Agent TWO's widow, to be allowed to help with the mass of ciphering work. Madrid responded with enthusiasm. Incredibly, they also accepted GARBO's suggestion that all future communications should be written in English, to assist Mrs Gerbers.

One agent who had excelled was J(3), the unconscious source who worked at the Ministry of Information. As Tommy Harris had already pointed out, this individual could have been identified as the head of the Spanish section and, purely by chance, the real person actually went to Madrid early in May 1944. GARBO reported his departure, and MI5 requested that the British embassy send him home at the earliest opportunity, before the Germans took any initiative. Nothing untoward happened to the entirely innocent official, and on 22 May GARBO described a conversation he had had with him on his return:

> Result of interview today with J(3). He returned from Madrid for reasons connected with propaganda preparations of the second front. He proposed that I should help him, offering good remuneration for work which I could do at home. I accepted provisionally, telling him that I wanted to consult with my family, in order to allow time to receive approval from you, since it concerns work for the enemy which I could only accept as a sacrifice to be compensated by getting important information.

Not surprisingly, when tempted with such an attractive prize, the Germans wasted no time in telling their star agent to take up the MOI official's tantalising offer. They radioed the next day:

> Have studied carefully the question of J(3). Am of the opinion that you should accept the offer as apart from his being able to facilitate good information, this work assists your cover in every respect.

On 28 May, GARBO announced that he had taken the job ... and had been made to sign a special document in which he had undertaken not to breach the Official Secrets Act.

I attach much importance to this because I learned that only
people who may get to learn details which may compromise
secret plans are obliged to sign this.

Even forty years later it is not difficult to imagine the fun that
GARBO and his case officer had while compiling this particular
message. But there was also a serious side to the Abstelle's
signal of 22 May. Madrid Abstelle had also inquired about
FORTITUDE's fictitious units in Scotland:

I am particularly interested to know urgently whether the
52nd Division is still in the camps in the Glasgow area after
finishing the manoeuvres on the 11th, in accordance with the
message of BENEDICT. I should be grateful to have your reply
as soon as possible. Please take every measure to ensure that
you are notified of every movement of that division by the
quickest possible means. I should be grateful if you would tell
me how much time will be lost from the moment the division
starts its embarkation operation until the news reaches you for
the transmission to us by message.

One interesting aspect to this text was the final sentence concerning the delay involved in passing on news of any embarkation.
MI5 knew, from the ISOS intercepts, that this exact question had
been put to the Madrid Abstelle by the Berlin Abwehr; M
had promised Berlin that the information about embarka
would reach the Spanish capital within forty-eight hours.
23 May GARBO offered to send it on within twelve hours, which
must have pleased Madrid.

This request was also convenient because it offered an
excuse for GARBO to demand that the German receiving station
in Madrid stay on the air later than its current closedown of
eleven o'clock at night. MI5's motive for obtaining longer hours
from the enemy's wireless service lay in a controversial plan
to warn the Abwehr that the Normandy invasion had begun

shortly before the landing craft really did hit the beaches. Both
GARBO and Harris were adamant that the network's credibility
would be enhanced greatly if it could send a message to Madrid
in time. The Abwehr would then be more likely to believe that
this first attack was a feint and would then listen to GARBO's
information about preparations for the main landing in the
Pas-de-Calais area. With GARBO's increased reputation, Harris
had argued, he would be an even more effective weapon of
deception. He also pointed out that if the warning was received
a few hours before the invasion started, it would still be too late
for the Germans to do much about it. MI5 knew from ISOS that
it would take the Abwehr about three hours to relay the warning
to the relevant sectors via Berlin, so there was no danger of actually betraying or endangering the operation itself. Naturally, this
extraordinary proposal got a mixed reception from the services
responsible for conveying the troops across the Channel safely.
Some thought that what Harris was suggesting was uncomfortably close to treachery. After lengthy negotiations with General
Eisenhower's staff, the supreme commander eventually gave
his consent for a transmission to be made on condition that
it should go out no more than three and half hours ahead of
the attack. The idea of signalling just before eleven the previous evening was vetoed. The master plan for D-Day had the
first troops landing on enemy territory at exactly 6.30 on the
morning of 5 June 1944, so GARBO was authorised to make his
signal at about three o'clock in the morning. Unfortunately, the
Abwehr operators went off the air between eleven and seven,
so GARBO was obliged to find an excuse to keep them up all
night. His scheme was particularly ingenious and involved the
creation of a spurious crisis concerning his Greek agent.

On the evening of 26 May GARBO reported that he had
summoned his last agent in Scotland, the Greek seaman, 3(3),
down to London. At a debriefing session, 3(3) had confirmed
that the ships assembled for the forthcoming invasion of
Norway were still moored in the Clyde.

3(3) is in London having been called here by me by telegram. He says that the 52nd Division is at present in camps in the areas Saltcoats, Kilmarnock, Prestwick and Ayr. The entire division is concentrated there. He also saw there a large number of the insignia of the pilgrims' shell, which he had previously mentioned in the area of Dundee. Since it was impossible for him to keep a check on the fleet and the 52nd Division at the same time, as they were no longer both in the same place, he was told that he should not lose contact with the fleet, as troops could not embark without ships, thus, while controlling one you control the other.

3(3) was promptly sent back to Glasgow with instructions to send a single code word when the ships steamed out of the Clyde. But at 8.20 on 3 June, GARBO reported that he had just received a telegram from the Greek, announcing his arrival in London at eleven that night. This was obviously a significant development:

Something must have happened which cannot be explained in the code which had been agreed between us for announcing the sailing of the Clyde fleet. Therefore you should be listening tomorrow morning at 0300 hours.

GARBO later sent a message explaining that the Greek had blundered and had simply come down to London to report in person. Now, apparently, he understood completely the code word arrangements and had gone straight back to Glasgow. GARBO recommended that to avoid further delays the Madrid operator should maintain a night watch. To MI5's delight, the Abwehr agreed, and the scene was set for a secret warning to be transmitted in the early hours of 5 June, three and a half hours before the Normandy landings.

GARBO had also manoeuvred himself into what was supposedly a sensitive position in the Ministry of Information. In theory, GARBO would report on the advice the MOI was offering in connection with propaganda for the invasion. If GARBO claimed that the MOI had forbidden any newspapers to speculate on a further invasion after D-Day, the Germans would inevitably conclude that a second attack was likely. The possibilities were almost limitless and, in order to acclimatise the Abwehr to their new source, GARBO described on 29 May how he had been reading the material used for the North African and Italian campaigns:

> What I was clearly able to get out of it and what I consider to be of the maximum importance is the intention to hide the facts in order to trick us.

A little later the same evening GARBO sent a lengthy (and accurate) account of the political warfare executive's role. This was an exercise intended to dazzle the Abwehr with GARBO's grasp of the intricacies of the British establishment's bureaucracy. It was also supposed to ensure that Berlin took proper account of his messages, which, in the coming days, would be of vital importance.

> It is the executive body for all foreign propaganda and it coordinates directives issued which are based on policy recommendations of the Foreign Office, War Cabinet and Supreme Headquarters of Allied Expeditionary Forces. The latter is known by the initials 'SHAEF'. Thus PWE is the propaganda mouthpiece of Eisenhower, Eden and the British chiefs of staff. ... In view of the fact that this department's work is secret, it is very possible that Berlin is not aware of these important facts and I therefore recommend that steps should be taken to notify the competent chiefs in Berlin so that experts can evaluate and interpret the strategic plans behind the propaganda directives which are issued, hitherto unknown to us but which, through my present position, will be available

to you in future. I am convinced that, knowing the intentions behind these directives, together with the reports from my agents, we will know the future intentions of the enemy.

GARBO was now ready to assist in the second phase of Operation FORTITUDE, which began on 29 May with a massive fighter attack on the Pas-de-Calais area. A total of sixty-six squadrons took part in the exercise, which was observed and reported on by DONNY, the leader of the Aryan World Order, who was living in Dover. He identified a number of airfields in Kent and Sussex which had been used by the planes, although most had in fact been based in Hampshire. The Luftwaffe was known to be aware of the various aerodromes around Southampton that were crammed with aircraft waiting to provide air cover over Normandy. By suggesting that these concentrations were merely awaiting dispersal to operational sites nearer north-west France, the enemy was distracted from the most obvious conclusion: that planes in Hampshire meant an attack on Normandy. During the exercise on 29 May hundreds of fighters landed on unfamiliar airfields in Kent and Sussex to rearm and refuel. DONNY made the necessary observations (which were, of course, confirmed by such German aircraft as ventured into the sky) and the operation achieved the desired result.

On 3 June GARBO raised the temperature a little further by relaying an interesting snippet of information from DORICK in Harwich:

Sign, not previously seen, of a yellow shield with three blue mountain peaks outlined in white. This newly arrived division from USA.

The following day GARBO transmitted a long despatch from his Greek agent in Scotland, adding further pressure on the eve of the planned invasion:

3(3), having received news of the landings in Scotland of a large contingent of troops coming from Ireland, disregarded my instructions that he should not leave the Clyde in order to investigate this information. He discovered the entire division had, in fact, arrived and was encamped in the Locherbie area. Insignia is the red rose on a white ground. He believes it to be the 55th English Division. Returning to Glasgow, on arrival at Motherwell he discovered that vehicles and men in full equipment in large numbers were assembling there and in the surroundings belonging to the stags antler divisions and the one with the sign of the fish in red on blue and white waves. The road in direction of Hamilton was controlled by CMP.

Monday 5 June had been earmarked as D-Day, but bad weather forced a temporary delay of twenty-four hours. So instead of transmitting a warning early on 5 June, GARBO had to content himself with forwarding a brief message from the wretched Agent 7(6), who claimed to have spotted a division of US assault troops assembling in Liverpool

> destined for an attack on the South Atlantic French coast in cooperation with a large army which will come direct from America to the French coast.

GARBO did not attach much importance to this message, especially as he had already characterised the self-styled Welsh Fascist as an incompetent. In any case, there were more important matters at hand. His chief concern was the elaborate warning message which had to be transmitted at exactly three o'clock on the morning of the D-Day landings. The timing was to be explained by a complicated text from CHAMILLUS, who was supposed to have reported to BENEDICT. The resulting message had been encoded by the long-suffering widow Mrs Gerbers, who had then sent it straight to ALMURA in time for him to begin transmitting at exactly three o'clock. Its content was intended to tell the Germans that the invasion had already begun, but GARBO was too subtle to say so in so many words:

> Still no news from 3(3) but, meanwhile, CHAMILLUS has hastened to London, having broken camp together with two American deserters who had arrived in the camp on Friday. Discovering the plans of these two men, he decided to join them in view of the important news which he would otherwise have been unable to communicate in view of the complete sealing of the camps for the past week. En route, he tried to communicate by telephone, using the password prepared in case of emergency, but found that only official calls were being accepted. He therefore continued his journey clandestinely to London in order to report to me personally. He arrived after a difficult journey created by the steps he took to slip through the local vigilance. He told me that three days ago cold rations and vomit bags had again been distributed to troops of the 3rd Canadian Division and that the division had now left the camp, its place now taken by Americans. There were rumours that the 3rd Canadian Division had now embarked. The American troops which are now in the camp belong to the First US Army. The two Americans who escaped with him through fear of embarking belonged to the 926 Signal Corps. The situation of this agent is very compromising for the service because his absence must have been noted owing to the many hours which have elapsed since he left the camp. In order to protect the service, I have taken a decision which I think you will approve, which is to put him in hiding, taking advantage of the fact that DAGOBERT is here, who says that he can arrange this with absolute safety and without danger of compromise. Therefore, tomorrow, they will both leave for the south of Wales.

Charles Haines, masquerading as ALMURA, the conscientious objector, tapped out this historic message and was watched by

GARBO, Tommy Harris and Tar Robertson, who had driven up to Crespigny Road especially for the occasion. The Germans had begun transmitting to GARBO at 7.29 p.m. and had continued until about midnight. Most of it was for relaying on to Cyril Mills in Canada, and there were one or two items concerning GARBO's call signs. Evidently, the Abwehr had little idea of the offensive which was about to open. GARBO, Harris and Haines continued the cipher work until the time arrived for them to start transmitting to Madrid. Haines switched on his set and keyed in his call sign, but he got no reply. Instead of the agreed answer Haines heard nothing but static. He tried again at regular, fifteen-minute intervals for the next five hours, but the Abwehr only came up on the net at eight in the morning. After so many heated arguments about the advisability of giving a specific warning to the enemy, the entire plan had flopped. Madrid finally acknowledged GARBO's message more than two hours after the first Allied troops had landed in Normandy. Understandably, everyone concerned was profoundly disappointed, although some consolation was taken in the slightly altered text which was eventually transmitted. This implied that ALMURA had actually tried to reach Madrid rather earlier than three o'clock. Thanks to the Abwehr's inefficiency a tremendous opportunity had been lost, but it was now too late to alter the plans. The long-awaited invasion had begun, and it was up to GARBO to persuade the enemy that this was a mere feint to divert attention away from the major cross-Channel attack which had yet in take place.

Shortly before dawn on 6 June 1944, 1,213 warships gathered off the coast of Normandy and began disembarking more than 120,000 Allied troops. It was the first phase of history's biggest amphibious operation, involving some 13,000 Allied aircraft, flying a total of 1,1,600 sorties and dropping 5,200 tons of explosives. Yet the enemy was caught entirely unprepared.

The sheer scale of OVERLORD was breathtaking. The statistics were almost incomprehensible in their magnitude. In all, counting the small assault craft, more than 5,333 ships would be deployed off the French beaches, having made the Channel crossing in fifty separate convoys. Approximately 2,000,000 Allied personnel were concerned either directly or indirectly with the plan. The logistical problems of landing and maintaining the invaders without the benefit of a fully equipped deep-water port were so immense that extraordinary arrangements had been made to build an entire harbour offshore and lay a fuel pipeline across the widest part of the Channel. Twenty thousand vehicles were to be driven ashore and supplied, including 900 armoured vehicles and 600 guns in the first few hours. Therefore, the southern half of England had been transformed into a vast military camp with armour clogging every country lane.

The preparations had been going on for months, and yet the German high command was sufficiently confident that the German commander in the field, Field Marshal Rommel, was authorised to return to his home near Ulm on leave ... to celebrate his wife's birthday, which happened to be on the sixth of June. At the headquarters of the Seventh Army in Le Mans, Colonel General Friedrich Dollman had chosen 6 June to hold an indoor war game. His instructions specified that all divisional commanders were to attend and that they should each bring at least two of their regimental commanders. For his part, General Spiedel read the forecasts of high winds and rain and gave his permission for the troops of both his two armies to reduce their state of readiness and get some rest. In the first twenty-four hours of the invasion the Germans suffered 6,500 casualties.

Incredibly, the first serious Allied loss of D-Day was a single Norwegian destroyer, sunk by a group of torpedo boats, which made a brief counter-attack before returning to Cherbourg. Not even the German coastal radar stations had been able to alert the defenders to the armada's imminent arrival. Most had been destroyed by the RAF, and the lone installation near Caen that did spot the force was unable to persuade the military to take the warning seriously. Even after the bridgehead had been established, the enemy was thoroughly confused about its significance, and a majority of the senior Wehrmacht officers in France were convinced that a further attack was likely further north in the Pas-de-Calais area. In fact, Rommel actually signalled to von Rundstedt on 19 June that 'a large-scale landing is to be expected on the Channel front on both sides of Cap Gris Nez or between the Somme and Le Havre'. He even repeated the message eleven weeks later, thus preventing the German Fifteenth Army, which was being held in reserve to resist the expected second assault, from launching a counterattack. As Winston Churchill later observed (*The Second World War*, Vol. VI, p. 10):

> Our deception measures both before and after D-Day had aimed at creating this confused thinking. Their success was admirable and had far-reaching results on the battle.

While the supreme commander and his staff waited anxiously throughout the day to hear of the progress being made on the five target beaches in Normandy, MI5 prepared themselves for GARBO's evening transmissions. Would the Abwehr be full of recriminations or congratulations? In the radio contacts with Madrid early in the morning of 6 June (and the complete text of his warning message had been repeated no less than five times), the Germans had shown no particular concern. Nor, the previous evening, had they betrayed any signs of anxiety which might have indicated that they had been aware of the significance of the date. GARBO, Harris and the rest of the team were satisfied that the enemy had been duped, but what would their reaction be to the news from the beachhead? GARBO's main objective now was to build up FORTITUDE SOUTH, the projected deception for the Pas-de-Calais area. Unfortunately, his job was not made any easier by some highly indiscreet remarks made by the prime minister during his afternoon statement to the House of Commons. All ministers and all the public commentators had been asked not to speculate on the possibility of further landings on the Channel coast, so that the Germans would accept GARBO's line, but Churchill evidently got a little carried away with himself and announced that during 'the early hours of this morning the first of a series of landings in force upon the European continent has taken place'. This indiscretion was entirely contrary to MI5's advice, for if there really were to be more attacks, the prime minister would hardly announce them in advance. Furthermore, the statement seemed to be in contradiction with GARBO's prepared text, which was due to be communicated later that day.

That evening, at 8.05, exactly on schedule, Haines began signalling to Madrid:

After the crisis last night with CHAMILLUS I was summoned early this morning to the Ministry of Information. I arrived to find the department already in a complete state of chaos, everyone speculating as to the importance of the attack which had started this morning against France. All the sections were handed copies of a directive, distributed by PWE to the ministry. I find it very significant and more still if compared with the speeches of the Allied chiefs. I transmit an exact copy of the directive.

Special Directive on the Offensive against Northern France, Political Warfare Executive. Central Directive.
1. The offensive launched today by General Eisenhower forms another important step in the Allied concentric attack on the fortress of Europe.
2. It is of the utmost importance that the enemy should be kept in the dark as to our future intentions.
3. Care should be given to avoid any reference to further assaults amid diversions.

4. Speculation regarding alternative assault areas must be avoided.

5. The importance of the present assault and its decisive influence on the course of the war should be clearly stated.

Together with the directive, J(3) handed me copies of the speeches which had, at that moment, not been broadcast. After reading these documents I asked him for a further interview and told him that, as a basis for propaganda, I considered that the directive was in complete contradiction with the speeches, as it was inevitable that these speeches would be quoted and used as the basis of propaganda by the world press. I pointed out that these speeches gave a latitude which is denied by the directive. For instance, in Eisenhower's speech, which says: 'A premature uprising of all Frenchmen may prevent you from being a maximum help to your country in the critical hour. Be patient. Prepare!' … and still more important, the following: 'This landing is but the opening phase of the campaign in western Europe. Great battles lie ahead.' The Belgian prime minister said: 'Preliminary operations for the liberation of Europe have begun. The first assault is the certain signal for your deliverance.' And also: 'The moment of supreme combat has not come.'

J(3) told me, in confidence, that I had spotted the one inevitable weakness in the policy which had been directed. He explained that, in the first place, it was essential that Eisenhower should keep the people from rising too early in areas which were yet to be involved in operations but, at the same time, it was equally necessary to try to hide all this information from the enemy. He said he did not think the enemy would be able to draw any definite conclusions from these speeches but he thought that they, nevertheless, constituted such a contradiction to the directives as to create a difficult situation internally. He went on to say that the director-general had himself raised my point. Nevertheless, he felt that, if the work were done intelligently, he believed it possible to focus public attention on the present attack and thus detract from any other suggestion of future plans, this being precisely the work with which he was entrusted.

Although he did not refer to it directly, GARBO was actually attempting to explain away the prime minister's gaffe. He was to return to this embarrassing subject the following day when, at 9.58 on the evening of D+1, GARBO explained that the Political Warfare Executive had now agreed to alter its directive so that 'certain limited speculation in general terms as to future operations' might be included. As for the prime minister, GARBO gave a reasonably plausible explanation:

> In spite of recommendations made to Churchill that his speech should contain every possible reserve, he based it on the consideration that he was obliged, on account of his political position, to avoid distorting the facts and would not permit that his speeches should be discredited by coming events.

This message is particularly remarkable, bearing in mind that it is, in effect, a German spy claiming that Winston Churchill had failed to adhere to his advice!

In the meantime, while GARBO was wriggling out of the discrepancy between his messages and the prime minister's ill-timed speech, he had to report a distinct lack of activity elsewhere. Agent 3(3), the Greek seaman, could still see the fleet in the Clyde, so there was not much going on there, although there was apparently a continuing state of alert. GARBO had, therefore, decided to call all his subagents to London for a conference.

> For the present, I can only state a definite argument based on the studies and appreciations which my work in the ministry has facilitated, and it is that the enemy are biding their intentions behind this first action.

GARBO concluded his second transmission of the evening with the following observation:

> Fortunately, the first action was robbed of the surprise which they wished to create through the information from CHAMILLUS as, from the hour at which the assault is said to have started, I am able to prove, with satisfaction, that my messages arrived in time to prevent the action coming as a surprise to our high command. There is no doubt that CHAMILLUS has accomplished through his action a service which, though it will make it impossible to use his collaboration in the future, has justified a sacrifice by his last report. CHAMILLUS left this morning accompanied by DAGOBERT who will arrange for him to be hidden in a safe place. For myself, and counting on your approval, I intend to take care of this friend and give him every consideration in order to make him aware of our recognition.

Once this text had been transmitted, GARBO pretended to have received a visit from Mrs Gerbers, who had informed him, for the first time, about the delay in getting his signals acknowledged the previous morning. GARBO was suitably indignant, and his tone changed from self-congratulation to simulated outrage:

> On handing over today's messages, ALMURA told the widow that he was not able to send the urgent messages until 0800 hours since you had not been listening. This makes me question your seriousness and your sense of responsibility. I therefore demand a clarification immediately as to what has occurred. If what I suspect is the case and ALMURA has failed in his duties, then I am absolutely decided in this event to abandon the radio service until I can find some other solution. I am very disgusted; in this struggle for life or death, I cannot accept excuses or negligence. I cannot swallow the idea of endangering the service without any benefit. Were it not for my ideals and faith I would abandon this work as having proved myself

a failure. I write these messages to send this very night though my tiredness and exhaustion, due to the excessive work I have had, has completely broken me.

The transmission had begun at 11.55 p.m. on D-Day, and Madrid's reply came through at 8.10 p.m. on D+1, 7 June:

I have read your last two messages of yesterday and I perfectly well understand your state of morale and feel moved to answer you the following. It would be difficult, if not impossible, to find out who is to blame if a culprit really exists with regard to the delay in the transmission of CHAMILLUS. After finishing on Monday at 2350 hours, having received your message, CENTRO was listening according to plan every hour up to 0300 hours and again from 0700 hours on Tuesday, getting the message of CHAMILLUS at 0800 hours. It is possible that, in spite of the staff having been listening properly, due to bad conditions having set in, there would have been no other calls from ALMURA during the night. Let us know at what time ALMURA tried to call us without success. But, even supposing the worst and ALMURA did not call, you must remember that ALMURA, according to what you have told us, is not aware of the true significance of your mission, and it is possible that he, after his day's work and having been transmitting that night for nearly three hours, should have felt very tired and, considering that he had fulfilled his duties, he could not imagine that the message was one of such importance that it could not have been delayed for a few hours. I wish to stress in the clearest terms that your work over the last few weeks has made it possible for our command to be completely forewarned and prepared, and the message of CHAMILLUS would have influenced but little had it arrived three or four hours earlier. Thus I reiterate to you, as responsible chief of the service, and to all your collaborators, our total recognition of your perfect and cherished work, and I beg of you to continue with us in the supreme and decisive hours of the struggle for the future of Europe.

Clearly the absurd amateur psychology exercised by GARBO and Harris had paid off handsomely. The Abwehr were anxious to cover up their own blunder and, at the same time, were desperate to maintain contact with their best source. But GARBO was not going to let the matter drop and, when he replied on 12 June, D+6, he pressed home his advantage:

> ALMURA communicated that on the night of the crisis he called at 0300 hours for half an hour and that he repeated his calls at 0700 hours without any result. With regard to the belief that ALMURA would not imagine the extreme urgency of the message handed to him, this I can dispel, as whether or not he knew its contents is nothing to do with the fact that he had his instructions given to him by the widow, which were to tell him that it was of extreme urgency that that message should be sent that night. I cannot, therefore, accept negligence, even if he were tired from his long hours of transmission. I am also exhausted but I know to fulfil my duties. Furthermore, the payment he receives is the highest of the network and it would, therefore, be unwise for him to accept the possibility that the atmospheric conditions were bad but, on future occasions, I intend to take my security measures in urgent cases as in the one mentioned and will endeavour to see that the widow remains present at any important transmission.

The next item on MI5's deception agenda was GARBO's much vaunted conference of subagents. In general, his messages had fallen into three categories: those that expressed his own opinion (which, of course, expressed well-judged scepticism when the occasion suited); those that contained his own, first-hand observations (and were, therefore, verifiable and accurate); and, finally, those that summed up the combined wisdom of several agents. This latter group were reserved for matters of crucial importance and were only used for items which were required to be delivered with weight. The conference of 8 June was just such an opportunity, because three of DAGOBERT's best agents had been called to London. The idea for the gathering had been Tommy Harris's, and he had justified it in his secret master plan for GARBO's contribution to FORTITUDE, dated 4 May 1944. In this historic document Harris observed:

> With the approach of D-Day and even after, until the nature and full significance of NEPTUNE (the landings in Normandy) is discovered, there will almost inevitably be a certain divergence of opinion as to Allied intentions, even in the German high command. There will, we hope, be among the leaders of Germany some who will draw the conclusion we are trying to inspire through FORTITUDE. If we can continue through GARBO and the Abwehr to supply those Germans who are already inclined to believe in our cover plan with further ammunition for our arguments … it may well be that we shall be helping those elements in Germany to influence plans in our favour during the few critical days of the post-assault period.

Accordingly, those members of GARBO's network who were reasonably available to come to London held a unique meeting to discuss the strategic implications of the events of the previous forty-eight hours. DONNY had travelled up from Dover; DICK, the Indian, had arrived from Brighton; DORICK had rushed over from Harwich; and BENEDICT had arrived late the previous evening. GARBO had set the scene just after midnight, imparting the first definite intelligence the Germans had received since the invasion had begun:

> I found BENEDICT awaiting me after a short interview he had had with DICK. Urgent points communicated; he learned that

the 3rd British Battalion landed in the first assault and has identified it as the one with the insignia of the inverted triangle. The Guards Armoured Division will enter in action three days after initiating the first attack. The division has left the area.

At 7.28 p.m. GARBO sent the following message to whet the Abwehr's appetite further.

I have had an extremely agitated day today, but I have the satisfaction of being able to give you the most important reports of my work. As I have not got all the messages ready, I hope you will be listening tonight at 10 GMT.

GARBO was finally ready to start sending at seven minutes past midnight, and the resulting message was sent by Charles Haines for the next 122 minutes. The transmission was easily GARBO's longest and by far his most important, for it encapsulated the entire FORTITUDE deception:

From the reports mentioned, it is perfectly clear that the present attack is a large-scale operation but diversionary in character, for the purpose of establishing a strong bridgehead in order to draw the maximum of our reserves to the area of operation and to retain them there so as to be able to strike a blow somewhere else with ensured success. I never like to give my opinions unless I have strong reasons to justify my assurances, but the fact that these concentrations, which are in the east and south-east of the island, are now inactive means that they must be held in reserve to be employed in the other large-scale operations. The constant aerial bombardments which the area of the Pas-de-Calais has suffered and the strategic disposition of these forces give reason to suspect an attack in that region of France which, at the same time, offers the shortest route for the final objective of their illusions, which is to say, Berlin. This advance could be covered by a constant hammering from the air since the bases would be near the field of battle and they would come in behind our forces which are fighting at the present moment with the enemy disembarked in the west of France. From J(5) I learned yesterday that there were seventy-five divisions in this country before the present assault commenced. Supposing they should use a maximum of twenty to twenty-five divisions with which to attempt a second blow. I trust you will submit urgently all these reports and studies to our high command, since moments may be decisive in these times and before taking a false step, through lack of knowledge of the necessary facts, they should have in their possession all the present information which I transmit with my opinion, which is based on the belief that the whole of the present attack is set as a trap for the enemy to make us move all our reserves in a hurried strategical disposition which we would later regret.

This single message is of extraordinary historic significance, and the decrypters watched its progress through the enemy's military intelligence structure. From Madrid it was relayed to Berlin and then delivered to Hitler's headquarters at Berchtesgaden, where it was received by Colonel Friedrich-Adolf Krummacher, the head of the Wehrmacht High Command's intelligence branch. By that time it had been edited several times and code names had been slightly corrupted in the process, but it is entirely recognisable when compared to MI5's original version, and the central theme remained intact:

After personal consultation on 8 June in London with my agents JONNY, DICK and DORICK, whose reports were sent today, I am of the opinion, in view of the strong troop concentrations in south-eastern and eastern England, which are not taking part in the present operations, that these operations are a diversionary manoeuvre designed to draw off enemy reserves in order then to make a decisive attack in another place. In view of the continued air attacks on the concentration area mentioned, which is a strategically favourable position for this, it may very probably take place in the Pas-de-Calais area, particularly since in such an attack the proximity of air bases will facilitate the operation by providing continued strong air support.

After the war the actual document summarising GARBO's opinion was recovered intact, and a further assessment had been added:

The report is credible. The reports received in the last week from the ARABEL undertaking have been confirmed almost without exception and are to be described as especially valuable. The main line of investigation in future is to be the enemy group of forces in south-eastern and eastern England.

When Krummacher received the summary he underlined the sentence characterising the Normandy landings as 'diversionary in nature' and added the written comment: 'Confirms the view already held by us that a further attack is to be expected in another place (Belgium?).' Before being handed to Hitler, this paper was passed to Field Marshal Jodl, who initialled it and underscored the words 'south-eastern and eastern England'. Evidently, GARBO's poison had proved particularly efficacious on him.

It was later established that this single message had a devastating effect on the German high command and led to the cancellation of a major armoured counter-attack in Normandy, using seasoned units from the Pas-de-Calais area. Instead, the troops en route were ordered to return to their bases. The much-feared armoured thrust simply never materialised, and credit for this coup can be given to GARBO and his notional conference of D+2.[1]

This news did not filter through to GARBO or Harris for some considerable time, so the ARABEL network continued its routine, reporting numerous Allied troop movements to support the FORTITUDE master plan. On D+3, DICK and DORICK submitted their observations from Dover and Harwich respectively:

> DICK reports that the following divisions are to be found in his area without indication of embarking at present ... Southern Command ... 47th Division ... DORICK reports that the activity in his area has greatly increased, giving the following divisions stationed in the area without indications of embarking for the moment ... 47th London Division.

Later the same day, GARBO sent a further signal to hammer the message home:

> Amplification and notes on the messages sent yesterday; Looking over the messages I see that I omitted to include, in the list of troops in the area of DONNY, the units 2nd Canadian Division and 2nd Canadian Corps. DORICK has learned through a well-informed channel that there are more than a hundred tank transport barges capable of transporting about five hundred tanks ... which have gradually been concentrating in the ports of Yarmouth, Lowestoft and in the rivers of the Debenham and the Orwell.

The invasion was now just seventy-two hours old, and the need for the Allies to consolidate their position before the enemy could amount a counter-offensive was greater than ever.

Every day that the Germans could be persuaded not to send additional reinforcements to the Normandy front gave

---

1   See Appendix.

the Allied troops a greater chance of victory. All the Allied commanders were only too well aware of their vulnerability during the first few days ashore. GARBO's message of D+2 was to have immense implications for the German defenders, but FORTITUDE called for continuous deception until well into July when, it was conceded, there would be no further advantage to pursuing the campaign. The next priority was to persuade the Abwehr that the non-existent First United States Army Group (FUSAG) had not yet been committed to Normandy and, therefore, constituted an immediate threat around the Channel.

Although GARBO himself had played an exceptional role in the overall FORTITUDE plan, his agents had not contributed much to the existence of FUSAG. This had been left largely to two of MI5's other double agents, BRUTUS and TATE. BRUTUS was a Polish air force officer, Wing Commander Roman Garby-Czerniawski, who had been imprisoned by the Nazis during the occupation of Paris. He had subsequently 'escaped' from their custody and made his way to England, where he revealed the true nature of his mission for the Abwehr. His dramatic escape had been stage-managed by them to give him cover and encourage the British to accept him at face value. After he had been turned into a double agent by his MI5 case officer, Hugh Astor, the Abwehr had been successfully duped into believing his reports, and he had made many of the notional observations which had created FUSAG. His contribution had worked well, and BRUTUS was held in high regard by the Abwehr.

Roger Hesketh later commented that,

> of all the British controlled agents, it is evident that GARBO, BRUTUS and TRICYCLE enjoyed reputations of a high order throughout the whole period of FORTITUDE deception. This came as a surprise to us. We never doubted GARBO's position. We knew that BRUTUS had attained something at least approach-

ing GARBO's stature by midsummer, but we had supposed that
he had risen during the spring from comparative obscurity.

Unfortunately, the same could not be said of TATE, a German
spy who had parachuted into Cambridgeshire in September
1940. He been taken into custody quite quickly and had been
persuaded to play his wireless back with what had seemed,
initially at least, a degree of success. It had proved more difficult to double-check on his standing with the enemy because
he reported direct to an Abwehr wireless station in Hamburg,
which relayed his messages on to Berlin by a secure landline.
The lack of wireless messages made interception impossible,
but those relevant signals that were decrypted indicated that
the enemy was not taking TATE's messages too seriously. Ml5's
problem lay in the parts of the FORTITUDE campaign, and in
particular various sightings of FUSAG units in Kent, which
had been allotted to TATE. In fact, the Abwehr's poor opinion
of TATE threatened to jeopardise FUSAG's very existence in
the minds of the enemy because the Hamburg Abstelle was
consistently failing to pass on key pieces of intelligence. It
was, therefore, decided to move GARBO onto the scene. On
D+6, GARBO reported on a conversation he had had with the
American sergeant, 4(3):

> I attempted to find out from 4(3) where the headquarters of
> General Bradley are to be found, but as he is at present under
> Montgomery's orders at 21 Army Group, 4(3) had been unable
> to say where this headquarters might be. I asked him who,
> then, was in charge of FUSAG, to which he replied that it was
> General Patton who had taken over the command which had
> temporarily been held by Bradley during the first phase of its
> formation. In the conversation held, I was able to find out that
> the headquarters of General Patton, that is to say of FUSAG
> … is situated near Ascot.

GARBO was now committed to FUSAG's continued presence in England, and further efforts were made to reinforce the idea of an impending further attack across the Channel by bringing elements of FORTITUDE NORTH further south. After BENEDICT's arrival in London to assist his chief, GARBO only had one remaining subagent left in Scotland, the Greek seaman known as 3(3). At the time of BENEDICT's summons at the end of May, the Abwehr had expressed some anxiety:

> If you consider it advisable to call BENEDICT to help you, please ask him to consider carefully if in this event the north will be well covered by 3(3), since it is very possible that some action will start up from those ports.

GARBO had covered the gap by ordering the Greek from Methil to Glasgow, and just before D-Day he had reported the 58th British Infantry Division and the British 2nd Corps in Motherwell apparently heading south. Other units also seemed to be on the move. On 16 June GARBO submitted several reports from DAGOBERT's agents:

> DICK: Brighton. The situation has changed little, with the following exceptions. Troops with the insignia of the knight on horseback have left the area. They left for Normandy. US troops with the insignia of a blue circle cut in four have arrived in the area of Lewes. The insignia was reported by DORICK on his last journey to London as having been seen in his area. DONNY has also seen some troops with the insignia of the red fish on waves and the stag's antlers. I have written to DONNY telling him that he should let me know urgently if he sees there ... troops of the 55th Division, which 3(3) also reported in the concentration at Motherwell.

In fact, DONNY was to 'discover' the genuine 55th Division a few days later in Dover, apparently preparing to cross the

Channel. The following day, on 17 June, GARBO made a further attempt to keep the FORTITUDE threat alive. The reference to training exercises involving landing craft was intended to be interpreted as a sign that further amphibious landings might be in the offing:

> DORICK communicates that the American division at present occupying the camps in which the 28th US Division has been before they left for the south, is the division which has the insignia of a serpent which the Americans call a rattlesnake. The division recently arrived in England. In his letter he sets out in detail the manoeuvres which the 28th US Division carried out on the beaches of Felixstowe.

When the unreliable agent 7(6) had claimed to have seen American assault troops massing in Liverpool on the eve of the real invasion, GARBO had sent DAGOBERT to check. DAGOBERT had found nothing to confirm 7(6)'s alarmist suggestion of an impending attack on Bordeaux, but he did see a lot of American soldiers in the dock area. GARBO commented on 15 June:

> Further evidence of the arrival of a new American formation over and above the number already mentioned is at present lacking. Nevertheless, reports of the arrival of fresh American transports deserve attention. We must therefore reckon with an early increase in the number of American divisions in England.

The following day GARBO received a message from DONNY in Dover, identifying the shoulder flashes of both the units known to have recently left Scotland. GARBO remarked:

> I attach the greatest importance to the reference by this agent to these insignia, as it is an indication that all the troop concentrations seen by 3(3) in Motherwell have been moved south.

Three days later, on 20 June, GARBO returned to the subject of the increase in the American presence, courtesy of his indiscreet US army sergeant:

> In conversation with 4(3), I today learned some very important news. I casually asked him which division his uncle was in. He replied, in the 48th US Division. To my question as to whether this division belonged to the First US Army Group, he replied that it did not, nor did it belong to 21 Army Group, thereby drawing the conclusion that there are many American troops here who belong to other large units. As is natural, I will investigate this matter as much as possible.

GARBO did not have a chance to pursue the sergeant until 2 July, when he reported:

> Today I lunched with 4(3) and brought the conversation around to the subject which interested me, which is to say about the American units which have recently arrived in England. He told me that FUSAG will undertake a more important task and that in order to be able to accomplish it, four American divisions have recently arrived in this country under the command of another American army. These divisions are stationed in the Liverpool area. He insinuated that the war was about to enter a new and decisive phase. In view of this interesting news, I intend to send DAGOBERT immediately to investigate what is going on in the western area, which I am not controlling at the moment. I intend to clarify this matter and will invite 4(3) out frequently.

The Greek seaman followed up his report with a further message on 22 June, D+16, noting an exercise conducted by the British Fourth Army in Ayrshire. In his twenty-second letter, dated 20 July 1944, GARBO finally disposed of the threat posed by these non-existent forces in Scotland and killed

FORTITUDE NORTH after a long and useful life, taking credit for the scepticism which he had expressed earlier:

> There is something important which I want to stress. If I recall correctly, the British Fourth Army was in Scotland with the formations observed by 3(3), that is to say, together with the 2nd Corps, the 55th and 58th Divisions. If, therefore, the British Army moves down, the only division to effect the proposed attack against Norway will be the 52nd Division. I therefore consider that an attack against Norway is impossible for the moment. My present observation goes to show how right I was when I expressed the opinion against the views of BENEDICT and 3(3) that the operation would not then come off at that time of the year. I therefore consider that a state of alarm in Norway need no longer be maintained.

This, at a stroke, removed FORTITUDE NORTH, but GARBO was still heavily involved with FUSAG and FORTITUDE SOUTH, and the operation's time was still running out. It was accepted that the deception could not be maintained indefinitely, and some of the real forces in Kent obviously had to move off to France in due course. With DONNY in Dover, it was a little difficult to avoid reporting genuine troop movements, and the 21 Army Group's security group were especially keen to conceal the number of reinforcements going to France. Their main strategic task had been to persuade the enemy to underestimate the strength of their forces in Normandy so as to avoid attracting a massive counter-attack. FUSAG was destined to be eliminated, but not at the cost of the Germans believing that the FUSAG units had gone to reinforce the Normandy bridgehead. One solution was for the spy to travel to Tenterden, where both British and American units were known to be based awaiting their departure to Normandy. On 30 June GARBO described how DONNY had travelled to Tenterden by train, but had been turned back at the station because he was not equipped with the required documentation. When the 21 Army Group finally gave their consent to the reporting of various troop movements, GARBO sent the following from DONNY, which implied that the units were heading in the opposite direction:

> Many troops of the 2nd Canadian Division have been leaving the area. Have seen large convoys of this division moving north on the London road. The 28th US Division is said to be leaving Tenterden.

On 3 July GARBO made his last contribution to FORTITUDE, with a short message from DORICK, who had seen the 80th British Infantry Division in Ipswich.

10

ESCAPE

The FORTITUDE operation had now entered an exceedingly dangerous stage, GARBO had initially been brought into detailed communication about FUSAG (as opposed to the overall Pas-de-Calais deception plan) because TATE's lack of credibility might have endangered the entire campaign. Having participated directly in putting FUSAG across, MI5 were left with a dilemma. GARBO's subagents were spread generously around the countryside and had begun to make genuine observations. BRUTUS, for example, presented none of these difficulties because, as a Polish officer, he could be posted elsewhere and, in fact, he was sent away to Scotland. But there were no such easy options available for GARBO's network. This situation, if left unattended, would bring GARBO and Harris into direct conflict with the 21 Army Group. A quick resolution was required, and it was found in GARBO's sudden arrest by the police in London on 4 July 1944.

MI5's easiest solution to the crisis over FUSAG's demise lay in GARBO's removal from the stage for a convenient period, but there was another, equally pressing, reason for his temporary elimination. This latter motive dated back to a mysterious message received from Madrid on 15 December 1943:

> Circumstances dictate that you should carry out your proposition with regard to setting up your home outside the capital. This warning is strictly confidential for you and, in taking the necessary measure, the collaborators must on no account suspect your reasons. Should the threatened action commence, in making your preparations, leaving to your judgment their

execution, you must ensure that your collaborators maintain
their contact with you.

What was this 'threatened action'? At that time only a few
people on the Allied side had any idea of Hitler's 'vengeance
weapons', so GARBO sought further information. On one occasion, on 22 February, GARBO complained that CHAMILLUS had
narrowly escaped death when his rooms sustained a hit during
an air raid:

> I would be grateful if you would let me know immediately that
> these are the preliminaries of other, more intense attacks so
> that I can take immediate protective measures for the service.
> Let me know immediately, therefore, whether one is to know
> whether one is to expect other, graver developments such as,
> for example, the rocket, as if this were so I would remove the
> present radio apparatus to a safer place, taking the precaution
> to make it appear as if the present bombardments were the
> motive for my doing so, thus avoiding comment by the agents
> and, at the same time, without alarming them, being able to
> make them change their residences.

These none-too-subtle attempts to acquire advance warning of
any major secret weapon offensive failed, although various ISOS
intercepts indicated that GARBO was being groomed as a kind
of advanced observation post, apparently to guide the V-1s
onto their targets. ISOS showed that once the attack had started
GARBO's wireless messages would pass directly from Madrid to
Arras, the German centre of operations in control of the V-1
launching sites. This new arrangement was planned to bypass
Berlin and demonstrated, once again, GARBO's high standing
with the enemy.

The various problems presented by the V-1s remained
academic until 13 June 1944, when the first 'buzz bomb' or
'doodlebug' fell on a railway bridge in Grove Road, Bow, in

London's East End. Six people were killed and nine were injured. GARBO was suitably indignant three days later:

> We had not been informed by headquarters about this project, owing no doubt to the fact that all attention had been absorbed in the operations in France.

Later the same evening he remarked:

> It has upset me very much to have to learn the news of this arm having been used from our very enemies when I had hoped to have heard about it in advance from you in order to be able to leave the city.

The Abwehr replied the following night:

> Today headquarters has notified us that it has been impossible for them to warn us in advance as to the date on which the new arm would be employed, since they themselves were not informed on account of an order from the high command that the secret should only be disclosed to those people who had to be told in order to put it into operation.

There was no arguing with the logic behind this explanation, but the Abwehr's request for his assistance in the bombing led to some agonising debates in St James's Street. The Germans in Madrid asked GARBO to record the exact time and the exact position of as many V-1 hits in London as possible. Their purpose was obvious. The time of each V-1 launch was carefully recorded by its crew, and the time and place of impact gave the enemy an invaluable method of checking their calculations and improving their aim. The V-1's navigation system was fairly straightforward, in that the unmanned craft was simply launched off a ramp aligned on a point in the heart of London, but the device which governed the duration of the flight was rather more complicated. A small propeller on the nose turned in flight and, after a predetermined number of rotations, cut off the engine's fuel supply. The bomb then plunged to the ground in an eerie silence. The launch crews could only establish the required number of rotations by trial and error, and therefore depended heavily on a reliable observer close to the point of impact. With a definite time and location, they could work out exactly which aircraft had been successfully on target and could adjust the others accordingly. Suddenly, GARBO had been transformed into a human bombsight, and the realisation made the Twenty Committee distinctly uneasy.

At first there were plenty of opportunities to delay reporting the hits. GARBO reported that he had moved away from Hendon and had found lodgings at a small hotel in Bray, a picturesque village on the river Thames in Berkshire. This was indeed true. He moved into a hotel owned by a Spanish couple from Valencia named Terrades, and each morning he commuted up to London on the train from Taplow to go to work at MI5's little front office in Jermyn Street. For his part, Tommy Harris left Chesterfield Gardens and took temporary refuge at the Bull, a well-known hotel at Gerrards Cross, to the north-west of London. These logistics disrupted GARBO's traffic, and other reasons were found to justify the prevarication. One excuse concerned the grid selected for GARBO's use by the Abwehr. It was only to be found in a street map of London published by Pharus of Berlin in 1906. Eventually, after a time-consuming search, a copy was borrowed ... from the British Museum! Once that matter had been sorted out GARBO tried to prevaricate further by delegating the task of spotting the V-1s to BENEDICT, his Venezuelan deputy. His initial results were poor, and GARBO justified his disappointing performance by insisting that 'the area affected is so extensive that it embraces a semicircle from Harwich to Portsmouth'. This was not entirely true, and it became clear that GARBO would have to take on the job himself. 'As BENEDICT is a little timid, I am going to do this work myself and make the observations starting from tomorrow,' said GARBO in a message at 9.15 p.m. on 30 June.

Thoroughly alarmed, the Abwehr responded forty-five minutes later:

> I wish to repeat again that the news about troop movements, units, locations etc. continues to be your principal mission and you should add information about the objectives hit only to the extent that circumstances permit.

Characteristically, it was Tommy Harris who dreamed up the solution while the bureaucrats and politicians fumbled with the moral issues of directing the flying bombs from one part of London to another. Harris suggested that GARBO undertake the enemy's bidding and then get himself arrested. This would isolate GARBO from the field, thus giving everyone a short breathing space in which the matter could be considered, and would also teach the Abwehr not to jeopardise the liberty of their star agent on such risky missions. Harris's solution also had the virtue of closing down the entire network at the crucial moment of FUSAG's disappearance. The scheme was very attractive and the Twenty Committee gave it their approval.

According to the Harris plot, GARBO had visited a pub on the evening of 3 July and had heard about the massive damage caused by the V-1 in Bow. The following afternoon he had paid a visit to the site in the East End and had started asking questions in the locality to determine the exact time of the impact. He had also taken notes of the bomb damage. As luck would have it, one of the onlookers at the bomb site had turned out to be a plain clothes detective, who had become suspicious of the inquisitive foreigner. GARBO had taken fright at the police officer's interest in him and had stuffed his notes into his mouth in a futile attempt to swallow evidence of his mission. The detective had promptly arrested him and had escorted him to the police station, where he had been questioned briefly

by the local chief inspector. GARBO had protested his innocence and had claimed to have been gathering material for the
Ministry of Information, following a conversation he had had
the previous day with his section head, J(3), concerning the
apparent inadequacies of the capital's air defences against the
V-1. The police had taken their time checking his story and
had left GARBO to sit in the cells for nearly three days. GARBO
had eventually been released through the intervention of the
contact J(3), who had confirmed GARBO's tale, but in the meantime he had received the benefit of some advice from a petty
criminal who was something of a barracks-room lawyer. Both
men had shared the cell for a while, and the crook had pointed
out that GARBO had been detained illegally because only the
commissioner could sanction the detention without warrant
of a prisoner for more than forty-eight hours. As soon as he
had been released, GARBO had written to the home secretary
to complain about his treatment. On 10 July the secretary of
state had sent him an impressive apology, which GARBO then
forwarded on to the Abwehr in triumph. In due course, they
returned it to him, through the Espírito Santo bank in Lisbon,
in case it came in useful again.

The true story, of course, was rather different. At 8.44 p.m.
on 1 July BENEDICT reported that GARBO had gone missing.

> ARABEL did not turn up yesterday; he also has not appeared
> for daily meeting today ... to avoid delay am sending reports
> which have not been sent by him.

The next day there was still no sign of GARBO and BENEDICT was
showing signs of panic:

> I fear that any investigations of the police or civil defence
> might turn out disastrous, as knowing his methods it is quite
> likely that he has gone off on some new track which has taken
> him to a prohibited area from where he cannot communicate.

On the evening of 7 July the Abwehr made a half-hearted attempt to calm BENEDICT, although the net result actually shows that a degree of panic had already set in at Madrid:

> I am very much puzzled indeed about what you told me about ARABEL. Of course, it might be possible that he left London on a special mission, although it appears rather strange that in this case he should not have informed you. It is very difficult for me to advise you as there are a lot of details which I ignore as regards the inner construction of the service. I think the first condition is to keep calm and quiet and to give anything you undertake the fullest consideration. If the worst has happened and ARABEL has been arrested, BENEDICT must do what he can to save the service and take all measures to protect its members and prevent clues of any kind from falling into the hands of the police.

While Charles Haines was taking down this message from Madrid, Tommy Harris was preparing BENEDICT's next text, which included a reference to 'red documentation', the Abwehr jargon for forged diplomatic papers:

> Widow reports alarming news just learnt. Police went to Taplow today to investigate and collect red documentation. ARABEL was arrested on Tuesday. No details known. Consider situation critical. Am immediately breaking communications to and from all agents.

It was not until 12 July that the Abwehr were put out of their misery by BENEDICT:

> Widow just reported surprising news that ARABEL was released on the 10th and is back at his hotel … My instructions from him are to give ARABEL ten days' holiday and return immediately to Glasgow and await orders there.

GARBO himself waited a further two days before writing a typically dramatic account of his arrest and detention in a letter, his twenty-first, containing the home secretary's apology. The Abwehr acknowledged it in a radio message received on 23 July, which instructed him to 'cease all investigations of the new weapon' forthwith:

> In my possession all your documents announced. Shocked by the story of your detention. We send cordial congratulations for your liberation. The security of yourself and of the service requires a prolongation of the period of complete inactivity on your part, without any contact with collaborators. For urgent and important military information, BENEDICT should be able to take charge of communicating with us.

This order to suspend operations was exactly what GARBO and Harris had been hoping for, and they both took a brief vacation, the first that either had had since GARBO's arrival more than two years earlier. GARBO went on a motor tour of the British Isles, chauffeured by Jock Horsfall, while Tommy and Hilda Harris stayed with Sarah Bishop's parents at Chisbury in Wiltshire. Naturally, Tommy took his easel and paint brushes, and he completed several pictures of the farmyard animals.

All the players in this bizarre pantomime were just recovering from the arrest when, on 29 July, Madrid sent their own congratulations:

> With great happiness and satisfaction I am able to advise you today that the Führer has conceded the Iron Cross to you for your extraordinary merits, a decoration which, without exception, is granted only to first-line combatants. For this reason, we all send you our most sincere and cordial congratulations.

Suitably humbled, GARBO answered:

I cannot at this moment, when emotion overcomes me, express in words my gratitude for the decoration conceded by our Führer, to whom humbly and with every respect I express my gratitude for the high distinction which he has bestowed on me, for which I feel myself unworthy as I have never done more than what I have considered to the fulfilment of my duty. Furthermore, I must state that this prize has been won not only by me but also by Carlos[2] and the other comrades, who, through their advice and directives, have made possible my work here, and so the congratulations are mutual. My desire is to fight with great ardour to be worthy of this medal which has only been conceded to those heroes, my companions in honour, who fight on the battlefront.

Being informed of the decoration was one thing, but actually taking possession of it was quite another, and both GARBO and Tommy Harris were keen to receive their trophy. On 12 August GARBO made further inquiries in a letter, his twenty-fifth:

I want also today to amplify my message with regard to the Iron Cross which I have been conceded. From the time of knowing this, I have carried the series of reverses which I have suffered with greater resignation and, I can now say, with greater courage than previously; my fervent desire is to possess this and hold it in my very hands. I know that this desire is difficult to fulfil, as I cannot glorify myself with it when I have it. But for my personal satisfaction, I should certainly like to have it by me, even though it be hidden underground until I am able to wear it on my chest, the day when this plague which surrounds us is wiped off the face of the earth. Can you possibly send it camouflaged via the courier?

---

2   ARABEL's deputy, the Venezuelan student BENEDICT, Agent THREE

MI5 were later to learn, via the ISOS intercepts, that GARBO's request was to create some serious problems for the Abwehr. The matter was still being raised some six months later when, on 12 December, the following ISOS decrypt was passed to Tommy Harris:

In re award of Iron Cross II to ARABEL and the discussions in Berlin. In our message of the 17 June we applied for the award of Iron Cross II to ARABEL, emphasising that he was a Spanish national, but giving as justification the fact that activity of ARABEL constantly at the price of his life was just as important as the service at the front of the Spanish members of the Blue Division. We were informed in your message of 24 June that this award was agreed to and that the submission of the prescribed proposal had been put forward. On the basis of this information, we at this end were under the impression that no difficulties were to be expected in [obtaining] the eventual award and this was reported to ARABEL, who was at that time, as a result of very great difficulties, in a state of mental depression for psychological reasons. The communication of this news about the award had the expected result and evoked from ARABEL a written expression of his special pride at the distinction. Difficulties in maintaining and extending the ARABEL network have been constantly increasing recently, but were mastered by ARABEL with an utter disregard for all personal interests and by giving all he was capable of. ARABEL has himself been in hiding for weeks, separated from wife and children. The extraordinary successes of ARABEL have been made possible by his constant, complete and express confidence in the Führer and our cause. He regards the award of the Iron Cross II, as reported to him, as final and as coming from the Führer. It seems psychologically impossible now to inform him that the award will not be made without exercising the most adverse effect on him and his organisation. For the reasons stated, please support the award from your end with all possible means. Would it not be possible to classify ARABEL retrospectively as a member of the Blue Division? Please report to us by w/t results of your efforts, as ARABEL has already asked for the decoration in question to be sent to his next of kin to be kept for him.

Evidently, GARBO's case officer had run into a few bureaucratic obstacles in his attempts to have the Iron Cross actually awarded to someone who was not a member of the regular armed forces. The compromise suggestion that GARBO should be enrolled in the Spanish Blue Division, then fighting on the Russian front, was the solution that was eventually adopted. When the question arose about a British decoration, an honorary award of Membership of the Order of the British Empire, no such obstacles were placed in GARBO's way. It was recommended by Tommy Harris (who was himself decorated with the CBE for his role in the GARBO case), Colonel Robertson (another CBE recipient for his war work) and the director-general of the Security Service, Sir David Petrie. Normally, the MBE is given only to British subjects, and a public notice naming recipients is placed in the *London Gazette*, but on this occasion, owing to the obvious security considerations, no such announcement was made and a special exception was allowed for GARBO to receive his medal. His name was placed in a secret annex at the central chancery of the orders of knighthood, with instructions that any inquiry concerning Juan Pujol should be referred immediately to MI5. That rule is applied strictly to this day. The medal itself, which GARBO still treasures, was presented by Sir David Petrie at a special luncheon in GARBO's honour, held shortly before Christmas 1944. It was a highly emotional affair and was attended by all the senior MI5 staff who knew of the GARBO case.

The setbacks GARBO had referred to in his letter the previous August centred on his decision to reorganise his network. CHAMILLUS had been out of commission for the entire period since his desertion from Hiltingbury, and had spent much of the time in hiding on a remote hill farm owned by an elderly couple in South Wales. He was apparently at the end of his tether, so GARBO arranged for DAGOBERT, the seaman from Swansea, to smuggle him aboard a merchant vessel bound for Canada. DAGOBERT had been unnerved by DRAKE's imprisonment in Exeter and his retirement seemed inevitable. He was, GARBO reported, considering returning to the sea. GARBO now promoted BENEDICT and left him in charge of the day-to-day running of the entire network. He also promoted DONNY and brought him back from Dover. DORICK, still in Harwich, was given responsibility for all the east of England, and the Greek was placed in charge of all future Scottish activities. With the removal of DAGOBERT, CHAMILLUS and DRAKE, GARBO was ready to begin operations again.

GARBO restarted with a letter, his twenty-second, on 20 July, in which he speculated on the question of FUSAG and its command:

> Patton was removed from his command of FUSAG and given, instead, the command of the Third US Army, giving over the command of the Twelfth US Army Group to General Bradley, who is Eisenhower's 'yes man', who, at the same time, has the experience of the battles he has led in France. The command of FUSAG was unfilled for a few days and was then given over to another of Eisenhower's favourites called McNair, who has just recently arrived from America. Patton is at present commander-in-chief of the Third American Army.

Although SHAEF may not have approved of GARBO's choice of words, there was a strategic purpose to the gossip. A number of the genuine units designated as being under the command of Patton's FUSAG had been sent to the Normandy front and, sooner or later, the Germans would interrogate a few prisoners. Only a relative handful of staff at SHAEF and elsewhere were privy to all FUSAG's secrets, and it would not take long for the enemy to suspect a deception campaign if individual prisoners expressed ignorance of their own supposed army group. Furthermore, the Abwehr would certainly want to know why FUSAG units apparently destined for the planned second offensive had been committed in France. The explanation was characteristically elaborate: extra reinforcements were unexpectedly required at the beachhead and Eisenhower had therefore transferred elements of FUSAG to Normandy. Patton had objected to the loss of some of his officers and had been replaced by General McNair, formerly commander-in-chief of the land forces in the United States. Patton had been sent to France in disgrace, and a US Twelfth Army had been formed under General Simpson (in reality the commander of the US Ninth Army) to bolster the FUSAG remnants. This all sounded reasonably plausible, especially given Patton's many recently publicised indiscretions, but unfortunately General McNair was killed by bombs dropped in error by US aircraft when he visited Normandy a few days after his arrival in England. Accordingly, on 29 July, GARBO reported McNair's demise, and other channels were used to communicate Simpson's new duties at FUSAG.

GARBO's resumption of duties took care of a substantial backlog of messages that had built up in his absence. DAGOBERT's were probably the most outdated, although DORICK had been sent on a mission some time before GARBO's arrest and none of his lengthy material had been passed on. Nonetheless, GARBO relayed all these reports so as to prove that his network had not been idle in his absence. He now relied on the ever-faithful DONNY, DICK and DORICK, from DAGOBERT's ring; J(1), his long-serving courier the Greek seaman, who continued to report from Scotland, and his various unconscious helpers: J(3) at the Ministry of Information; his mistress in Whitehall, J(5); and 4(3), the talkative American sergeant. All now communicated with Madrid through BENEDICT, who had taken over from GARBO in case the police pursued their inquiries into his detention. Meanwhile, the Canadian operation was progressing well with BENEDICT's brother in Ottawa, and DAGOBERT's Wren managed the occasional letter from her distant post at Peradenyia in Ceylon.

Throughout August 1944 GARBO relied increasingly on DAGOBERT's network to supply him with information. A signal dated 16 August is typical of one from DONNY:

> DONNY on return from south-west tour. Identified following units in Bristol area from vehicle markings: 691st Field Artillery Battalion, 184th Medical Battalion and 172nd Engineer Battalion, all belonging to the Ninth US Army, with the markings '99A' in addition to the unit number. Troops have no army insignia, though, from conversations with a soldier, I was able to confirm that the Ninth Army identification is correct, though he could not explain the reason for the absence of army insignia. Same contacts said that three more divisions are due to arrive from USA to be put under the command of the Ninth Army.

DORICK also had a contribution to make, on 23 August:

> Urgent. DORICK. The entire 59th, rattlesnake, American Division has started to leave Ipswich area, moving toward the south. Other divisions also preparing to leave. Agent is investigating and will send detailed reports as soon as possible.

Three days later DICK reported in:

> DICK. Saw many units with sign of white St Andrew's cross on circular background in red and blue, which I discovered belongs to the 17th US Division, which have been arriving in the Brighton area. Headquarters of this division is in Stanmer Park, about four miles from Brighton on Lewes Road. Have identified following units of this division: 293rd Infantry Regiment, 114th Engineering Battalion.

DORICK finally sent his observations to GARBO on 28 August:

> DORICK. Numerous rumours that entire American army in this area is leaving for south. Troops of the 11th US Division, previously seen in Stowmarket, have left the district. Few troops of XXXIII US Corps seen in Bury St Edmunds. Many troops of this corps left recently for unknown destination. Many convoys of the 17th US Division seen moving south. Advanced units of this division moved south some time ago. DICK recently reported arrival in Brighton area of units of this division. Blackwall tunnel, under the Thames, was closed for three days for passage of American troops.

In spite of their many preoccupations on the continent of Europe, the Germans were still mesmerised by GARBO's signals and they responded to all these messages with detailed questionnaires. All provided MI5 with valuable intelligence and betrayed highly significant areas of weakness in the enemy's knowledge of the Allied order of battle. Together, GARBO and Tommy Harris constructed suitable replies, like this item transmitted on the evening of 30 August:

> To investigate your questionnaire about airborne and armoured troops, I sent DONNY for a short trip to Larkhill-Bulford area where airborne and armoured troops were located before the landing. He discovered the following troops in this area: DONNY. 2nd British Airborne Division, with sign of winged horse, also saw American armoured troops and tanks of 25th US Armoured Division, just arrived from Norfolk, also some men with sign of 8th Armoured Division without vehicles. These both have unusual US armoured division sign with the number superimposed to identify the division. Also saw US infantry troops and convoys with the following sign: a blue oval with the letter 'V' in white interlaced with the number '9' in red and a circle divided diagonally, with the number '9' in

black on white in the white semicircle. Had no time to identify
but believe latter is the 94th US Division.

At the end of August 1944 BENEDICT was authorised by the
Twenty Committee to bring FORTITUDE SOUTH to a swift conclusion and concentrate on short-term operation deception plans
for 21 Army Group as the Allies headed for the Rhine. In
order to facilitate communications and liaison between the
commanders in the field in France and Ml5's case officers who
had previously been based in St James's Street, an offshoot of
the Twenty Committee was introduced, designated the 212
Committee. The essence of the 212 Committee's new scheme
was contained in BENEDICT's major transmission on 31 August:

> Important! The following obtained at meeting between
> myself, ARABEL and 4(3) yesterday, in reply to your question-
> naire about airborne army and also explains the moves of
> the Fourteenth US Army from the east coast. 4(3): He says
> that the original FUSAG plan for attacking Pas-de-Calais
> had been definitely cancelled, and the FUSAG forces are
> again being organised in the following way: the Fourteenth
> US Army and the 9th US Army are now under the direct
> command of SHAEF, as SHAEF strategic reserve. This
> force will be at the disposal of SHAEF for Eisenhower to
> be able to reinforce the Allied armies in France if they want
> assistance in the advance which is now about to be driven to
> prevent the German army from escaping to Germany. The
> Fourteenth US Army is being replaced in FUSAG by the new
> airborne army, which has now been given the name of the
> First Allied Airborne Army. With this rearrangement, a great
> part of FUSAG is now composed of airborne troops and will
> be used for special operations; in fact, FUSAG will become a
> sort of modern version of combined operations. For instance,
> they will carry out large-scale airborne operations anywhere
> in France, Belgium or Germany to attack the enemy lines of

communications. They will also be used to occupy any areas or countries which the Germans give up unexpectedly, and this will avoid the necessity of having to make sudden dispersals of forces in the battle at the expense of carrying out their original plans. Following just arrived, urgently, from ARABEL. This morning I happened to be present at an interview between J(3) and a war press correspondent of SHAEF, at M of I. He told us, in confidence, that a large attack in France is imminent. He was recently at advanced HQ of SHAEF in France, where he learnt about the following discussions. 21 Army Group demands that Patton's advance should stop. They want him to make a feint attack toward the east, keeping back the weight of his forces to turn north to attack the German flank, whilst the 21 Army Group, reinforced by FUSAG, makes a definite attack against the Pas-de-Calais to occupy that zone. On the other hand, Patton requests that all reinforcements and supplies are put at his disposal to attack into the centre of Germany, asking, at the same time, that the British armies should make a deceptive attack against the Pas-de-Calais to maintain all the German forces there, leaving Patton's troops with freedom of action. The correspondent said that it would, therefore, be absurd to speculate without knowing what personal decision Eisenhower will eventually take as to which of the two attacks is the feint attack and which is the one destined to make the advance.

On 9 September GARBO received the following letter from the Abwehr, which was dated 31 August 1944, from Lisbon. As one might expect, GARBO and Tommy Harris were fascinated by its contents:

It has, for a long while past, been my desire to deal in brief with your various collaborators or, that is to say, to let you know how we here judge the quality and importance of their reports.

I can say with satisfaction that all of these who are regular informants show that they have understood their mission owing to the logic of the good instructions which they have received from you. Outstanding in order of importance are the reports of your friend 4(3), who, owing to the position he occupies, is the best placed for facilitating details with regard to the organisation of the army in general, about its large units and its composition, the arrival of new American divisions, plans of the high command etc. Though I imagine that in this connection you are dealing with an unconscious collaborator, it is necessary to cultivate this friendship by all possible means, as you yourself have pointed out. The last report of this friend of yours about the reorganisation of FUSAG was excellent. Nevertheless, it is necessary to proceed with the greatest care so as not to arouse his suspicion through the questions you ask him.

The informants DONNY, DICK and DORICK we consider to be perfect military observers and we have no further observation to make. If they continue to work as they have done up till now, then we are more than satisfied!

As to 7(1), it is a long time since we had news of him, possibly you can get some information through this channel about the present location of the 9th British Division, a matter which interests us as we have already stated by message.

The work of DRAKE did not last long and we could not judge his good qualities. We are happy that the difficulties that he experienced did not bring more serious consequences. I realise that this agent must have been influenced by this incident. Nevertheless, I consider the Swansea area to be of great importance. Even though there are not, at present, large contingents of troops there, it is [important] from other aspects of war and therefore I do not think that you should break contact altogether with this agent. I think you should use him for work which is not dangerous, as I do not think that he will be able to work free from fear, but he might be of some minor use. I leave the final decision to you.

I am completely in agreement with your decision in regard to agent 7(6), who has shown no signs of intelligence. We have had practically no news about 7(3) since she has been in your employment. We hope for good results from her new place of residence.

DAGOBERT is the one who has the greater merits, since he has organised his large network and has at the same time acted himself as an observer and military informant of great precision and accuracy. He has also supplied us with several reports of extraordinary merit. We should be very upset should we ever have to lose this friend who has overcome so many difficult situations. It was undoubtedly he who gave so much help in cases which had to be resolved with urgency, such as the case of CHAMILLUS after he had left the camp. I hope, therefore, that we will be able to continue to count on the collaboration of DAGOBERT, and should he not wish to remain here we would like to have him in the new organisation in Canada, which I will deal with more fully later in this letter.

With regard to BENEDICT, who is undoubtedly your best collaborator, there is no need for me to say anything more since we have expressed, above, our opinion of him.

As to 3(1) and 3(2), it is a long time since we have had news of them. (Possibly your friend who was in contact with them is no longer able to maintain this contact.) If this is the case, please let us know so that we can remove them from our list.

The same applies to 3(3) as has been said about DRAKE, DICK and DORICK, though I think that this is a case where the informant might intensify his work a little, since it is undoubtedly the case that a lot of important military activities are taking place in the north, in spite of the fact that the possibility of an embarkation from there appears, for the moment, to have disappeared.

I shall deal more fully with CHAMILLUS, together with the Canadian project. The effort which he made when the invasion was about to take place merits the highest recognition and praise. I perfectly well understand that what he is doing now and his present situation must be intolerable, and I consider that we should please him as quickly as possible.

ALMURA continues to carry out his mission with all perfection and reliability. He has acquired a great deal of practice since he has been transmitting. The transmissions have sometimes been very difficult, owing to atmospheric conditions and other disturbances. Should he be able to modify his set, increasing the frequency bands from 5,000 to 9,000 Kcs, for example, we should be able to adapt more favourable frequencies to the general conditions and times of transmission. If he cannot do it, it does not matter, because we have managed to get along like this and will continue to do so.

4(2) is another of the agents about whom we have had no news for some time. I therefore hope that you will also let me know in this connection whether we may remove him from our list or whether this agent is collaborating with you in some other connection.

With regard to your friends J(3) and J(5), I do not think they call for any special mention. This information from the MOI, which you have obtained through J(3), has on many occasions made it possible for us to be able to draw important conclusions and this friend has, furthermore, served your cover magnificently.

With reference to J(1), I can tell you that the sending of correspondence has worked recently to perfection. Some letters have been in my possession within a week.

This historic document was the best confirmation of the success that GARBO and his network had achieved. There were no complaints, no recriminations for all the misinformation that had been conveyed over the previous two and a half years.

Every plausible word of the deception campaign had been swallowed whole by the enemy. DAGOBERT's ring was held in such esteem that MI5 were determined to wring every last advantage from it. DONNY was singled out in more than one ISOS decrypt as a 'hitherto particularly reliable source', so he was exploited further:

> Southampton and surrounding areas. Most military camps in the area are occupied by US troops. All roads extremely busy with large convoy movements. Saw following troops and vehicles: Fourteenth US Army, XXXIII US Corps, US Division with the sign of the letter 'VV' in white interlaced with the number '9' on a blue oval, 11th US Infantry Division, SOS SHAEF, 48th US Division, 59th US rattlesnake Division, 9th US Armoured Division, 25th US Armoured Division, 2nd British Airborne Division. General impression: great activity and movement of troops, vehicles, armour and supplies. Fourteenth US Army was recently reported by DORICK as having left his area.

All these assessments turned up, sooner or later, in the ISOS material intercepted by GCHQ. The Abwehr and the Wehrmacht high command seemed oblivious to the huge scale of the deception, and perhaps the ultimate irony lay in the fact that GARBO was receiving constant praise and funds from the victims of his imaginative duplicity. But just as GARBO and Tommy Harris were congratulating themselves on their triumph, disaster suddenly loomed large. The head of the British Secret Intelligence Service station in Madrid reported that a locally based Abwehr agent had offered to betray his organisation's chief agent in Spain. The news caused consternation in St James's Street.

SIS's man in the Spanish capital was Captain Hamilton-Stokes, who ran the British passport control office from the first floor of the British embassy annex in the Monte Scinta. On the floor above him the Section V representative, Jack Ivens, ran a small counter-intelligence department to monitor the enemy's activities in and around Madrid. Suddenly, in mid-August 1944, Ivens received a telephone call from the embassy's press attaché calling him to a meeting with a German who had walked into his office without warning. The German was a low-level Abwehr case officer named Fritz Guttmann, who made an intriguing proposition: he would give details of a major German spy ring run by a Spaniard in Britain in return for protection and help in getting to London. He was also prepared to trade his own star agent, an officer of the Dirección General de Inteligencia (DGI), Franco's intelligence service. The latter item was of no great interest to SIS, but Section V judged that the first would certainly intrigue MI5. Ivens agreed to communicate Guttman's suggestion to headquarters, and suggested that he return once he had received his instructions. Apparently satisfied, the German left the embassy by the front door.

Since the Security Service were confident that all the enemy's agents in Britain were operating under their supervision, it was clear that Guttman was actually offering to identify the man known to him as ARABEL, and to MI5 as GARBO. Somehow the Abwehr man had to be prevented from carrying out his plan, as it would be impossible to maintain GARBO if the Germans suspected that he had been betrayed by a defector. Fortunately, Ivens had stalled for time and Guttman had declined to go into any detail for fear of showing his hand before a deal had been struck. This enabled Tommy Harris to dream up a characteristically ingenious solution to the problem. Early in September, GARBO reported that his courier had recently met someone in Lisbon who had mentioned that Guttman was planning to defect to the Allies. But instead of eliminating Guttman, which might suggest to the British that there had been a leak, the traitor should be allowed to continue his work. However, Guttman should be informed that GARBO had recently fallen under police suspicion (which was partly true) and that he had been obliged to flee England. This manoeuvre would reduce GARBO's value to the British should Guttman defect and, in all probability, would prevent Guttman from making a further approach. The Abwehr was delighted with the scheme and GARBO promptly wrote a number of letters as though he had made good his escape to Spain. At the Abstelle in Madrid word was circulated to Guttman that ARABEL had fled the country and the police in London were now resigned to the fact that he had escaped and had given up calling at his lodging.

The plan worked, and Guttman failed to make a second appearance at the British embassy. Evidently he did not have much confidence in the value of his DGI source to the British. It was later reported that Guttman committed suicide rather than face interrogation.

This narrow escape, similar to the ARTIST crisis earlier in the year, highlighted the danger that GARBO was facing in London. As he was notionally under police suspicion, at the end of September 1944 it was agreed with Madrid that he should go into hiding at the remote Welsh farmhouse that had been used by the deserter CHAMILLUS before his departure for Canada. But life in the rugged countryside did not suit GARBO. On 3 October he wrote a long letter, his thirtieth, describing his rain-sodden surroundings and his uncongenial companions:

There were three of us, the Welsh couple and a Belgian. The former are both fairly old, each of about sixty years of age. They work all day long in the fields looking after the farm, which consists of four herds of cattle and about a hundred fowls. The house is miserable and poor and it only has electricity through a miracle, since the electricity supply happens to pass through some mountains and goes to a village which is only ten miles away. The old man is a Welsh Nationalist who, in his youth, worked a great deal for the party. His English is worse than mine and I mostly do not understand what he says. They speak Welsh when they are talking together. He is now no longer mixed up in politics. He is a friend of DONNY and it is in this farm that the group which was formed by those who are now working for us used to print their propaganda leaflets. They used to hide their documents; they had, and still have, a secret cellar which leads out of the basement of the house. It is a sort of shelter where the Belgian and I would hide should there be an unexpected visit from one of the neighbours. This, however, is very unlikely, since in this corner of the world no one will ever turn up, and secondly, because the nearest neighbour lives two and a half miles away from the farm. The Belgian is a man who is a little simple. I do not know whether his brains are atrophied. On studying him, he seems to be abnormal. We spend the day on our own, listening to the radio and reading books.

The Abwehr were suitably distressed by GARBO's plight and, on 1 January 1945, he received the following from Lisbon, dated 12 December 1944:

My dear friend and colleague, the days are approaching which, in normal times, would be days of good cheer for us all. We are living through the decisive hours for the future of humanity and the civilisation of Europe and surely for the whole world, and the thoughts of the tremendous unhappiness which this evolution has, to some extent, brought with it for millions of human beings does not allow conscientious people to enter into the good atmosphere of these festive moments. Thus, during these days we will devote ourselves with more intensity, if this should be possible, to thinking about our companions who, in the performance of their duty and in defence of their ideals, are now in a dangerous situation, terrible and very disagreeable. I should like to be a writer in order that I should have facility to find the words which might fully give you to understand the high esteem which we all have for you and the desire we and our headquarters have to collaborate with you.

We have, in your personality, your character, your valour, all these virtues which become a gentleman. I hope, nevertheless, that from what I have written to you, you will have been able to feel that which perhaps through lack of ability to express myself in the written word I have been unable to impress adequately. We here, in the very small circle of colleagues who know your story and that of your organisation, talk so often about you that it often seems as if we were living the incidents which you relate to us, and we most certainly share, to the full, your worries. On account of them, I know that with the approach of Christmas you will be suffering many bitter moments at having to spend these days separated from the people who mean most in your life. I trust, nevertheless, that the satisfaction of being able to contribute, through the mediation of the organisation which you have created, to a sacred cause, which is that of the struggle for the maintenance of order and salvation in our continent, will give you comfort and moral strength to be able to go ahead with us until we have overcome our obstacles.

At the termination of this year of truly extraordinary struggles, I wish to express to you our firm and absolute conviction that next year will bring us further along our none too easy road, at the end of which we will find that which has been awaiting us as a worthy recompense for all the sacrifices which this temporary task has imposed upon us.

For you, personally, my dear friend, you already know that my greatest wish is to see you soon free from your present critical situation and united once more with your family. We pray to the Almighty that He may give them and you His protection as He has done up till now, and that He may inspire those who direct the destination of countries to avoid the final catastrophe in the world. What is now taking place in many countries in Europe is perhaps the first way of light which He has shown us to illuminate and demonstrate what would occur if wise judgment is not shown in time, in order that it should be appreciated where the true danger lies.

These thoughts are also, to some extent, directed to all the companions of your organisation. I trust that it will be possible for you to pass them our thoughts, our good wishes and our gratitude for their magnificent work, and, in particular, to those who have helped you to resolve the present situation as true friends, to BENEDICT, DAGOBERT, the courier, DONNY etc. We hope very sincerely that one of these days it will be possible for us to express to them all our feelings in a more concrete form.

I know, my dear friend, that it is not possible to recompense materially all that you and your organisation are doing; nevertheless, I wish very sincerely that all your colleagues should have the possibility of being able to do something during the days of Christmas which will remind them that our thoughts are with you. Were it possible, I would send from here something to each of them as a small token. In view of the circumstances, I have no alternative but to confine myself to money, which, I trust, they will be able to accept as an expression of personal attention. I should be grateful to you, therefore, if you would take the necessary measures to effect this, and I leave it to your judgment to decide the amount which should be given to each of them in accordance with your knowledge of the various friends. I think that maybe the equivalent of a month's payment might be suitable, but as I have already said, you have absolute freedom to take the decision in this connection.

I purposely have not dealt with service matters in this letter. This I shall do when I have received your personal letter, which, I hope, will give me details about your plan for escaping, which I asked for by message, which will enable me, forthwith, to reply regarding all the possibilities in this connection.

I enclose, with this letter, a remittance of $3,000.

With our most cordial regards and a firm handshake.

The $3,000 brought the total paid to GARBO's network up to $20,000, enough to finance most of Ml5's other double agents. As usual, the money was paid to a Spanish fruit merchant in pesetas in Madrid. He then made the dollar equivalent available to GARBO at his London office. The enclosure of $3,000 referred to in the letter was simply a note authorising the fruit merchant to release the Abwehr's funds to their spy in London. The scheme had been code-named, appropriately, plan DREAM by MI5. In spite of German optimism, GARBO's mind had already been turning increasingly to the notional question of escape. The following month he grew a beard and sent a photograph of himself (referring, for security, to his 'friend') to the Abwehr in Madrid. They were not noticeably impressed with the disguise. In a letter from Lisbon dated 20 March, but received 1 April, the Abwehr commented tactfully:

> Having examined the photographs of the friend I must assure you that the camouflage is perfect. On the other hand, if I am to be quite frank about expressing my opinion I must say that this camouflage presents quite a lot of difficulties on account of the by no means usual shape of the friend's beard, since I think I can say with certainty that one can see very few people nowadays who wear a beard of that shape, with the exception of those beards which are rather more developed and one connects with people advanced in years.

GARBO ignored these adverse remarks and, even in the last weeks of the war, gave no hint that his entire network had been an elaborate sham.

In the last of some 2,000 messages GARBO broached the subject of the future of his own network. DICK and DORICK had remained particularly loyal, in spite of the adverse military situation on the continent. Throughout the winter months of 1944 these two sources had been active, although the signals must have made depressing reading for the Abwehr. On 23

November, for example, DORICK had liaised with BENEDICT and reported:

> DORICK. Sudbury: Saw large convoys of 58th Infantry Division moving direction of Cambridge. BENEDICT: This confirms that the troops of this division seen by me in Glasgow were on leave ... Have ascertained that 80th Infantry Division has been stationed in area between Ipswich and Stowmarket but that it left this district again between 10th and 15th of this month. Am proceeding to Yorkshire to investigate on basis of information received from my contact that 5th Armoured Division was moving to that county.

Once DORICK had reached Yorkshire, he maintained a steady flow of information:

> DORICK reports from York: has discovered that Fourth British Army has moved here but can find no sign of other divisions reported moving north in this area as yet. He is continuing investigations, though he states there is no sign of preparations for embarkation and has been told that Fourth Army and Northern Command are being amalgamated and will control any future landings in Germany, whether to help the present offensive or to occupy areas which you abandon, in the same way as other commands have been given similar roles; for instance, Norway in the case of Scottish Command and the Channel Islands in the case of Southern Command ... 80th British Infantry Division has left Canterbury area.

Even at this late date DORICK was still sufficiently keen to indulge in a little detective work to achieve his objectives. On 6 December GARBO gave this account of his activities in the north:

> DORICK. York. Agent has finally discovered that 58th Division is stationed in the areas surrounding Leeds. He discovered this

division by following the direction of very large convoy of
brand-new heavy trucks with divisional sign painted, which
were being delivered to the division. Have discovered that 80th
Division is stationed in the areas of Bedale and Catterick. ...
Agent assures me there is no immediate danger of an embarkation since 80th Division is undergoing training.

Ten days later DICK demonstrated that he too was still active in
the south of the country:

DICK. Bournemouth. Saw considerable number of newly
arrived American troops which are starting to occupy camps
near here. These wear the sign of red shield divided horizon-
tally, the main, lower portion in red, the smaller, upper portion
blue. Superimposed on blue portion is white design like a
telephone receiver. Have not been able to identify this yet but
am continuing investigation.

By the New Year of 1945 it was impossible to avoid the truth
– that the Third Reich was crumbling – and DAGOBERT's agents
became increasingly anxious to disband. In GARBO's thirty-ninth
letter, dated 8 April 1945, he explained:

These individuals are inspired by other ideas and their ends are
different from ours. They have helped us because they believe
and hope that with the assistance that they were giving us we
would one day be able to help them and the ends of their
party. Now that they see that our situation is itself difficult
and they cannot hope for anything from us, they wish to get
out without compromise from the promise of loyalty which
they have expressed.

DONNY was prepared to carry on, in spite of a severe asthma attack,
as was BENEDICT, but DORICK and DICK had already announced
their intention to resign. DORICK was not convinced that his

continued involvement would help the Welsh Nationalists, and DICK, the Indian, claimed that he had only helped in order to assist his mistress and, anyway, intended to return to India at the end of the war. Eventually, on 1 May, the Abwehr were forced to admit that GARBO should cease operations altogether:

> The rapid course of events and the confusion reigning all over the world makes it impossible to see ahead with clarity the future developments of the general situation or to take decisions in this connection. We thank you with all our hearts for the offer from BENEDICT and yourself for your continued collaboration, understanding and fully appreciating the motives which animated this. On the other hand, you will understand that in a situation which does not allow one to look ahead it is our greatest wish and duty as colleagues to arrange matters in such a way, taking as a basis the present events, so as to ensure generally for your safety and that of the collaborators, giving them an opportunity to return to their private activities.

On 3 May GARBO himself admitted defeat and requested Madrid to burn any compromising files they may have accumulated on him or his network. He added:

> I have absolute confidence, in spite of the present crisis, which is very hard, that our struggle will not terminate with the present and that we are entering into what is developing into a world civil war which will result in the disintegration of our enemies.

The Abwehr were suitably impressed with his expressions of undying loyalty and seemed prepared to entertain GARBO's latest idea, that he go back to Spain and start a new spy ring to penetrate the Soviets. Madrid replied on 6 May:

> Grateful for your latest messages and, especially, your offers of unconditional collaboration. The heroic death of our Führer

clearly points the course which must be followed. All future work and efforts, should they be carried out, must be directed exclusively against the danger that is threatened by a coalition of the east. Only a close union of all the sane peoples of Europe and America can counteract this tremendous danger, against which all other questions become unimportant. You will understand that, in view of the very rapid evolution of the situation during the past week, it has become completely impossible for us to be able to tell you now whether we will later be able to dedicate ourselves to the work, the basis of which is indicated above. Should we do so, we hope that we will be able to count on your proven friendship and the enormous experience in service matters. We, therefore, fully approve your plan to return to Spain where, once you have arrived, the plan for a new organisation directed against the east can be dealt with.

Two days later, in his penultimate wireless communication with the Abwehr, GARBO received specific instructions on how to renew contact on his arrival in Madrid. He was to go to La Moderna bar at 141 Calle Alcalá every Monday evening and carry a copy of the *London News* under his arm. Between eight and half-past he would be approached by 'a friend of Fernando Gomez'. This intermediary would give further instructions.

In his final transmission GARBO said:

I understand the present situation and the lack of guidance due to the unexpected end of the military struggle. News of the death of our dear chief shocks our profound faith in the destiny which awaits our poor Europe, but his deeds and the story of his sacrifice to save the world from the danger of anarchy which threatens us will last forever in the hearts of all men of goodwill. His memory, as you say, will guide us on our course and today, more than ever, I affirm my confidence in my beliefs and I am certain that the day will arrive in the not too distant future when the noble struggle will be revived, which was started by him to save us from a period of despotic barbarism, which is now approaching.

Some months later, when GARBO finally returned to Spain after a brief visit to the United States and South America, he followed the instructions he'd been given and managed to track down his Abwehr case officer to the small Spanish town of Avila. A broken man, desperate not to be deported to Germany, he begged GARBO to help his escape to South America. GARBO's reply? He promised to consult BENEDICT or DAGOBERT.

11

VICTORY

The last stages in life are always sad. Memories readjust biography,
the past outweighs the present and the future outweighs nothing.
Francisco Umbral, in his foreword to
Miguel Delibes's *La Hoja Roja*

From the moment I set foot in England in 1942 until I left after the war, I gained great pleasure from the beauty of the countryside, from the lush greenness of London's gardens and from the great variety of trees which lined the streets and filled the parks. I arrived in April, when the country was just about to appear at its best; the days were getting longer and the sun, the little sun that there is at that time of year, came peeping through the cloudy skies, welcoming me with its warmth and friendliness to a land which was to be a most hospitable host, a land which received me with open arms and often made me feel extremely happy, especially when it allowed me to associate myself with its joys and sorrows.

Although it was April, I found England cold. The day after my arrival I asked Tommy Harris if he would come with me to help me buy some warm clothes, but that had to wait. First I had to undergo a long and detailed interrogation. Mr Grey led the cross-examination, with Harris interpreting.

My English was not just poor, it was almost non-existent, so they suggested that I should, as a matter of priority, have some lessons so that I could learn the basics of the language of Shakespeare. However, I thought it much more important to make immediate contact with the Germans, sending them some really useful information, for I had been silent for some weeks. Three days later, after consulting various sections of MI5, we sent the Abwehr a juicy letter that, for the first time, included true information about England.

As soon as Colonel T. A. Robertson, who was responsible for Ml5's B1(a) section, dealing with counter-espionage through double agents, and his fellow officers had given me their full backing, Tommy Harris and I concentrated hard on drawing up a short-term and a long-term program of action.

Tommy Harris had endeared himself to me right from the start, not just from the firm way he had shaken my hand but because he had also put his arm around my shoulders in a gesture of protection and friendship. We soon began to confide in each other and I always trusted him completely; my trust was never misplaced. Together, we invented the role of GARBO, a creation that afforded us both great pleasure. Someone has said that GARBO without Harris or Harris without GARBO would have been unthinkable, for both were crucial to the other in carrying out the work that had to be done!

Tomás Harris, or Tommy as we affectionately called him, must have been thirty-five or forty then. Although he loved art and although painting was his dominant passion and his peacetime livelihood, he was no unkempt bohemian but an extremely sensible and capable individual, who always dressed impeccably in an elegant sports jacket, which he wore with a most distinctive air. He smoked like a chimney and the fingers of his right hand were almost chestnut coloured as he never put out a cigarette until it was about to burn him. Always cheerful, he had a most attractive smile. His wife Hilda, whom he adored, was also charming and very loving; both were gourmets who enjoyed good food and an excellent bottle of wine. Tommy owned an impressive art collection, which included paintings by Velázquez, Goya and Rubens, as well as those by more recent innovative artists. He also painted himself; his early works leant towards the El Greco School but, in the later part of his life, he was influenced by Goya. But he painted almost nothing during the war as his time was fully taken up with our mutual task. Tommy became a very great friend and a most hard-working and indefatigable colleague for whom I had the greatest admiration.

I continued to live in Hendon, travelling into the office in Jermyn Street, off St James's, every day. Once in the office I would sit down and write letters in Catalan hour after hour, leaving wide spaces between the lines so that I could then insert whatever Tommy and I had concocted in between in invisible ink. When the V-1s began, I went to live at a hotel near Taplow in Buckinghamshire owned by a Spaniard who came from Valencia. There were about twenty-five other guests there, including a red-haired girl of Jewish extraction who was always asking me for Spanish lessons, and I also remember a Spanish vice-consul and a Czech couple. It wasn't a bad existence. I told them all I worked for the BBC and I commuted up to London every day by train. When I returned in the evening, we would sometimes have a party and I would dance. At that time I was very good at the paso doble and the foxtrot.

V-2s were more frightening than V-1s. On 8 September at 6.43 p.m. there was a screaming noise followed by a great explosion, which shattered about twenty buildings in the centre of London. Sixteen seconds later a whole block disappeared in another part of London, literally falling down like a house of cards. No one had heard the characteristic whine of the V-1's engine nor seen any plane in the sky. This was the beginning of the V-2s.

The first V-2 fell on a school and killed seventy-eight children. No one knew where it had come from. It seemed to fall straight out of the stratosphere and it left a crater over eight metres deep. Everyone was surprised to find ice in these craters, a by-product of the rocket's stratospheric route. There was no possible defence then known against these flying bombs.

Soon the Germans wanted to know exactly where the point of impact was for each V-2, so we sent them false information in order to make sure that the rockets fell on the outskirts of London and not on the most densely inhabited areas, but doing this pricked my conscience. It was not easy to find areas of low population density near London and I was all too well aware that the least error could cost thousands of innocent lives. The Germans became more and more insistent with their demands for details and I became increasingly nervous, as they could easily discover that I was giving them false information.

Then on a glorious – though for many people also tragic – day, 6 June 1944, British and American troops landed in Normandy and were eventually victorious; and so we were able to bring Western democracy back to Europe and to end hostilities with the least possible number of casualties.

The work Tommy Harris and I did was hard at times because it meant having to solve complex problems and make difficult decisions. All the messages we sent exist on file, and I hope that one day they will all be published in full. For the time being, MI5 keeps them secret, even though some of them have leaked out. I was very proud to be given the MBE during the war; although it had to be presented to me privately, I had prepared a little speech for the occasion and, when I had been given it, all those present began to bang on the table to congratulate me. It was a very moving moment.

In my last message to the Germans I told them that I would try to go to South America by boat as soon as I could. Then, on 7 May 1945, London exploded with joy: people invaded Piccadilly Circus and Regent Street, and traffic came to a standstill; everyone was drinking beer, singing and dancing to celebrate the arrival of peace. Our office was disbanded; GARBO had no more messages to send and the whole team was broken up. I lost touch with most of them except for Tommy Harris, who had always been my best friend in MI5. They didn't want me to leave the country and even offered me a managerial job with the Eagle Star Insurance Company, but I had made up my mind to go to South America because I believed that the pact

between the Allies and the USSR was not going to last and I
feared that another war would soon follow.

I left Great Britain in June 1945 on board a Sunderland
hydroplane for the United States, accompanied by Tommy
Harris, for MI5 were determined to look after GARBO right to
the end. The British were always marvellous to me and, at the
end of the war, MI5 gave me £15,000 as a reward for my work;
they arranged for this money to be sent to Caracas through the
Banco de Londres y Sud América.

We left from Southampton and landed in Baltimore after a
twenty-four-hour flight. From there we went to Washington,
where I had an interview with J. Edgar Hoover, the boss of
the FBI, who wanted to meet me personally. He invited both
Tommy and me to his house, where we had dinner in an underground room. Hoover showed great interest in my activities as
a double agent and was most affable throughout, but he never
asked me to work for him.

Tommy Harris and I then stayed in New York for a few
days, after which I left him there while I went on to visit Cuba,
Mexico and several other countries in South America. I was
looking for somewhere which appeared safe and comfortable,
free from nationalist extremism, and whose future looked prosperous and likely to become democratic, a country where I felt
I could settle down permanently; finally, I chose Venezuela.

In 1945 Caracas, a true 'Sultana del Avila', had about
400,000 inhabitants and was a peaceful city, except for the
appalling traffic. The traffic was so bad, even then, that when
President Roosevelt's wife was asked what she thought of the
city by a local journalist, she replied: 'Caracas? Oh, it's just a
huge garage.' General Medina was governing the country,
although he had originally been a member of the dictator
General Gomez's government, but he was gradually allowing
the country to become more democratic.

The first thing I did on arrival was to go to the Spanish
consulate in Caracas and obtain a resident's permit, an identity

card, a driving license and all the other essential documents which would enable me to settle down there for good. I wanted to be forgotten, to pass unnoticed and to be untraceable. I therefore pretended that my passport had been stolen and asked if I could have a new one. I did this so that I could destroy my old passport; then no one would be able to see all the visas in it and so find out where I had come from. The Spanish consular offices in Caracas quickly furnished me with a brand new passport and, armed with this and all my other documents, I embarked on a liner for Barcelona. I wanted to see my family again and I had arranged to meet Tommy Harris in Madrid.

The ship was called the *Cabo de Buena Esperanza* and, after various stops, it eventually reached Barcelona. I found that my brother Joaquin had married after the civil war and now had two sons. Sadly, he never lived to enjoy the company of his grandchildren for he died at sixty-two, a victim indirectly of the privations he had undergone during his months in the front line, spent wandering up and down the mountains with his Republican unit, retreating toward France. Elena was still single, while Buenaventura was still happily married to the most sensible, hard-working, honest and affectionate man ever to be wished for by any woman. Although she and Frederic had no children, God had blessed this union from the start with love and harmony.

I then went to Madrid to join Tommy Harris, who now introduced me to Desmond Bristow, an MI6 officer who had spent the war in Gibraltar and North Africa. Both of them now put forward a new project which they had thought up: they suggested that I renew my contact with members of the German Secret Service still in Spain and offer to continue to work for them, so that eventually I could get in touch with those Germans who were in Soviet-occupied Germany. At that time all the Allied intelligence services were on the lookout for German intelligence officers who were thought to be roaming around Europe, the idea being to penetrate the Soviet Secret Service through those Germans whom the Soviets had recruited. I volunteered to go ahead with this plan though, thinking back, it showed alarming temerity on my part, for no one knew how the Germans in Madrid would react to seeing me again. But, anyway, I agreed to do it: I made contact again.

In the end I telephoned Madrid 333572 and asked for Gustav Knittel – the real name of the Abwehr agent Federico – who lived at Plaza Aunos 6. A voice answered that he wasn't there, but now lived outside Madrid, and the person to help me was Eberhardt Kieckebusche, who lived in Calle Sil 5 in the El Viso quarter of Madrid.

I had never had direct contact with Kieckebusche but, when I arrived at his house, he seemed very pleased to see me and invited me in for a meal. He looked like a Prussian, had been a commander in the Abwehr and a very good friend of Admiral Canaris. Kieckebusche had been in Spain ever since the civil war; he'd arrived at the same time as the Kondor Legion.

We shut ourselves in his office and he began to show me the greater part of all the messages I had sent him; he even produced the book which we had used for sending objects in, which had had its centre pages cut out in order to turn it into a secret box. He talked to me about 'our great task' and explained to me that things were difficult for the Germans in defeat. He told me that he was running an import/export business, which was doing quite well, and offered to help me in any way he could; he then handed me 25,000 pesetas in gratitude for all that I had done for the Reich. He also gave me Federico's address and told me that he was hiding in a little village in the Guadarrama Mountains.

Federico was not at all at ease when I met him. He gave me the impression that he was a very frightened man. Spain was a relatively safe country for Nazi officers to hide in, but many members of the intelligence service seemed to fear that they might be kidnapped or eliminated by their opposite numbers on the Allied side. Federico was greatly saddened by Germany's defeat, so I continued to play my role of a Nazi sympathiser and told him that better times lay ahead. I offered my services and said that I would be glad to continue to work for him. He fell for it completely – he believed me – and advised me to tie everything up with Kieckebusche.

I went back to Madrid and had another meeting with Kieckebusche, during which he said that all the members of the German Secret Service in Spain were either disbanded or out of touch with one another. He said that his old friend Canaris had been executed by the Nazis themselves and that most of his superior officers were either dead or had been arrested. It was therefore difficult for him to plan anything at the moment, as there was no organisation left; he would have to wait a while. I told him that I was thinking of settling down in South America and he gave me the Barcelona address of some people he thought I might find helpful, should I think of importing Spanish goods. Federico had been quite critical of Hitler and his conduct of the war, but Kieckebusche was much more prudent and suggested that the Nazis had been defeated by bad luck.

From Madrid, I went on to Lisbon. No doubt thanks to Risso-Gill's careful handling of the Portuguese authorities when I had left the country so precipitately in 1942, I had no difficulties with the Portuguese border police. Once in Lisbon I rejoined Tommy Harris, who took me to see Gene Risso-Gill. Neither of them could believe that I had really just been to see my German contacts in Madrid; they found it utterly incredible and were amazed at my audacity. To me, it had been final irrevocable proof that my double identity, ARABEL–GARBO, had been an impeccably kept secret right to the end.

I found Lisbon as charming and welcoming as ever, filled with happy memories and of people I will never forget. Portugal has always been England's faithful ally and has always cooperated loyally. I like saying this for I believe it and it is true.

While I was away, political changes were taking place in Venezuela. A military triumvirate overthrew General Medina and, after a failed attempt at democracy, Brigadier General Marcos Pérez Jiménez set up a dictatorship which lasted for seven years. Jiménez directed all his hatred against the very politicians with whom he had joined forces in order to overthrow General Medina, which was a hard lesson to swallow for all those who believed in democracy; but it was a lesson which the present political leaders have learnt well, since Venezuela has been living in peace now for some thirty years.

During Jiménez's dictatorship I was never harassed, questioned or harmed in any way, thanks to my customary stand of never, ever interfering in politics. I did not have to live the life of a recluse, but could continue with my job as a language teacher for Shell Oil on the eastern shores of Lake Maracaibo. I was never molested. No one knew about my past. Nobody knew what I had done during the Second World War.

Sometime around 1948 I made a trip to Spain to see my old friend Tommy Harris at his villa in Camp de Mar in Majorca, where he was living with his wife Hilda. It was to be the last time I saw him before he died. He told me that he had written a book about all our MI5 activities and that he had kept a copy for me should I decide one day to publish my memoirs, but I begged him to tell anyone who asked after me that I had died, leaving no trace, as I still wished to be protected from the Nazis. He obeyed me to the letter, for after this visit of mine MI5 spread a rumour that GARBO had emigrated to Angola and had eventually died there from malaria.

For the next thirty-six years I lived peacefully in Venezuela; it was a quiet time for me, for my life of action, of fighting for freedom, for my ideals, was over. Then in 1984, when I was least expecting it, Nigel West broke the cover that I had so successfully maintained and, through painstaking research and careful investigation, tracked me down.

A few days before the fortieth anniversary of the D-Day landings, he called on the telephone from London. He said how glad he was to be able to talk to the person whom everyone had thought to be dead.

Even though I wanted to forget all about the war, he was so insistent that I relented; he persuaded me that I would enjoy seeing old colleagues again and I was flattered at the thought of being introduced to HRH the Duke of Edinburgh, who, he said, was very keen to meet me. So many promises and offers were made that I agreed to think it over. After I was sure that all my German contacts had either disappeared or died, I decided that the time had come for my family to learn about my past, to hear about that part of my life which I had concealed from them up until now for security reasons.

And so I returned to London to receive personal thanks from the Duke of Edinburgh at Buckingham Palace, my acknowledgment from the people of Britain of all that I had done to help them retain their democracy and their freedom, and an example of their gratitude for backing their courageous fight against the Nazis. For it was their resolute stand and their humane conduct which had driven me all those years ago to offer to help, so that we could work hand in hand for victory in the battle of good against evil.

But my main pride and satisfaction, now I look back, has been the knowledge that I contributed to the reduction of casualties among the thousands – the tens of thousands – of servicemen fighting to hold the Normandy beachheads. Many, many more would have perished had our plan failed and the Germans counter-attacked in force.

EPILOGUE

The entire GARBO episode gave an eloquent demonstration of the value of strategic deception. The use of double agents was well established as a vital part of any sophisticated operation to mislead the enemy. Certainly, the British and the American intelligence agencies had learned all the relevant lessons through the FORTITUDE campaign, and had achieved extraordinary success by carefully coordinating the differing elements involved: signals intelligence, camouflage and the overall manipulation of the opposition's information-gathering networks.

At the conclusion of the war in Europe the various participants went their separate ways, GARBO himself to Caracas, where employment was found for him as a language teacher for an international oil company. Tommy Harris left MI5 at the end of hostilities and retired with Hilda to paint at his luxurious villa at Camp de Mar in Majorca. His sister, Violetta, remained in the Security Service for a further twenty years. Desmond Bristow also stayed in the intelligence field, and was eventually appointed head of the SIS station in Madrid, with responsibility for operations in his old stamping grounds of Spain, Portugal and North Africa.

It was not until 1951, when GARBO had settled down in his new life, that certain members of the British Intelligence community who had been involved in his wartime operation came under suspicion of having worked as Soviet spies. Neither Burgess nor Maclean, the two foreign office diplomats who defected to Moscow in May of that year, had played any part with GARBO during the war, but a number of their closest friends had. Principal among the remaining suspects was Kim Philby, who had headed Section V's Iberian subsection until late in 1944. He had been intimately involved with the GARBO case, especially after Desmond Bristow had been posted to Algiers. By 1951 he had been promoted in his chosen career, and had been posted to Washington, DC, as head of the SIS station at the British embassy. While in that sensitive position, he had been informed that Donald Maclean was under investigation by MI5. Philby communicated a warning to Guy Burgess, thus enabling Maclean to make his escape at the very last moment before he was due to be interrogated. A slight departure from the plan was Guy Burgess's decision to accompany him. It was immediately obvious that both had been tipped off by a fellow conspirator, and Kim Philby was one of the few people who had the necessary advance knowledge. Also high on MI5's list of possible Soviet spies was another close friend of Guy Burgess, the art historian Anthony Blunt. He had not been privy to the closely guarded secret of Maclean's impending arrest, but he might have acted as a conduit for the warning message. Documents left in Burgess's flat in London eventually incriminated another Cambridge graduate and former MI6 officer, John Cairncross, who was then working as a civil servant in the Treasury. He steadfastly denied having committed any offense, but wisely decided to resign and live abroad. The MI5 investigators were convinced that both Blunt and Cairncross were, or had been, important Soviet agents.

Apart from being covert Soviet agents, Burgess, Philby and Blunt all had another thing in common. They had been close friends of Tommy Harris, who, in an act of characteristic generosity, had actually paid for the education of one of Philby's sons. Although there was insufficient evidence to arrest and charge either Philby or Blunt, the Security Service remained convinced of their guilt. Harris was simply regarded as an innocent acquaintance of all three, for he had no known connection with Donald Maclean and, unlike the others, had not been educated at Cambridge, where the Russian recruiters had been so active. But, at the end of July 1953, the situation was to alter dramatically.

Even though it was generally believed that Burgess and Maclean had gone to live behind the Iron Curtain, there was no definite news of their whereabouts until April 1954, when Vladimir Petrov, a Russian diplomat and undercover NKVD officer, defected in Australia. Petrov confirmed that the two missing diplomats had led a secret life since leaving Cambridge. In the meantime, while there was still considerable speculation on the subject, Donald Maclean's American-born wife Melinda suddenly disappeared.

When Maclean had fled in May 1951 his wife had been expecting their third child, and she had been left behind. The following year, after the birth of her daughter, Melinda Maclean went to live in Geneva, to escape the intrusive attentions of the British press. She remained in Geneva until the summer of 1953, when she planned to take a vacation on the Spanish island of Majorca in the Mediterranean with her three children and her wealthy American mother, Mrs Dunbar. All five were supposed to travel to Majorca, where they were to be the guests of an American widower, Douglas MacKillop. The party was booked to travel via Barcelona on 1 July 1953, but shortly before the end of June Melinda Maclean suddenly changed her plans and took her children to Saanenmoser, a small mountain resort above Gstaad. She announced that she intended to stay at Saanenmoser for a fortnight, and then go on to Majorca, but she reappeared in Geneva just five days later. The out-of-season village had not suited her. The original plan, to stay with Douglas MacKillop, was reinstated, and eventually, on 23 July, Mrs Dunbar took her daughter and three grandchildren on their much-delayed trip to Majorca. For the next five weeks they stayed in the tiny seaside village of Cala Ratjada, on the other side of the island from Camp de Mar, and then returned to Melinda Maclean's flat in Geneva. On 11 September 1953, just three days after her return from Majorca, Mrs Maclean suddenly disappeared, together with her three children. She had made elaborate arrangements to conceal her hurried departure, and the authorities tried in vain to discover where and how she had received her complicated travel instructions. She eventually turned up in Moscow, reunited with her fugitive husband, and it became clear that her own departure to the east had been as carefully orchestrated as that of her husband two years earlier. The investigators noted the coincidence of her recent vacation in Majorca, and the possibility that she might have kept a secret rendezvous with a Soviet courier in Palma.

After her return from Majorca, Mrs Maclean had told her mother that she intended staying the weekend 'with some old friends from Cairo', Robin Muir and his wife, at their villa in Territet, near Montreux. In fact, Muir did not exist, and Mrs Maclean only drove her children as far as Lausanne, where they all boarded a train for Zurich. On arrival she connected with the Vienna express, but was met by a car at Schwarzach St Viet, some ten miles from Salzburg. From there, evidently, she was driven into the Soviet zone of Austria. When Mrs Maclean had not returned to Geneva by Monday, 14 September, Mrs Dunbar raised the alarm. Three days later she received a telegram, allegedly from her daughter, claiming her absence was only temporary. Subsequent inquiries showed that the telegram had been handed in at Territet by another woman who did not answer the description of Mrs Maclean, who, predictably, was by then reunited with her husband in Moscow.

Mrs Maclean's exit from Switzerland had been carefully planned, but how and when had she received her instructions? Her mother, Mrs Dunbar, had been with her constantly since the brief trip to Saanenmoser in July, and had denied knowledge of any long-standing escape plan. Presumably the information detailing the rendezvous and confirmation of the train times had to have been passed on shortly before her departure. Her mother had been with her constantly in Geneva, so had she been contacted in Majorca, and why had she cut short her trip to Saanenmoser? It rather looked as though Mrs Maclean had been spirited away from Geneva, right under the noses of any security agencies who were anxious to discover her husband's fate. After this further embarrassing humiliation, MI5 redoubled its efforts to identify all the members of what appeared to be an increasingly large and powerful Soviet spy network.

The key figure in the ensuing investigation was Kim Philby, who had been sacked from the Secret Intelligence Service in 1951 and had eked out a living as a journalist in the Middle East ever since. Late in 1962 evidence came to light which confirmed his close collaboration with Burgess and Maclean and, in January 1963, he was confronted. In return for formal immunity from prosecution, Philby admitted his treachery and agreed to give a detailed confession. A few days later, on the evening of 23 January 1963, he suddenly vanished from his apartment in Beirut, and was not heard of until he surfaced in Moscow some considerable time later.

Philby's guilt again raised the spectre of an extensive, deep-rooted network of ideologically motivated Soviet agents in the very heart of the British establishment. A massive molehunt followed, but inevitably, and in the absence of Kim Philby, MI5 was forced to return to its first suspects after the defection of Burgess and Maclean: John Cairncross and Anthony Blunt. Cairncross underwent a further interrogation at his new home in the United States late in March 1964, and was a lot more forthcoming about his own activities, although he denied knowledge of any other Soviet agents. That left only Anthony Blunt. Coincidentally, Michael Straight, Blunt's former pupil at Cambridge and a one-time recruit, volunteered a highly incriminating statement to the FBI in Washington, which finally led to the interrogation and confession of Sir Anthony Blunt on 22 April 1964. Then the keeper of the Queen's pictures, he had not had access to any official secrets since his retirement from MI5 in 1945, but he did confirm that a large spy ring had been created by Soviet recruiters in the mid-1930s, and that many of its members had achieved positions of authority within Whitehall and the intelligence community. Although he knew the names of many Oxford and Cambridge undergraduates who might have been approached, he merely confirmed the guilt of those like Cairncross who were already well known to the Security Service. In the months that followed dozens of leads were pursued, and two more friends of Tommy Harris came under suspicion: Lord Rothschild and Peter Wilson.

Lord Rothschild had been a member of the famous Apostles, the secret society at Cambridge that had nurtured so many Soviet agents. Among them had been Guy Burgess, Anthony Blunt, Leo Long and Alistair Watson. The latter two had been identified as Soviet spies by Blunt. Long had been a wartime military intelligence officer and, after a fruitless attempt to join MI5, had worked for a film company in London. Alistair Watson, on the other hand, had been an admiralty scientist specialising in antisubmarine warfare. He later gave a partial confession: he admitted being a covert communist and having conducted covert meetings with Soviet intelligence officers, but denied ever having passed on classified information from the admiralty. He was promptly moved into a less sensitive position.

In 1940 Rothschild had joined the Security Service, and had subsequently recommended Blunt for a transfer into MI5, but had returned to scientific research at the end of hostilities. When questioned by MI5 in 1964 he had 'felt it essential to help them in every possible way' and successfully cleared himself of any suspicion.

Before the war, Peter Wilson had been appointed a director of the art auctioneers Sotheby's, and had later served in MI6. He had been a regular visitor to Tommy Harris's gallery home in Chesterfield Gardens and had known Philby, Blunt and Burgess both professionally, while a serving MI6 officer, and socially. Like Blunt and Burgess, he was an active homosexual. But had he also been a Soviet spy?

The one person who seemed to be at the centre of these

events, Tommy Harris, was killed in a car accident in January 1964, a year after Philby's escape from Beirut and three months before Blunt was induced to confess his treachery. Harris had been driving Hilda from Palma, where they had been seen to argue at a restaurant, and both had consumed a great deal of alcohol. Instead of heading toward his home at Camp de Mar, Harris had turned inland in the direction of a pottery which he had commissioned to glaze some of his latest ceramics, and he lost control of his new, powerful Citröen on a humpback bridge on the notorious Lluchmayor Road. The car had spun off the road and had hit an almond tree, killing Harris instantly. Miraculously, Hilda had been thrown clear and had suffered only minor injuries. A discreet but necessarily superficial investigation had followed, and such evidence as could be found had pointed toward the crash having been entirely accidental. However, not everyone had been convinced, and more than one intelligence officer has commented on the fact that Harris had driven along the Lluchmayor Road many hundreds of times before the crash occurred. Although the road has some tortuous bends, the bridge where the car ran off the road is actually quite straight. Was it likely that such an experienced driver would lose control of his car on a perfectly straight road? Or had alcohol, combined with a domestic argument, stolen his judgment?

Of the very few Allied intelligence officers who were allowed to learn GARBO's full story, it is extraordinary that at least two, Kim Philby and Anthony Blunt, should have turned out to be very senior Russian spies. The fact that Tommy Harris, the genius who masterminded the operation, should have been killed in such circumstances and at such a time is remarkable. Although Hilda survived the car crash, she never fully recovered her health and, unable to live alone, died not long afterward. Forty years after GARBO's departure for Venezuela, most of the principal participants have either departed to Moscow or died, and the conundrum remains as insoluble as ever.

APPENDIX I

By Colonel R. F. Hesketh OBE TD

The aim of Operation FORTITUDE, the cover plan for the invasion of occupied Europe in June 1944, was to convince the enemy that the landings on the Normandy beaches were a feint and that the main attack would be made in the Pas-de-Calais region. Largely thanks to the code breakers at Bletchley and the efforts of the British Security Service, MI5, there were no genuine German spies in England to betray our intentions. In fact, the only Abwehr sources at large were those who were the double-cross agents operating under the control of MI5's B1(a) section, headed by Colonel T. A. Robertson. He and his team provided us with a ready-made channel for passing our fictitious story to the German high command.

The deception staff at SHAEF, under Colonel Noel Wild and known as Ops B, was divided into two sections. One, under Colonel Jervis Read, dealing with physical deception, such as camouflage, and the other, generally known as the special means section, for which I was responsible, dealing with all forms of controlled leakages. Events proved that the only consistently effective conduit for passing false information to the enemy was that provided by the double agents, and it was to feed this channel that, within the overall framework, a succession of special means plans were prepared and put into operation, each being designed to meet changes in the situation. There was at all times a close liaison with Colonel David Strangeways, who was in charge of deception at 21 Army Group, largely to ensure that there should be no conflict between the cover plan and the operation itself.

When the implementation of FORTITUDE first began, an MI5 officer from B1(a) was seconded to us to help in the task of passing the story to the enemy through double agents. It must be explained here that every double-cross agent had a case officer who looked after his affairs generally and, as there was a strict rule that there should be no direct contact between the SHAEF deception staff and the agents themselves, it was invariably the case officer who visited our office at Norfolk House to receive the information that was to be conveyed through his agent, and then made sure that the message was passed correctly.

From the start, it was thought likely that GARBO would provide one of our best channels. Unlike many of the other double-cross agents, GARBO's sympathies had lain all along with the Allied cause. GARBO's status was amply confirmed by an examination of the German intelligence reports for the year 1944, made after the war had ended. Because of his high standing with his Abwehr masters, much of the burden of communicating the FORTITUDE plan fell to GARBO and his case officer, Tommy Harris. German faith in him hardly faltered, even after the beachhead in Normandy had been well established. The post-war analysis demonstrated that, during the period of the FORTITUDE campaign, no less than sixty-two of his messages were quoted in the German high command's intelligence summaries.

As the date for the invasion drew near, General Eisenhower was asked when the all-important message might be transmitted which would specifically affirm that the Allied attack in Normandy was merely a feint and that the main assault was destined for the Pas-de-Calais. This part of the cover plan had been supported by an apparent concentration of troops in south-east England. Eisenhower replied, at any time after the first landings had taken place.

Because of his reliability and his standing with the enemy, GARBO was chosen for this task, but his case officer insisted on a three-day delay before sending the message. He pointed out that if the Germans could be persuaded to recall troops who were already on the move, there would be little chance of them changing their minds again. Accordingly, GARBO's crucial text was not sent until D+3, when Berlin had already authorised the immediate transfer of forces to the west.

Within hours of the D-Day forces coming ashore, certain German armoured and infantry divisions received orders to move from the Pas-de-Calais to spearhead a German counter-attack in Normandy. But at 0730 hours on the morning of 10 June, the day after GARBO's wireless transmission, Field Marshal von Rundstedt issued a countermanding order recalling these troops to the Pas-de-Calais, and there they remained. Indeed, there were more German forces in that region at the end of June than there had been on D-Day.

When the war ended I decided to find out whether GARBO's message had contributed to the issue of the countermanding order. It was important that no time should be lost since, with the war crimes trial approaching, delay might result in some of our best witnesses being no longer with us.

I sought and obtained permission to interview von Rundstedt and his chief of staff, General Blumentritt, who were then being held in a prisoner-of-war camp near Bridgend in Wales. I took with me my brother Cuthbert (who has since died), who had worked with us in SHAEF and had a better command of the German language than me.

When asked why the order had been issued recalling the reinforcements then on their way from the Pas-de-Calais, they both, without hesitation, answered that it had been issued on instructions from the OKW, the supreme command of the German armed forces. It was therefore arranged that my brother should interview field marshals Keitel and Jodl, who were by then awaiting trial at Nuremberg. In the meantime, I was able to find, among captured enemy documents that had been brought to London, GARBO's message of 9 June. This my brother took with him. On 18 April 1946 I received the following letter from him, which I quote in full:

BRITISH WAR CRIMES EXECUTIVES (E.S.)

April 18th, 1946

My dear Roger,

I saw Keitel last night. He agreed that the halting of 1 SS Pz Div would have been an OKW decision as they were very hesitant and nervous about moving anything from the P-de-C at that time. He could not, however, recollect the incident, nor could he say for certain what the 'bestimmte Unterlagen' were. He suggested that it might have been air recce of shipping movements on the south coast, so some other report from the Marine or Luftwaffe. When he saw the RSHA message he as good as said, 'well there you have your answer'. He read through the comment at the end and explained to me that it would have been written by Krummacher and that it exactly represented the frame of mind of the OKW at that moment, which was such that the RSHA report in question would have had just the effect of persuading them to countermand the move of those forces. He added, 'This message proves to you that what I have been telling you about our dilemma at that time is correct.' Later he said, 'You can accept it was 99 per cent certain that this message was the immediate cause of the counter order.'

This morning I managed to get hold of the OKW war diary and I enclose an extract from it which I think will interest you. The rest of the sheet is a list of things which have recently been sent to London, the first one being in fact the war diary, which I will try to get hold of when I get back as it covers the whole of 1944.

I am going to Regensburg tomorrow and return here on Monday to pick up a note which Keitel has promised to write in amplification of what he said yesterday. Then I hope to get the airplane on Tuesday to London.

With love from Cuthbert

Not surprisingly, GARBO's code name can now be found in virtually every manual on the subject of strategic deception, and his achievements have been well documented in books such as J. C. Masterman's *The Double Cross System in the War of 1939–1945*. But although I had worked with GARBO, via MI5's intermediaries, throughout the latter part of the war, I never discovered his real identity and did not actually meet him in person until May 1984, when he suddenly emerged from his self-imposed obscurity abroad. A few days before the fortieth anniversary of the D-Day landings I was invited to attend a private reception at the Special Forces Club in London where GARBO, who was introduced to me by his real name, Juan Pujol, was reunited with his surviving wartime MI5 colleagues. None had seen him in the intervening years. It was an emotional gathering, and one I shall never forget.

APPENDIX II

GARBO's Agents

GARBO's Close Contact No 1 – known as: J(1) or THE COURIER

NAME: Not mentioned.
NATIONALITY: Presumably British.
OCCUPATION: Employed as an official of one of the airline companies running a service between UK and Portugal. (Note:- From the regularity of the service it would appear more likely on analysis that the actual carriers of the letters were members of the KLM rather than BOAC.)
ADDRESS: Not mentioned.
RECRUITED: Prior to 15.7.41.

From the early information about this character, it would have appeared that he was a rather accommodating individual who, taking advantage of his position in a trans-continental airline company, was prepared to facilitate the sending of correspondence to Portugal without passing through Censorship, pretending he thought he could justify his conscience by the knowledge that the writers were political refugees, while increasing his income by so doing.

Though he was never definitely identified with SMITH JONES, the person who received the incoming correspondence for GARBO (and presumably the other characters in England whom the courier was facilitating) the Germans nevertheless frequently referred to him as 'THE COURIER SMITH'.

It was not advisable that the Germans should believe that the courier carried the correspondence to and from Portugal personally, lest they requested that he should be put in contact with them. Therefore, we took pains to impress upon them that though he did at one time make the journey as a member of the plane's crew, he later made use of various friends of his who were members of the crew to cooperate in this and the other business of smuggling.

It is a fact that the crews of planes became notorious through the press for engaging in smuggling, and though these activities were mostly confined to the smuggling of watches purchased in Portugal for sale in England, it was reasonable that the Germans should imagine that they engaged in other traffic.

As time went on, the courier developed into a very sinister character who, it became apparent, was trafficking in the sale in Portugal of Bank of England notes, the proceeds of robberies in the UK, which were exchanged in Lisbon for other Bank of England notes which, when brought into circulation in the UK, were no longer traceable to the robberies.

It subsequently became apparent that in order to engage in this very dangerous business the courier made use of a number of rather well placed British subjects in Portugal, one of whom at least was in direct contact with a person either employed by, or used as, an outside agent by SIS.

By means which were never disclosed, the courier came to discover that one of the cover addresses to which GARBO had been writing in Lisbon was a German cover address that had become the subject of investigations by the British in Lisbon.

With this valuable information in his possession, and realising that GARBO was therefore a German agent and not a refugee, he decided to blackmail him. We informed the Germans of this situation. They reacted to it as if it had been news of good fortune rather than bad and promptly authorised GARBO to pay the courier the sum of £2,000, which he was demanding far his silence, pointing out to GARBO that once he had accepted this blackmail money he would be entirely in GARBO's power.

Though the courier could never be induced to supply the Germans with military information against his country he did, in the interests of his self-protection, produce valuable counter-espionage information for GARBO, which enabled him to escape the vigilance of the British Security Service when, towards the last stages of the case, the Germans were made to realise that the British had become aware of his activities and identity.

GARBO's Close Contact No 2 – known as: J(2) or
GARBO'S AVIATOR FRIEND

NAME: Not mentioned.
NATIONALITY: British.
OCCUPATION: Officer in the RAF.
ADDRESS: British Overseas Club, London, and Bentley Priory,
Headquarters of Fighter Command.
RECRUITED: Operated as an unconscious informant from 12.4.42.

The first piece of genuine information supplied by GARBO after his
arrival in the UK, which was a report on the rocket batteries in Hyde
Park, was attributed to this contact. He was quoted as a source at
infrequent intervals throughout the case and was primarily instru-
mental in serving as a build-up for GARBO.

GARBO's Close Contact No 3 – known as: J(3) or
GARBO's FRIEND AT THE MINISTRY OF
INFORMATION

NAME: Not mentioned. (By a careful examination of the traffic and check on the movements of W. B. MCCANN, head of the Spanish
section of the Ministry of Information, while in Spain, the Germans
would have been bound to draw the conclusion that J(3) and MCCANN
were identical.)
NATIONALITY: British.
OCCUPATION: A high ranking official in the Spanish department of
the Ministry of Information.
ADDRESS: Not mentioned. (Address in Madrid given as Palace Hotel.)
RECRUITED: Was first mentioned as being in contact with GARBO on
16.5.42.

This character has certainly been the most important of GARBO's
contacts. He was represented as having been increasingly indiscreet
as his confidence and his liking for GARBO grew. GARBO firstly worked
as a part-time employee in the ministry on J(3)'s recommendation,
and a great deal of important deception material that was passed over
shortly after D-Day was attributed to this source. MCCANN was told
in confidence about GARBO's activities and informed that one of the
notional characters in the GARBO case had been built up around him.

GARBO's Close Contact No 4 – known as: J(4) or
CENSOR AT THE MINISTRY OF INFORMATION

NAME: Not mentioned.
NATIONALITY: British.
OCCUPATION: Employed at the Ministry of Information.
ADDRESS: Not mentioned.
RECRUITED: Was first mentioned as a contact of GARBO
on 10.4.43.

This character was created primarily with the object of building him up as a source for deception material. It was planned that this source should eventually provide GARBO with 'STOP' and 'RELEASE' notices issued to press censors. Thus, by indicating a complete press 'STOP' on all mention of a certain area, the enemy would be expected to deduce that the area indicated was likely to be a target area for operations.

To implement this plan, the Germans were told that the censor had introduced himself to GARBO in the ministry and, after they had become acquainted, he disclosed to GARBO that he was extremely left wing and had been passing certain secret information to the British Communist Party. It happened that at this time the press had raised the question of certain secret information having been passed to Mr ['Manny'] Shinwell [MP] by someone, unidentified, employed by the Ministry of Information, and questions were raised in the House. The censor, therefore, assumed the role of the source of these leakages and told GARBO that he was now lying low since the question had been given so much publicity. He offered to assist the Spanish 'Reds' in a similar capacity if GARBO would act as his cut out.

Although the character was built up on these lines, it was not found necessary to use him in any serious role to implement the cover story for OVERLORD, so that after March 1944 the censor was allowed to fade out of the picture.

GARBO's Close Contact No 5 – known as: J(5) or
THE SECRETARY AT THE MINISTRY OF WAR

NAME: Not mentioned
NATIONALITY: British
OCCUPATION: Secretary in the Secretariat of the 'Ministry of War'. A
more precise definition of the nature of her work was never given.
ADDRESS: Not given.
RECRUITED: This contact was first referred to on 4.9.43.

This character was mainly created as build-up for GARBO and it was
proposed that she should play an important role in the final deception
story. We built her up by passing over relatively high-grade, general
information, attributed to her indiscretions.

Domestically, she was represented as having fallen in love with
GARBO.

GARBO was authorised by the Germans to spend money on her as
lavishly as he wished in the hope that he could extract more valuable
information from her. She supplied GARBO with information about
the Moscow Conference in 1943, attributing her source to a colleague
who had attended the conference as secretary to the Chief of the
British Military Mission.

She was given as the source for a certain amount of high-grade
chicken food[1] about the movements of important British Service
chiefs. She was used to implement PLAN BODYGUARD.

In the spring of 1944 the Germans were very much on edge and
apprehensive about the possibility of an imminent attack, and J(5) was
used until early May to reassure them that there was no possibility of
an immediate invasion. Although at that date this information should
have served her as a good build-up, it did not in fact do so as the
Germans, in reply, warned GARBO that he should not place too much
confidence in her word, as it was common practice in government
offices to mislead the subordinate personnel lest they should, through
knowledge of the true facts, cause a leakage through indiscretion.

She was, however, used again immediately after D Day to support
the build-up of the notional FUSAG, by confirming that there were
seventy-five divisions in the UK prior to the Normandy landing,
whereas there were in fact less than fifty.

---

1   Genuine information designed to make an agent appear well-informed
without causing damage to operations

This character was then allowed to fade out of the scene, on the assumption that GARBO did not think it prudent to continue to forward her information in view of the warning which he received from the Germans.

Agent No 1 – known as:
THE PORTUGUESE COMMERCIAL TRAVELLER

NAME: CARVALHO
NATIONALITY: Portuguese.
OCCUPATION: Commercial traveller.
ADDRESS: Newport, Men.
RECRUITED: Prior to 17.8.41.

This character was the first to be created by GARBO while he was still in Portugal. Though he lived in Newport, the majority of his reports were on the counties of Devon and Cornwall. He was alleged to remain, throughout his career, a rather colourless individual who worked regularly but without great zeal, presumably picking up information, mostly about airfields and military camps, which he came by in the course of his commercial travels.

He was eventually given secret ink and a cover address in Lisbon, to which he corresponded directly, receiving his questionnaires and replies through GARBO. The writing was done by a member of this office.

In view of the fact that there was no one in the office to whom we could delegate the work of writing who had fluent Portuguese, it was decided to make him write in French. The Germans were given the excuse that although a Portuguese he had fluent French. Since there were a lot of Belgians and Frenchmen in the area where he was living, we said that to write in French would serve as perfect cover should one of his letters be detected by the British Censor, since they would undoubtedly look for the author among these nationals and be unlikely to suspect a Portuguese.

This agent was sent to Northern Ireland with commercial cover, in place of another agent who had originally been intended to be sent there. He was one of the principal sources used in support of Operation STARKEY, during which period he covered the area of Southampton.

We realised that though he was required on that operation, his presence in south-west England would be undesirable during Operation OVERLORD, as he would see too much in this part of England. It was, therefore, decided to have one of his letters supposedly discovered in censorship during the time of Operation STARKEY, with the result that several Belgians were detained in the Southampton area and all non-residents, including the agent, ordered to leave.

Though the agent himself was not discovered, the incident greatly shook his confidence, and when GARBO accordingly came to realise that his morale was seriously shaken he decided a few months later to pay him off and allow him to resign from the service.

Agent No 2 – known as:
THE SWISS BUSINESSMAN

NAME: William Maximilian GERBERS
NATIONALITY: British (of German-Swiss descent.)
OCCUPATION: Not mentioned.
ADDRESS: Bootle, Liverpool.
RECRUITED: Prior to 17.8.41.

This agent, one of GARBO's creations during the period he was working in Lisbon, was perhaps one of the most colourful characters
of the organisation, though he came to an untimely end. Not only
was he responsible for the Malta convoy report but for numerous
other Naval reports of a rather high grade, which were forwarded
after GARBO's arrival in the UK. He worked well until the preparations for Operation TORCH had commenced, when it was realised
by the Admiralty that his presence in Liverpool was most undesirable.
The agent was therefore reported as having fallen ill and to be about
to have an operation for what appeared to be cancer. Three months
went by, during which time the agent was paid, though due to his
illness he was unable to contribute any information.

On visiting Liverpool during November 1942, GARBO discovered
that the agent had died on the 19.11.42 and an obituary notice, which
was inserted at our request in the *Liverpool Daily Post*, was forwarded
to the Germans in evidence.

Agent No 2's Subagent No 1 – known as: 2(1) or THE WIDOW

NAME: Mrs William Maximilian GERBERS.
NATIONALITY: British
OCCUPATION: Housewife
ADDRESS: Bootle, Liverpool.
RECRUITED: Prior to 10.4.43.

Following the death of her husband, Agent No 2, she found herself in a very difficult financial situation and stated her willingness to do anything to help GARBO in return for employment. GARBO, realising that she was not well suited to engage in espionage, decided, nevertheless, not to abandon the loyal wife of an ex-collaborator and that it would be wise to employ her to look after his household, as, by having a woman of complete confidence about the house, there would be less danger of his activities being discovered. One or two low-grade reports were sent over as attributed to her, but they were so bad that GARBO decided to suppress any further reports she might submit to him.

She did, however, serve a very useful role in the organisation. When the volume of wireless traffic became great she assisted GARBO with the enciphering of messages, and later she was used as a cutout for contact between the agents, and finally as a contact between GARBO and Mrs GARBO, GARBO and Agent No 3, and between Agent No 3 and the operator after GARBO had gone into hiding.

Agent No 3 – known as:
THE VENEZUELAN

NAME: Not mentioned. (His letters to the Germans were signed PEDRO.)
NATIONALITY: Venezuelan.
OCCUPATION: Of independent means.
ADDRESS: Glasgow.
RECRUITED: Prior to 7.10.41.

This was the third and last of the agents recruited by GARBO while he was operating in Lisbon. He was represented as having been educated at the University of Glasgow and was still in the UK at the outbreak of war. Though his exact means of livelihood were never disclosed, the impression was given that he was a man of means whose family had properties in Venezuela, one near Comuna and another in Caracas.

From the outset, GARBO showed a preference for this agent and, being the oldest survivor of the network, after disposing of Agents Nos 1 and 2 it was natural that he should have finally gained the rank of deputy chief of the GARBO network.

He was the first to be given secret ink to write directly to the Germans, who furnished him with a cover address in Lisbon for this purpose. The letters were written in this office. They were written in English, a language which the Germans were told he knew as well as his native Spanish, if not better, since he had been absent from Venezuela for many years. His traffic was, on the whole, higher grade than that of any other agent during the first two years of the history of the network.

After GARBO's first arrest in 1944 the entire organisation was directed by this agent, and the Germans came to regard him as an able substitute for the chief of the organisation. The purpose of handing over the organisation to this agent and removing the control from GARBO was primarily with a view to being able to run the organisation entirely through this office, without the personality of GARBO entering into it, and this was achieved. Thus, during the last months of the running of the case, this office was in direct communication with the German Intelligence Service, utilising only officers of this department to communicate in English on a wireless transmitting set which was installed within our office building.

Agent No 3's Subagent No 1 – known as: 3(1) or
THE NCO IN THE RAF

NAME: Not mentioned.
NATIONALITY: British.
OCCUPATION: NCO in the RAF
ADDRESS: Glasgow
RECRUITED: First mentioned as a contact of Agent No 3 on 3.2.43.

This man was represented as a drunkard and gambler with whom Agent No 3 made contact, believing him to have been capable of parting with confidential information for a monetary consideration. We did acquire through this source an aircraft recognition manual, which helped considerably in building up the case. We also used this character as a means of demonstrating to the Germans the complete integrity of GARBO and his Agent No 3. When the opportunity first arose to acquire this book, GARBO decided that he should consult the Germans before parting with cash and ascertain from them the approximate sum which this information might be worth. He was authorised to pay up to £100 for it. However, when it came to discussing the price with 3 (1), Agent No 3 discovered that this man, contrary to his expectations, was very small-minded so far as financial matters were concerned, and thus he succeeded in getting the book for the small sum of £3. Through this incident the Germans were able to appreciate that GARBO and his Agent No 3 were honest: though they had been authorised to pay £100 for the book, they did not take advantage of the fact that they were able to purchase it for so small a sum as £3, which is what the Germans were charged.

This character was allowed to fade out of the picture in September 1944.

Agent No 3's Subagent No 2 – known as: 3(2) or
THE LIEUTENANT IN THE 49TH DIVISION

NAME: Not mentioned.
NATIONALITY: British.
OCCUPATION: Lieutenant in the 49th British Infantry Division.
ADDRESS: Not mentioned.
RECRUITED: First mentioned as being in contact with Agent No. 3
on 1.10.43.

Agent No 3 made contact with this rather talkative lieutenant on a train journey from Glasgow to London. In the first place, the contact was used to confirm and explain certain reports which Agent No 3 had made on his own observations in the Troon area, where a brigade of the 49th Division was represented as undergoing assault training.

In support of TINDALL, we implied, through this source, that the 49th Division, which had been trained in mountain warfare, would be an assault division in an attack against Norway. Thus, when the preparations for Operation TORCH were well advanced, this contact was reported as returning to Scotland to join his division. A great number of troops employed in the TORCH operation did in fact leave from the Clyde, and when it was later ascertained that the 49th Division had not embarked we were able to maintain the threat to Norway, instead of, perhaps, exposing it as a cover plan for the TORCH operation.

This source played a very small role henceforth. He was active as late as September 1944, when, after the 49th Division had entered operations in France and been identified by the Germans, we had an occasion to make contact with him again through Agent No 3. This officer, now promoted in rank, told the agent of all his adventures overseas and the routing of his division through France. This was passed back to the Germans, who, having taken prisoners, were in a position to prove the accuracy of the information.

Agent No 3's Subagent No 3 – known as:
AGENT 3(3)

NAME: Not mentioned.
NATIONALITY   Greek.
OCCUPATION: Seaman.
ADDRESS: Glasgow.
RECRUITED: Prior to 19.12.43.

When building up the network to implement FORTITUDE NORTH and
FORTITUDE SOUTH, though these cover plans for Operation OVERLORD
had not then been developed in detail, it was realised that at least two
GARBO agents would have to operate in Scotland: one on the west
coast, the other on the east coast.

Agent No 5, who had at one time worked with Agent No 3 in
Scotland, had left for Canada a few months earlier in order to build
up a sub-organisation for GARBO there. Therefore, this new character
was created to substitute Agent No 5.

He was a Greek merchant seaman who had been working on the SS
Bristol City at the time she was torpedoed by the Germans, in May 1941.
This experience caused him to decide to desert from the Merchant
Navy, and prior to his recruitment as our agent he had, for nearly two
years, been living on his wits and on small sums of money which he
would occasionally borrow from his friends, among whom was our
Agent No 3.

Recruiting him, however, was a difficult case, since he was a man
of strong communist sympathies. Apart from this he was ideally
suited. Therefore, it was decided to recruit him by deceptive means.
Agent No 3 approached him as if he himself were a secret agent of
the Russians, and stated that as the Russians were unable to get information from the Anglo-Americans about the Second Front they had
found it necessary, in the interests of their own operations, to try to
discover as much as possible about British plans by secret means. He
was promised good pay, and at the same time given the assurance that
he would be assisting the inter-Allied cause. After accepting, he was
warned that any indiscretion might lead to complications between the
British and the Russian governments, and that if he were indiscreet
the Russians would have no hesitation in liquidating him.

During the first few months of his activities he stayed close to
Agent No 3. They made joint reports. Thus, we were able to cut down
the volume of information passed over until we were due to imple-

ment FORTITUDE NORTH. They parted company and 3(3) was moved over to the east coast of Scotland.

His usefulness to us came to an end shortly after D-Day and so we allowed the standard of his reporting to deteriorate, until November 1944, when he asked Agent No 3 if he might be allowed to resign. GARBO had already commented on the very poor grade of his reports by this time and expressed a desire to be rid of him. It was, therefore, much to GARBO's relief that the suggestion to resign came from the agent.

Greece had by then been liberated, and the agent decided that he wanted to return to his native land, even if to do so meant handing himself over to the British authorities as a deserter and paying the penalty for this. After being further threatened by Agent No 3 as to the consequences if he were indiscreet about his work for the 'Russians', he was told that he might carry out his plan, and he was given the sum of £100 as a final pay-off.

His punishment for desertion was a fine and a few weeks imprisonment, after which he was given employment on a coaster prior to signing on a ship going to the Mediterranean, where he again proposed to desert on touching at the first port of call of his native country.

Agent No 4 – known as:
FRED

NAME: FRED.
NATIONALITY: Gibraltarian.
OCCUPATION: Waiter.
ADDRESS: Soho. Later, Whitelands Hotel, (Gibraltarian Centre)
Putney. Until burnt out by enemy action.
RECRUITED: Prior to 27.5.42.

On the 27.5.42 GARBO reported that, after having cultivated this man
for a long time and having satisfied himself as to his loyalty, he had
decided to recruit him as an agent.

The primary objective in this recruitment was to ascertain
from the Germans the area of England which they were most
interested to cover. It was also taken into consideration that the
Germans had instructed GARBO to build up a network, and as
seven months had passed since he had last recruited an agent
personally it was considered that a new recruitment was in
fact overdue.

After operating for three months on the east coast Agent
No 4 presented GARBO with the opportunity of acquiring a wireless transmitter which he had discovered was for sale on the
black market in Soho. GARBO used the agent as a cut-out for
making the purchases of the radios, as well as for recruiting
the operator.

In December 1942 GARBO decided that this agent might most
usefully be employed in a West End London hotel, where he would
be likely to pick up gossip. With these plans in mind, the agent went
to the Ministry of Labour where, to his great disappointment, and
in spite of his qualifications as a waiter, he was directed to take work
in a quarry, on the assumption that all Gibraltarians ought naturally
to be good at tunnelling. He was directed to take employment with
Highways Construction, on work which he at first believed would be
connected with the construction of underground factories. In fact,
he was sent to work in the Chislehurst Caves, where vast tunnelling
operations had commenced to convert the caves into a huge arms
depot. It was later to be discovered that the caves were connected
to the London underground railway system by a miniature electric
railway, and thus the depot was enabled to supply ammunition to the
various airfields defending London.

Agent No 4, through his friends in the hotel business, provided GARBO with an assortment of writing paper with the headings of the leading West End hotels, which provided excellent camouflage for those of GARBO's secret letters which were sent by air mail.

He also served as contact with the wireless operator and, from March 1943, he himself practised under the supervision of the operator so that he might later be qualified to substitute the regular operator in the event of his ever falling ill.

Reports on the development of the underground occupied a great bulk of the GARBO traffic between January and September of 1943. By this time, we were beginning to feel that the German reactions to the story about the Chislehurst Caves were none too good, and it appeared a little dangerous to push this story further with the knowledge that we might have to maintain it for another year if we were to be able to make use of it for deception purposes in connection with the Second Front. It was, therefore, decided to remove the agent from his employment in the caves. This was done by his making friends with someone in the canteen there, through whom he eventually obtained employment in the NAAFI. This gave him greater freedom of movement for a while, and more time to spend in his haunts in Soho. For several months he was posted by the NAAFI from one place to another, from where he sent military reports until April 1944, by which time the role he was to play in the implementation of FORTITUDE SOUTH had been settled. He was then requested by the NAAFI to sign a Military Security Certificate so that he might be posted to one of their canteens within a sealed area. Thus, he was situated in one of the most important concentration areas in the Southampton district. There he was allowed to collect very important information until he finally discovered the secret of D Day, which, by breaking camp, he managed to get to GARBO, who transmitted it to the enemy just too late for it to be of any use to them.

Having deserted from a sealed area at such a time, the agent was inevitably in danger, but he managed to escape arrest by taking refuge in a safe hideout in the south of Wales, which was provided for him by another member of the organisation.

Later, having furnished himself with false seaman's papers, he managed to sign on as a steward on a ship, which he deserted on its arrival in Canada. There he was protected by Agent No 5, who was already well established in Montreal.

By this time Agent No 4 had become proficient as a wireless operator, and he was therefore given charge of the wireless station for the Canadian network which had in the meantime been developed.

Agent No 4's Subagent No 1 – known as: 4(1) or
THE RADIO OPERATOR

NAME: Not mentioned,
NATIONALITY: British.
OCCUPATION: A wireless mechanic employed by the EKCO factory.
ADDRESS: London.
RECRUITED: Prior to 28.8.42.

It was through 4(1) that Agent No 4 heard of the transmitting apparatus which was for sale. Being himself of strong left-wing sympathies, 4(1) quickly jumped at the proposition put to him by Agent No 4 to work secretly for what he believed to be the Spanish Republican exiles in this country, and thus facilitate them to be able to maintain rapid and clandestine contact with their underground movement in Spain. He was to be well paid with a minimum salary of £6 per week, even when he did not transmit. During the long period over which he was operating, he was never given grounds to suspect that he was working for anyone other than the Spanish refugees, in spite of the fact that there was always a marked activity in the work at the time of every operation. The reason for the burst of activity was explained to him by GARBO, who made it appear as though it was always the hope of the Spanish refugees to bring the underground movement to revolt to coincide with an Allied success. Though the story was not very convincing, the operator never appeared to be inquisitive. During the periods of great activity he would earn upwards of £100 a month, and it became more and more apparent that he was working for this liberal award rather than for any true desire to help the unfortunate Spanish refugees. The messages were always handed to him enciphered and he was never aware of their contents. He was responsible for building the set which was later used by Agent No 5's network in Canada. He was told that it was to be used by the Spaniards in Mexico who also wished to establish wireless contact with London and Madrid.

Another inducement for him to work with enthusiasm was the fact that all the equipment which had been paid for by GARBO was promised to him as a gift on the termination of his services.

To avoid arousing the suspicions of the operator when, after VE Day, communications with Spain suddenly broke down, he was told that the Spanish underground movement, stimulated by the total defeat of the Germans, had come out into the open too soon, with the result that their leaders and their wireless station had been discovered by the Falangist Police, thus bringing their activities to an end.

Agent No 4's Subagent No 2 - known as: 4(2) or
THE GUARD IN THE CHISLEHURST CAVES

NAME: Not mentioned.
NATIONALITY: British.
OCCUPATION: Guard in the Chislehurst Caves.
ADDRESS: Not mentioned.
RECRUITED: First reported as a contact of Agent No 4 on 25.4.43.

The guard in the Chislehurst Caves was responsible for prohibiting the entrance of all unauthorised persons into the depots of the caves. Thus, he served as a source of information for Agent No 4 about the activities within the caves, without putting Agent No 4 in the position of having to give too much first hand information, which might have been the case had he been allowed access to all the underground workings. The information about the caves was intentionally always kept rather vague, in the absence of a concrete plan, and thus this contact served a useful purpose.

After Agent No 4 left his employment at Chislehurst, contact with the guard was not maintained regularly, and in September 1944 GARBO informed the Germans that they could consider this contact as no longer operative.

Agent No 4's Subagent No 3 – known as: 4(3) or
THE AMERICAN NCO IN SERVICE OF SUPPLY

NAME: Not mentioned.
OCCUPATION: US Citizen.
NATIONALITY: US Army Service of Supply.
ADDRESS: COMZ Headquarters, London.
RECRUITED: First reported as a contact of Agent No 4 on 5.11.43.

This character was created purely to assist in reporting on US formations in the UK in connection with the deception plan.

He was first represented as having met Agent No 4 (the
Gibraltarian) in Soho, and believing him to be a Spaniard he got into
conversation with him about the Spanish Civil War, showing that his
sympathies had been with Franco. He took advantage of the friendship which thus sprung up to practice Spanish with Agent No 4. He
showed himself to be extremely anti-British and a great boaster who
took delight in demonstrating how well he was informed about the
formation of the US Army and their operational plans.

In December 1943 he had occasion, in conversation with Agent
No 4, to mention the return of landing craft from the Mediterranean
theatre of war. This information was based on a Most Secret Source
message on information received through German observers operating at Algeciras. The information was accurate, but there was no
harm in it being repeated through GARBO channels since it was already
out of date and known to the Germans. In passing on this information, GARBO suggested that they should check with Berlin to ascertain
whether it was accurate or not and let him know, as, on their reply,
he would be able to estimate the potential future usefulness of this
new collaborator. The Germans, as was anticipated, replied that the
information was entirely accurate and that the contact should therefore be developed. This gave him a very good start. From then on,
he reported mostly on the build-up of American forces in the UK, in
accordance with the cover plan for OVERLORD.

Agent No 5
(The Brother of Agent No 3)

NAME: Not mentioned.
NATIONALITY: Venezuelan.
OCCUPATION: Of independent means. Later employed as a commercial traveller in Toronto.
ADDRESS: Glasgow and, later, Toronto.
RECRUITED: Prior to 34.6.42

He was first mentioned by GARBO during the period when GARBO was working in Lisbon. He was brought on to the scene in connection with a provocation by GARBO to ascertain whether the Germans were refuelling their submarines in the Caribbean. He then offered the services of this individual to set up a refuelling base near his parents' property in Venezuela. The offer was turned down. He was later used as bait to draw the Germans to disclose whether they were interested in having an agent in Northern Ireland. Finally, he was recruited in June 1942 as an active member of the GARBO network.

At that time the Germans were very interested in the Isle of Wight. It would, in fact, have been difficult, if not impossible, to have got an agent in there, but we decided to satisfy their request to send Agent No 5 to investigate activities there. To make it appear plausible that he should have been able to enter the island, we depicted this agent as an adventurous young man prepared to take any risks for his masters. We set out in great detail the story of his adventurous, clandestine entry to the island and the perilous experiences he had there.

Though the story told was similar to that which one might read in any spy novel, the Germans liked it and believed it to be true, and thus he rose in their estimation.

Having completed this dangerous mission and toured the south coast of England and Wales, the agent, a restless character, decided that he wanted a change.

With the help of Agent No 7 he eventually smuggled himself out of England to Canada, having received instructions from GARBO to endeavour to set up a sub-organisation there. This he successfully did, and, by August 19 he was already communicating in secret writing to a cover address in Lisbon provided by the Germans far this purpose. To avoid Censorship the letters were sent from Canada to a cover address in Scotland provided by Agent No. 3 on the assumption that there was no testing for secret writing in correspondence between these two countries. The letters were then handed by Agent No. 3 to GARBO who forwarded them to Lisbon by his courier service. After the arrival of Agent No. 4 a wireless station was established in Montreal. Communications from Montreal by wireless to Madrid were started up in February, 1945. Though trials were made to establish contact between Montreal and London the results were never successful.

In addition to Agent No. 5's correspondence with the Germans, all organisational matters were dealt with in direct correspondence between GARBO and the agent. GARBO would send a monthly report summarising their correspondence, and occasionally extracts of the original letters received from him by GARBO would be forwarded to the Germans to add colour.

The ink used by the agent for his correspondence with the Germans was [word censored on insistence of the intelligence services] ink, for which GARBO did not have the developer. Therefore, the long process of forwarding the letters to Lisbon, instead of developing them here and transmitting their contents by wireless, was necessary. GARBO was, of course, in possession of the developer for the inferior ink used for the service intercommunications in which Agent No. 5 used to correspond with him.

Agent No 5's Subagent No 1 – known as: 5(1) or
THE AMERICAN COMMERCIAL TRAVELLER

NAME: CON.
NATIONALITY: Not mentioned.
OCCUPATION: Commercial traveller.
ADDRESS: Buffalo, USA.
RECRUITED: Prior to 5.1.45.

Shortly after the arrival of Agent No 5 in Montreal he met his cousin who, though residing in Buffalo, used to travel frequently to Canada,

In the first place, Agent No 5 used to extract information from him, and in January 1945 he got his cousin to hand him espionage reports, periodically, knowing that the information he was supplying would be passed to the Germans. These reports, which were very extensive, were forwarded via GARBO to the Germans, where they were well received. In spite of the mass of detail and unimportant information which they contained (much of which had already appeared in the press in a different form), it was nevertheless seen to pass from Madrid to Berlin on MSS in its entirety.

It was envisaged at the time of recruiting this agent to increase the network of Agent No 5 that the Canadian organisation might have continued to operate against the Japanese after the collapse of Germany. The sudden German collapse made this impossible.

Agent No 6 – known as:
DICK

NAME: DICK.
NATIONALITY: South African.
OCCUPATION: Independent means. He had contacts in the Ministry
of Information and other Government Departments.
ADDRESS: London and, later, Algiers.
RECRUITED: Prior to 10.8.42.

Agent No 6 was violently anti-communist and worked for the
Germans for ideological reasons. GARBO had promised him an important post in the New World Order after the war. This agent was the
person responsible for introducing GARBO to J(3). He was a first-class
linguist, intelligent and capable. From the time of his recruitment,
the Germans were told that he did not like living in England and
proposed to take advantage of the first available opportunity to get
abroad. He had been GARBO's intermediary in Plan DREAM, and before
he left the UK he made the necessary arrangements for GARBO to be
able to continue to carry out these final transactions through a friend
of his, who performed in his role.

In October 1942, GARBO wrote to say that he was studying a plan
of the greatest importance for this agent. It later materialised, for
Agent No 6 managed to get himself recruited to go to North Africa
a few days prior to Operation TORCH. He was taken on by the War
Office on the strength of his linguistic abilities.

When his recruitment and departure from the UK materialised very
rapidly and unexpectedly, there was just time for GARBO to instruct him
in secret writing and supply him with the necessary inks, so that he was
able to maintain contact with GARBO through a cover address in London
and send him military and naval reports as soon as he was established in
the Mediterranean.

GARBO, who had no developer for the ink which he had supplied
for these communications, had to forward the original letters to one
of his cover addresses in Lisbon, and thus the Germans had the satisfaction of handling material which, to all appearances, had passed
through the censorship of Algiers.

Though there was frequently a delay of up to six weeks between
the date of the letter and the time of its arrival in German hands, they
were nevertheless delighted with their new agent. During the period
of his build up it was possible to pass the Germans very accurate

information which served them no useful purpose, as it was already very out of date by the time it reached them.

An attempt was made to get the Germans to send GARBO the developer for ink which he was using, so that the contents could be transmitted to them by wireless from London. This was not forthcoming, probably due to the fact that the development of ink is somewhat complicated and they were afraid that GARBO might have been unable to develop the letters successfully.

When the case of this agent had started to develop well a real misfortune occurred. The person in this office who had been acting as scribe for this notional agent met with an air crash while returning from leave in Scotland and was killed. It was considered inadvisable to take the risk of imitating his handwriting and so it was decided that the case would have to be brought to an untimely end.

GARBO reported that the agent had been killed in an accident in Algiers, having learned the news from the agent's mistress in London. Through her, GARBO was also able to discover that none of his espionage material had been discovered after his death. Thus, there was no risk of any developments as a result of this incident which might reflect on the security of GARBO or the rest of his organisation.

Agent No 7 – known as:
STANLEY

NAME: STANLEY.
NATIONALITY: Welsh.
OCCUPATION: Seaman.
ADDRESS: Swansea.
RECRUITED: Prior to 24.12.42.

During the period when we were first considering breaking down the airman courier system of communication, the alternative of using a seaman courier was considered. It was envisaged that a seaman courier in the organisation would permit bulkier objects to be sent out than would be possible by air.

Another consideration at the time was that after Agent No. had left for North Africa his letters, which would bear the Field Censor's stamp of North Africa, could not very well be sent on by the airman courier without arousing his suspicion.

Therefore, Agent No 7, a seaman, was recruited, and it was to transpire that he would have numerous friends in the Merchant Navy who, for a monetary payment, would be prepared to do a little smuggling of correspondence and parcels at his request. He was introduced to the GARBO network by Agent No 4, who guaranteed his loyalty. From the very beginning, GARBO pointed out that no one could be better placed to assist the work of his organisation than a member of the Merchant Navy. He then prophesied that this agent would facilitate the growth of the network. His prophecy was fulfilled a year later.

The recruitment of a seaman agent was at first frowned upon by the Admiralty because it was feared that the Germans would ask him a number of embarrassing questions about convoy routing and composition. We therefore emphasised to the Germans from the beginning that, on account of his long association with the sea, the agent had stipulated that he would not give information about the movements of ships which might lead directly to the death of his fellow seamen. He nevertheless gave a considerable amount of information about convoy protection which the Admiralty considered might be misleading to the enemy.

With time, it became obvious that the agent's primary consideration in helping the GARBO network was a monetary one. At the same time, he was a Welsh Nationalist and, as such, anti-British. He pestered GARBO a good deal for money, but in return gave him good service and, in particular, supplied him with numerous seamen couriers operating in ships which put in at South Wales and Portuguese ports. The agent was an ill man, suffering from a defect of the spine which had developed after an accident, and towards the middle of 1943 he was invalided out of the Merchant Navy,

Between then and December 1943 he operated mainly as a military reporter, and in December that year he brought to GARBO's notice an organisation known as the 'Brothers in the Aryan World Order'. This was composed of a number of fanatical Welsh Nationalists who had long ago abandoned the too moderate Welsh Nationalist Party. From this 'Order' no less than six operative agents were recruited who played an important role in implementing the cover plan for OVERLORD.

Agent No 7 thus became head of one of GARBO's sub-organisations until July 1944, when, shaken by the arrest of Agent No 7(5), a member of his network, he decided to return to the Merchant Navy. This did not result in his breaking with the network, for he offered to continue to serve GARBO to the best of his ability in his new employment.

He was responsible for hiding Agent No 4 after the latter had exposed himself to the danger of arrest. He later succeeded in smuggling this same agent to Canada.

He found a safe hideout for GARBO in South Wales after his activities had brought him to the notice of the British authorities. Finally, he operated as courier on the North Atlantic route, facilitating the clandestine communications exchanged between the GARBO network in the UK and his Canadian network.

Agent No 7's Subagent No 1 – known as: 7(1) or SOLDIER IN THE 9TH ARMOURED DIVISION

NAME: Not mentioned.
NATIONALITY: British.
OCCUPATION: Soldier in the 9th Armoured Division.
ADDRESS: Not mentioned.
RECRUITED: Prior to 16.9.43.

The 9th Armoured Division, frequently referred to in the traffic as the Panda Division (since its insignia was that of a panda) was built up as a first line formation by the GARBO organisation at the time of Operation STARKEY. The Germans took a lively interest in the activities of this Division. The association of the words 'panda' and 'panzer' seemed to register in German minds. They were prepared to accept this Division as a likely assault division for the Second Front.

In the absence of a directive, we built up the potential of the 9th Armoured Division until January 1944, after which period it was allowed to fade out since the plans then revealed that it was not among those Divisions which were to be used in the order of battle of FORTI-TUDE SOUTH. In fact, it never operated in France and was disbanded.

Agent No 7(2)

NAME: DAVID.
NATIONALITY: Welsh.
OCCUPATION: Retired seaman. Ex-Welsh Nationalist.
ADDRESS: Swansea.
RECRUITED: Prior to 6.12.43.

He was introduced to the GARBO organisation by Agent No 7 as a seaman who had left the sea seven years previously. He was a fanatical Welshman who had left the Welsh Nationalist Party to form the 'Brothers in the Aryan World Order'.

This agent started to report in January 1944 and was given the important area of Dover and district to cover during the period of build-up for the FORTITUDE SOUTH deception. He continued to operate from there until August 1944. He then travelled around the country for GARBO to obtain military reports and continued to be an important source until VE Day.

Agent No 7(3)

NAME: THERESA JARHCNE.
NATIONALITY: English.
OCCUPATION: Secretary to the 'Brothers in the Aryan World Order'.
From January 1944, leading WREN (Waiter) WRNS.
ADDRESS: From August 1944 – c/o DICA Headquarters, SEAC,
Ceylon.
RECRUITED: Prior to the 6.12.43.

To explain her strange association with the 'Brothers in the Aryan World Order' she was represented as the mistress of an Indian (Agent No 7(4)), a member of this Brotherhood.

No sooner had she been recruited than she found herself conscripted into the WRNS, and on account of her predilection for Indians she did all in her power to ensure that she would be posted to India. She was first sent to a WRNS Office in London and later to a training school at Mill Hill, and finally to the WRNS camp near Newbury, where she studied Hindustani, which she had already learned from her Indian lover, and was trained in secretarial work. This training covered the period from January–July 1944, when, during a period of embarkation leave in London, she was trained by Agent No 7 in secret writing and given a cover address in the UK, to which she was instructed to send her reports from Ceylon, where she was about to proceed.

Her first letter from Ceylon was forwarded by GARBO to his Lisbon cover address in September 1944. She continued to write until early in 1945, when she met with a car accident. It was then considered necessary to bring her activities to an end, since a close similarity in her reports and those of other agents controlled from Ceylon had been noticed by the enemy and aroused slight suspicion. The speedy termination of hostilities did not give us an opportunity to bring her case to a tidy close.

Agent No 7(4)

NAME:	RAGS.
NATIONALITY:	Indian.
OCCUPATION;	Poet.
ADDRESS:	Swansea.
RECRUITED:	Prior to 6.12.43.

This individual had joined the 'Brothers in the Aryan World Order' to uphold his fanatical belief in the superiority of the Aryan race.

Since his occupation was that of a poet, he was presumably able to win the affections of his English mistress, 7(3).

He was recruited together with the other members of this Brotherhood, and in February 1944 he was established in the Brighton area to operate as an observer for the GARBO organisation. He continued to send in a stream of high-grade military reports until April 1945, when he confessed that he had tired of his association with the Welshmen, to which he had been attracted mostly on account of their association with 7(3). On her instructions, £500 which had accrued to her for services rendered were entrusted to him to hold for her until they were able to meet again.

Agent No 7(5)

NAME: Not mentioned.
NATIONALITY: Welsh.
OCCUPATION: Employee of a commercial firm in Swansea.
ADDRESS: Swansea.
RECRUITED: Prior to 6.12.43

Though he was a member of the 'Brothers in the Aryan World Order, and a relative of 7(2), it became apparent that he was either less intelligent or less fanatical than the other members of this Brotherhood. This came to notice when he failed to establish himself in the Exeter/Plymouth area where he had been instructed to proceed as an observer. In fact, it was undesirable that he should have been successful, since the cover plan did not provide for reporting from this area, though it would have looked suspicious had no attempt been made to cover it. 7(5) did get as far as Taunton, from where he produced reports, and in May he entered the prohibited area around Exeter in spite of the continual police check-ups on documentation. He was, however, arrested a few days prior to D Day. He was only sentenced to one month's imprisonment for the offence of having entered a restricted area without permission. The true nature of his mission there was not discovered or suspected.

On his release he returned to his family in Swansea but his narrow escape had completely demoralised him; he had lost his nerve and he became useless as an agent. He was given a pension from September 1944 until March 1945, when he was finally paid off.

Agent No 7(7)

NAME: Not mentioned.
NATIONALITY: Welsh.
OCCUPATION: Treasurer of the 'Brothers in the Aryan World Order'.
ADDRESS: Swansea.
RECRUITED: Prior to 6.12.43.

As the Treasurer of the Brotherhood it was recommended that he should be given an important allocation in the GARBO network, and therefore he was situated in the Harwich area, which GARBO believed would become one of the most important areas at the time of the opening of the Second Front.

He established himself in residence in the Ipswich/Harwich area prior to the imposition of the coastal ban, and his first report, which GARBO received in April 1944, was one of ten pages of secret writing that, though unsubstantial in part, tended to show the importance of this area, which had for some while been relatively neglected by the GARBO network. The details contained in this report not only showed the thoroughness of the agent but also introduced a style that would permit the inclusion of apparently minor, though significant details in subsequent reports.

He continued to report from this area in considerable detail, in particular on the notional 34th US Army, which he, in due course, located in this area. Later, he extended the area of his control further north so as to cover Northern Command.

He was one of the agents who continued to operate until VE Day.

Agent No 7(6)

NAME:	Not mentioned.
NATIONALITY:	Welsh.
OCCUPATION:	Employed in an office in Swansea.
ADDRESS:	Swansea.
RECRUITED:	Prior to 6.12.43.

This agent, though recruited on the strength of his association with the 'Brothers in the Aryan World Order', turned out to be a very low-grade spy. Though he accepted his mission he did not want to leave his employment in Swansea to travel. Since an observer was needed in South Wales (which area the Germans had asked us to cover) his offer of services to operate from Swansea was promptly accepted. In fact, it was inconsistent with the cover plan for OVERLORD that we should pass reports on military activities in South Wales, and therefore it was admirably suitable that this agent should not only be working part-time, but also that he should turn out to be a low-grade reporter.

GARBO first pointed out the low category of his reports in March 1944. He was used in a rather half-hearted way to implement Plan IRONSIDE, a threat to the Bordeaux coast. When the operation did not materialise the information passed did not tend to discredit the GARBO organisation, since the Germans had been forewarned that this agent was not a high-grade reporter.

In January 1945 the agent was put on half pay and in March we finally terminated with his services.

**The above agent stories can be found at the
National Archives at Kew in file KV 2/41**

'The reader should bear in
mind that none of these
people actually existed.'

Sir Michael Howard

British Intelligence in the Second World War,
Volume V, Strategic Deception

Index

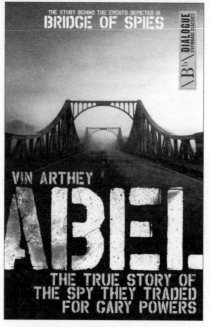

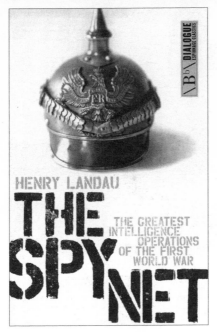